Better Homes and Gardens.

Low Carb
SLOW
COOKER
RECIPES

Better Homes and Gardens. Books
Des Moines, Iowa

Low-Carb Slow Cooker Recipes
Editor: Kristi M. Thomas, R.D.
Writer: Alice Lesch Kelly
Designer: Barbara J. Gordon
Copy Chief: Terri Fredrickson
Copy and Production Editor: Victoria Forlini
Editorial Operations Manager: Karen Schirm
Managers, Book Production: Pam Kvitne, Marjorie J. Schenkelberg, Rick von Holdt
Contributing Copy Editor: Maria Duryée
Contributing Proofreaders: Gretchen Kauffman, Susan Kling, Donna Segal
Indexer: Kathleen Poole
Editorial and Design Assistants: Karen McFadden, Mary Lee Gavin
Test Kitchen Director: Lynn Blanchard
Test Kitchen Product Supervisor: Jennifer Kalinowski, R.D.
Test Kitchen Home Economists: Marilyn Cornelius; Juliana Hale, Laura Harms, R.D.;
    Maryellyn Krantz; Jill Moberly; Dianna Nolin; Colleen Weeden; Lori Wilson; Charles Worthington

Meredith® Books
Editor in Chief: Linda Raglan Cunningham
Design Director: Matt Strelecki
Executive Editor, Food and Crafts: Jennifer Dorland Darling

Publisher: James D. Blume
Executive Director, Marketing: Jeffrey Myers
Executive Director, New Business Development: Todd M. Davis
Executive Director, Sales: Ken Zagor
Director, Operations: George A. Susral
Director, Production: Douglas M. Johnston
Business Director: Jim Leonard

Vice President and General Manager: Douglas J. Guendel

Better Homes and Gardens® **Magazine**
Editor in Chief: Karol DeWulf Nickell
Deputy Editor, Food and Entertaining: Nancy Hopkins

Meredith Publishing Group
President, Publishing Group: Stephen M. Lacy
Vice President-Publishing Director: Bob Mate

Meredith Corporation
Chairman and Chief Executive Officer: William T. Kerr

In Memoriam: E. T. Meredith III (1933-2003)

Our seal assures you that every recipe in *Low-Carb Slow Cooker Recipes* has been tested in the Better Homes and Gardens® Test Kitchen. This means that each recipe is practical and reliable, and meets our high standards of taste appeal. We guarantee your satisfaction with this book for as long as you own it.

All of us at Better Homes and Gardens® Books are dedicated to providing you with the information and ideas you need to create delicious foods. We welcome your comments and suggestions. Write to us at: Better Homes and Gardens Books, Cookbook Editorial Department, 1716 Locust St., Des Moines, IA 50309-3023.

If you would like to purchase any of our cooking, crafts, gardening, home improvement, or home decorating and design books, check wherever quality books are sold. Or visit us at: bhgbooks.com

Introduction

No one has to convince you of the ease of using a slow cooker. It's a busy family's answer to getting meals on the table quickly. With an exciting array of flavors, spices, and ingredients, the recipes contained in this cookbook will inspire and tantalize you. Additionally, they will keep you on your low-carb quest. But before you start cooking, these tips will help you get the most from your slow cooker.

What Size Do I Need?

Slow cookers range in size from 1 to 6 quarts. The recipes in this book specify the recommended size to use. Check the capacity of your cooker to determine whether it fits the recommendations in the recipe.

Fuss-Free Cooking

If you want dinner to cook all day, use the low-heat setting of your cooker. This allows the food to cook from 10 to 12 hours. For a shorter cooking time, use the high-heat setting, which cooks food in 3 to 6 hours (depending on the recipe). Cooking times may vary depending on the cooker, but the timings generally will work with all continuous slow cookers. *Note:* When a recipe recommends only cooking on one setting, do not use the other setting. Often, the other setting did not produce a satisfactory dish during testing.

Keep Food Safe

For food safety reasons, remove cooked food from the slow cooker before storing it. If you store the warm food and the liner in the refrigerator, the food may not cool down quickly enough. Cooling foods quickly is the key to keeping foods safe from bacteria. Place leftovers in a storage container and refrigerate or freeze.

Enjoy!

Slow cookers can produce a multitude of dishes. You'll never grow tired of using it because it can make everything from soup to pot roast. It's nice to come home to a great meal—and any extra time you'll gain because you didn't have to watch the pot.

Low-Carb Basics

Knowledge about health benefits of various foods has exploded during the past few decades. As scientists have worked to search out specific compounds in foods that fight disease, they have also sought to determine what combination of carbohydrate, protein, and fat is most beneficial. Not long ago, it was believed that the optimal diet was low in fat and protein and fairly high in carbohydrates. However, researchers have concluded that some of the healthiest cultures in the world owe their robust well-being in part to the considerable amounts of fish oils and monounsaturated fats that they consume. Today, many scientists agree that curbing carbohydrates and eating moderate amounts of lean protein and heart-healthy fat is the best way to fight disease and maintain ideal body weight.

Reducing carbohydrates in your diet isn't hard, but doing it healthfully requires some thought. Of course, you can cut down on carbohydrates by choosing an enormous steak for dinner instead of a bowl of pasta, but that won't help your cholesterol level or your weight. The secret is to replace starchy carbohydrate-rich meals with nutritious, delicious, low-carb dishes that will benefit both your health and your waistline. Those are just the kind of foods you'll find in this book. With these luscious, easy-to-prepare recipes, you'll reduce the carbohydrates in your diet while enjoying delectable meals that are packed with flavor and nutrients.

Why Choose a Low-Carbohydrate Diet?

Many Americans are adopting low-carbohydrate diets. People are tired of surviving on tasteless low-fat foods such as watery salad dressings and rubbery cheeses. They are thrilled with the idea of being able to eat more of the foods that have been discouraged in low-fat eating plans, such as meats and cheeses.

Stories abound of people who swear by low-carbohydrate diets as an effective way to lose weight. Not only do they drop pounds, but they are able to do so while eating foods they love. Because they enjoy their food, they are better able to stick to their diets. What's more, many people report (and studies support this) that low-carbohydrate diets leave them feeling less hungry than high-carbohydrate, low-fat diets.

Before you start reducing the carbohydrates in your meals, it's important to understand how to do it in a healthful way to lose weight and decrease your risk of disease. Read on and find out why eating fewer carbohydrates may make sense for you.

Building Blocks

Food is made up of three macronutrients: protein, fats, and carbohydrates.

Carbohydrates provide immediate energy. There are three types of carbohydrates: complex carbohydrates, simple carbohydrates (sugars), and fiber. Complex carbohydrates include foods such as whole grain breads and cereals, fruits, vegetables, and legumes. Simple carbohydrates include white breads, table sugar, and soft drinks such as cola or sweetened iced tea. Foods that are rich in fiber include fruits, vegetables, whole grains, and legumes.

Fats offer a concentrated source of energy, but they have other jobs as well. Fats transport fat-soluble vitamins through the blood, help maintain healthy skin, assist in maintaining cell structure, help manufacture hormones, and insulate body tissues. The fats in food are made of different types of fatty acids: saturated, polyunsaturated, monounsaturated, and trans fatty acids.

Protein supplies amino acids, the building blocks that erect, repair, and maintain your body tissues. It transports vitamins and minerals in the blood and helps build muscle. Protein also can provide energy when your body's supply of carbohydrates and fats is low.

Food also contains vitamins, minerals, water, and other nutrients such as phytochemicals. A healthful diet includes all of these elements of good nutrition. However, too much of one and not enough of the others can throw your body out of balance, foster weight gain, and boost your risk of disease.

Glucose and Insulin

Many people eat too many carbohydrates, particularly simple carbohydrates and sugars—mostly "white" foods such as sugar, white bread, bagels, pasta, rice cakes, pretzels, potatoes, cake, popcorn, cookies, and muffins, as well as sugary soft drinks. Although these foods taste good, they trigger a chemical reaction in the body that can, over time, cause damage. Here's how: When you eat a high-carbohydrate food, your body's level of blood sugar, or glucose, rises. In response, the pancreas releases a hormone called insulin, which has the job of ushering glucose into the body's cells, where it is either used immediately for energy or stored for future use. Insulin's function is to move glucose out of the blood and into muscle and fat cells as quickly as possible. If it lingers too long in the blood, glucose can harm blood vessels and other tissues.

Highly processed, high-sugar foods—for example, sugarcoated cereals—trigger a large, rapid dump of glucose into the blood. Minimally processed foods that are low in carbohydrates—scrambled eggs, for example—cause a slower, smaller release of glucose into the blood. The more high-carbohydrate foods you eat, the more glucose is released in the blood and the more insulin your pancreas secretes. A low-carbohydrate food, on the other hand, results in less glucose and, therefore, less insulin release in the bloodstream.

Large amounts of glucose and insulin in the blood can cause trouble for your cardiovascular system. Excessive amounts of insulin can raise blood pressure and triglyceride levels in the blood and can reduce HDL, also known as the "good" cholesterol. High blood pressure, high triglycerides, and low HDL all boost the risk of heart disease.

Over time, repeated surges in blood glucose and insulin can lead the body to become insulin-resistant, which means that the body must release more and more insulin in order to clear glucose from the blood. The American Diabetes Association (ADA) calls this insulin-resistant condition prediabetes." Someone with prediabetes has blood glucose levels that are higher than they should be, but not yet high enough to be considered diabetic. Prediabetics have a 50 percent increased risk of heart disease or stroke compared to people who have normal glucose levels.

People with prediabetes are at a very high risk of developing full-blown diabetes, a serious disease that can lead to heart disease, eye problems, circulatory problems, kidney disease, and death. More than 17 million Americans have diabetes, the sixth leading cause of death in the United States, and according to the ADA, an additional 16 million have prediabetes.

Carbohydrates and Weight Loss

Diets that are low in carbohydrates appear to foster weight loss. As several major studies have shown, people tend to get hungry sooner after a high-carbohydrate meal than they do after a low-carbohydrate meal. The reason for this relates, once again, to glucose and insulin. To illustrate, say you are hungry for a quick snack and you munch on a handful of pretzels, which are a starchy, high-carbohydrate food. Glucose floods into the bloodstream quickly, and the pancreas swiftly churns out insulin to escort the glucose out of the blood into the cells. The body burns the energy-producing glucose that it needs at that moment and stores the rest as fat. Once the glucose is either burned

or stored, your blood sugar drops quickly—often to below-normal levels—triggering the surge of another kind of hormone that stimulates hunger and cravings for more high-starch foods.

In other words, when you eat a high-starch snack, you feel satisfied for a while. Before long, however, you're very likely to be walloped with sudden hunger pangs that trigger cravings and send you searching for another high-starch snack that will restore blood sugar levels. Chances are, you'll be so hungry that you'll choose another high-carbohydrate snack or meal that will set the cycle in motion again.

Now, say you reach for a handful of low-carb, high-protein, high-monounsaturated-fat peanuts instead of those pretzels. After you eat the peanuts, glucose is released slowly into the blood, rather than quickly, which gives your body a steady source of energy and no glucose spikes. Your body responds by releasing insulin at a steady rate and in reasonable amounts. Your hunger returns gradually, not suddenly, and because it comes on slowly, you're more likely to satisfy it with a smart, healthful meal or snack rather than a binge.

Not all carbohydrates are alike, however. Starchy foods such as white bread, sugar-coated cereals, and sugary sweets trigger a sudden dump of glucose into the bloodstream. Such foods are said to have a high glycemic index, or GI. (A food's glycemic index is determined by how much glucose it releases into the blood.) Complex carbohydrates such as those found in some fruits and vegetables and whole grains trigger a slower, less intense glucose response and are described as low-GI foods. (See Glycemic Index vs. Glycemic Load, below.)

High-GI foods have been found to be less satisfying than low-GI foods. Studies at the Obesity Program at Children's Hospital in Boston, among other research centers, have found that several hours after eating high-GI meals, study subjects ate as much as 81 percent more than they did after low-GI meals with the same number of calories.

Some researchers believe that a low-carbohydrate diet promotes fat burning. This is a controversial theory, and so far, there is limited research to support it. However, there is some evidence to suggest that high insulin levels promote the storage of fat and restrain the release of fatty acids from fat cells.

In other words, when you eat foods that are rich in carbohydrates, the body is more anxious to store those calories as fat (and keep them stored!) than to burn them as fuel. On the other hand, when you eat a low-carbohydrate meal, the body is more apt to burn those calories as fuel than to store them in the form of body fat.

There is also some research that supports the theory that a low-carbohydrate diet boosts the metabolism, giving you more energy and enabling your body to burn more calories throughout the day, even when you're at rest. More study is needed to prove this, but anecdotal evidence from people who have adopted low-carbohydrate diets seems to back it up. Many people who cut down on carbohydrates report feeling more energetic.

Glycemic Index vs. Glycemic Load

The glycemic index (GI) is a score assigned to foods based on how high the food raises blood sugar levels compared to how high table sugar raises blood sugar levels (table sugar raises blood sugar more than any other food). Carbohydrate-containing foods that break down slowly release glucose into the bloodstream slowly, and, therefore, blood sugar levels don't rise quickly. These foods are assigned a low GI. Conversely, carbohydrate-containing foods that break down quickly cause a high increase in blood sugar levels and are assigned a high GI.

Many popular books recommend avoiding foods that have a high glycemic index. These recommendations have been challenged by some experts because a carrot, for example, has about the same GI score as table sugar. This translates into eating six or seven servings of carrots to match the blood glucose effect of one-fourth cup of sugar.

Many think the glycemic load (GL) scoring may be a better measure of a food's effect on blood sugar. This score is determined by multiplying the grams of carbohydrate in a serving of food by the food's glycemic index. A GL score takes into account how much carbohydrate is in a serving of food, rather than just how high a standard amount of carbohydrate in a food raises blood sugar levels. Carrots, for example, have a glycemic index of 131. When using the GL score, carrots drop to a GL of 10, which is more appropriate for carrots, say proponents of GL scoring. This score gives a more accurate picture of the effect foods have on blood sugar, whereas the GI score unnecessarily makes healthful foods look bad.

Alternate Choices

In a world where carbohydrate-rich foods so often take center stage, you may wonder what will fill your plate in a low-carbohydrate diet. Believe it or not, scientists recommend replacing some of the carbohydrates in your diet with heart-healthy fats. This may sound shocking, considering that we have been told for so long that a healthful diet is a low-fat diet and that all fats should be reduced. Recent research shows that monounsaturated fat, the fat found in foods such as nuts, olive oil, fatty fish, and avocados, is actually good for you.

In a landmark study conducted at Pennsylvania State University several years ago, researchers found that diets high in monounsaturated fats are superior to low-fat diets for heart health. Diets high in "good" fat actually improve risk factors for heart disease such as total cholesterol, LDL cholesterol, HDL cholesterol, and triglycerides. A diet rich in monounsaturated fats reduced the risk of heart disease by 21 percent, the study found, while the low-fat diet reduced it only 12 percent.

Monounsaturated fat can be an effective partner in a weight loss program, according to recent studies. For example, researchers at the Harvard School of Public Health and Brigham and Women's Hospital in Boston found that people in their study found it easier to stick to a moderate-fat, reduced-calorie diet than to a low-fat, reduced calorie diet. In that study, all subjects consumed between 1,200 and 1,500 calories per day. Half ate a moderate-fat diet (35 percent of calories from fat) and half ate a low-fat diet (20 percent of calories from fat). The moderate-fat group substituted high-saturated fat foods, like butter, with healthier monounsaturated fat foods such as peanut butter. They tossed almonds on their salads instead of croutons and poured small amounts of full-fat dressings on their salads instead of non-fat dressings. Both groups lost an average of 11 pounds. However, those in the low-fat group gained back most of their weight quickly, but the moderate-fat group maintained their weight loss for at least 2½ years.

It's important to remember, however, that although low-carbohydrate diets allow a more liberal intake of meat, you should continue to limit saturated fat-rich foods such as marbled red meat; full-fat dairy products; fatty cuts of pork, chicken, and other meats; along with tropical oils such as palm and coconut. Eating too much saturated fat raises your blood cholesterol level, which increases your risk of clogged arteries, coronary artery disease, and heart attack. Because saturated fat is associated with higher risks of heart disease, certain cancers, and stroke, it should contribute no more than 7 to 10 percent of daily calories. If you consume 1,800 calories a day, for example, no more than 180 calories—and ideally, less than that—should come from saturated fat.

You should also limit your intake of trans fats, the fatty acids that are created when unsaturated fats undergo the chemical process of hydrogenation. Hydrogenated fats have replaced animal fats in many manufactured foods because they contribute flavor and texture to foods such as cakes, cookies, crackers, donuts, and chips and extend foods' shelf lives too. Foods fried in partially hydrogenated fats, such as fast-food french fries, taste pleasingly crispy and are nicely browned. Margarines can also be very high in trans fats, although lately, many margarine manufacturers have reformulated their recipes to rely less on hydrogenated fats. If you use margarine, choose a brand with no trans fats.

The problem with trans fats is that they raise the LDL, or bad cholesterol, in the blood nearly as much as saturated fat. High blood levels of LDL are a major contributor to heart disease, which kills more than 710,000 people in the United States each year. Trans fats may reduce levels of HDL, or good cholesterol, in the blood as well.

A number of studies bear this out. For example, the Nurse's Health Study, a long-term look at the health habits of about 80,000 nurses, found that those with the highest intake of trans fat were 27 percent more likely to develop heart disease than those with the lowest intake. Unfortunately, trans fats are not currently listed on food labels, so you have to read ingredient lists to root them out. Look for the words "partially hydrogenated vegetable oil" or "vegetable shortening," which indicate the food contains trans fat.

What about Protein?

Cutting down on carbohydrates doesn't mean you can go wild on protein. Very high-protein diets force the kidneys to work overtime trying to get rid of the excess waste products of protein and fat, called ketones. A buildup of ketones in the blood (called ketosis) can cause the body to produce high levels of uric acid, which is a risk factor for gout (a painful swelling of the joints) and kidney stones. Ketosis can be

especially risky for people with diabetes because it can speed the progression of diabetic kidney disease.

That said, however, there is some research that suggests a diet that is higher in protein and lower in carbohydrates than what is currently recommended by the U.S. Department of Agriculture (USDA) Food Guide Pyramid may help people lose weight and keep it off. For example, at the University of Illinois at Urbana-Champaign, researchers put two groups of overweight women on a 1,700-calorie-a-day eating plan for 10 weeks. The control group ate according to the USDA pyramid—55 percent of their calories came from carbohydrates, 15 percent from protein (a total of 68 grams per day), and 30 percent from fat. The experimental group ate a moderate-protein diet consisting of 40 percent of calories from carbohydrates, 30 percent from protein (125 grams a day), and 30 percent from fat.

The average weight loss in both groups was the same—16 pounds. However, the higher-protein group lost more fat than muscle—seven times more. The higher-protein group lost 12.3 pounds of fat compared with the lower-protein group, which lost 10.4 pounds of fat. (Both groups did the same amount of physical activity.)

The University of Illinois researchers believe that eating more high-quality protein increases the body's stores of leucine, an amino acid that helps people maintain muscle mass and reduce body fat during weight loss. Although the body does make many amino acids, it is not able to produce leucine, which is found primarily in beef, dairy products, poultry, fish, and eggs. Subjects in the higher-protein group also had higher levels of thyroid hormones in their blood, which suggests a higher rate of metabolism. Additionally, their blood levels of heart-harming triglycerides were down, and their HDL ("good") cholesterol had risen slightly.

The women in the study ate more than just protein, however: Their daily diet included, in addition to 9 to 10 ounces of lean beef and other meats, three daily servings of low-fat dairy foods, five servings of vegetables, two fruits, and four servings of grains, pasta, and rice.

Following a Low-Carbohydrate Diet

Whether you choose to limit the carbohydrates a little or a lot, this book can help. In the following pages, you'll discover more than 200 tasty recipes for appetizers; snacks; beverages; beef, pork, poultry, and lamb dishes; plus plenty of quick side dishes that are all low in carbohydrates. Using these recipes, you'll be able to put together a delicious diet that will be just right for you.

How Do I Begin?

Switching to a low-carbohydrate diet requires more than just swapping meat for pasta, and eggs for your morning bagel. The following tips, suggestions, and advice will help ease the transition from a high- to low-carbohydrate diet.

- **Make every carbohydrate count.** When you eat carbohydrates, reach for complex carbohydrates such as wholegrain breads and pasta, legumes, and nonstarchy fruits and vegetables (see Carb Counts of Fresh Fruits & Vegetables, pages 12 and 13, for carbohydrates, serving sizes, and calories).

- **Pick produce that triggers lower glucose response.** Fruits and vegetables with the lowest glycemic index include apples, apricots, asparagus, broccoli, Brussels sprouts, cauliflower, celery, cherries, cucumber, grapefruit, green beans, lettuce, mushrooms, onions, plums, spinach, strawberries, sweet peppers, tomatoes, and zucchini. Moderate-GI produce includes cantaloupe, grapes, oranges, orange juice, peaches, peas, pineapple, yams, and watermelon. High-GI fruits and vegetables include bananas, beets, carrots, corn, potatoes, and raisins.
- **Read labels.** Food labels are required to show how many grams of carbohydrates are in each serving. By reading labels carefully, you can track how many carbohydrate grams are in all the foods you eat.
- **Skip the soft drinks.** Soda, sports drinks, sweetened juices, and other soft drinks are chockful of low-quality carbohydrates. For example, a can of ginger ale contains 36 grams of carbohydrates, and a serving of sweetened iced tea made from a mix has 19 grams of carbohydrates. What's more, sweetened drinks don't fill you up, according to a study at Purdue University. The study found that people who ate 450 calories per day of jellybeans adjusted their dietary intake during the rest of the day to compensate for the calories from the jellybeans, and their daily caloric intake stayed stable. But when they drank 450 calories' worth of soda each day, their daily caloric intake soared by 17 percent. When you're thirsty, choose diet sodas, sugar-free iced tea, or seltzer water with a splash of lemon.

continued on page 14

Carb Counts of
Fresh Fruits & Vegetables

Fresh Fruit	Serving	Calories	Carb (g)
Apple, with skin	1 medium (5 oz.)	81	21
Apricots	4 (1 oz. each)	68	16
Banana	1 small (6 inch)	93	24
Blueberries	¾ cup	61	15
Cantaloupe	1 cup, cubes	56	13
Cherries, sweet	13	62	15
Cranberries	1 cup	47	12
Figs, large	1 (2½ inch)	48	12
Grapefruit	½ large	51	13
Grapes, seedless	17	60	15
Honeydew melon	1 cup, cubes	59	16
Kiwifruit	1 large (4 oz.)	56	14
Mango	½ cup, sliced	54	14
Nectarine	1 (2½ inch)	67	16
Orange	1 (5 oz.)	62	15
Papaya	1 cup, cubes	55	14
Peach	1 large (6 oz.)	67	17
Pear	½ of a large	62	16
Pineapple	¾ cup	57	14
Plums	2 (2 inch)	73	17
Raspberries	1 cup	60	14
Strawberries, whole	1½ cups	65	15
Tangerines, medium	2 (3 inch)	74	19
Watermelon	1¼ cups, cubes	62	14

Fresh Vegetables (nonstarchy)	Serving	Calories	Carb (g)
Asparagus, cooked	½ cup	22	4
Asparagus, cooked	8 spears	29	5
Beans, snap green, cooked	½ cup	22	5
Bean sprouts, raw	1 cup	31	6
Beets, cooked	½ cup	37	8
Broccoli, cooked	½ cup	22	4
Broccoli, raw	1 cup	25	5
Brussels sprouts, cooked	½ cup	30	7

Fresh Vegetables (nonstarchy)	Serving	Calories	Carb (g)
Cabbage, cooked	½ cup	17	3
Cabbage, raw	1 cup	18	4
Carrot, raw	1 medium (2 oz.)	26	6
Carrot, cooked	½ cup	35	8
Cauliflower, raw	1 cup	25	5
Cauliflower, cooked	½ cup	14	3
Celery, raw	1 cup	19	4
Cucumber, raw	1 cup	14	3
Eggplant, cooked	½ cup	13	3
Greens, cooked			
Collard	½ cup	17	4
Kale	½ cup	21	4
Mustard	½ cup	10	2
Turnip	½ cup	14	3
Lettuce, iceberg	1 cup	7	1
Mushrooms, raw, whole	1 cup	24	4
Mushrooms, cooked	¾ cup	32	6
Okra, cooked	½ cup	25	6
Pea pods, raw	1 cup	61	11
Pea pods, cooked	½ cup	34	6
Romaine	1 cup	8	2
Spinach, raw	1 cup	7	1
Spinach, cooked	½ cup	20	4
Squash, summer, raw	1 cup	25	5
Squash, summer, cooked	½ cup	18	4
Tomato, cooked	½ cup	32	7
Tomato, raw, chopped	1 cup	38	8
Tomato, raw, whole, sliced	1 (2½ inch)	26	6
Turnips, cooked	1 cup cubes	33	8
Zucchini, raw	1 cup	17	4
Zucchini, cooked	1 cup	29	7

Fresh vegetables (starchy)	Serving	Calories	Carb (g)
Corn, sweet, yellow, cooked	½ cup	88	21
Peas, green, cooked	½ cup	67	13
Potato, white, baked	3 oz.	93	22
Potato, white, boiled	½ cup	68	16
Squash, winter	1 cup	82	22
Sweet potato, baked	½ of a medium (4 oz.)	59	14

Source: USDA Nutrient Database for Standard Reference

continued from page 11

- **Think ahead when dining out.** You can eat in restaurants when you're on a low-carbohydrate diet, but you'll succeed best if you choose wisely. First, pick a restaurant whose menu doesn't revolve around bread or pasta—a seafood restaurant is an excellent choice. Second, plan your day's diet around the restaurant meal. If you've got your heart set on a hunk of French bread at dinner, go light on carbohydrates at breakfast and lunch. Third, when you place your order, don't be afraid to ask the waitress to leave off the bun or breading. You're paying for the meal, after all, and it should be served the way you like it.
- **Stock your kitchen with low-carbohydrate foods and snacks.** Fill the pantry and fridge with non-starchy fruits and vegetables, fresh fish and shellfish, lean meats and poultry, dairy products, and low-carbohydrate snack bars.
- **Go nuts about nuts.** A variety of studies have shown that peanuts and other nuts, which are rich in monounsaturated fats, help contribute to weight loss and heart health. What's more, they are rich in magnesium, folate, fiber, copper, vitamin E, and arginine, all of which play an important role in the prevention of heart disease. Smear peanut butter on a sliced apple, sprinkle chopped almonds on a salad or in yogurt, or reach for a handful of nuts instead of a bag of potato chips.
- **Have an oil change.** Select heart-healthy monounsaturated oils such as peanut, olive, and canola oil for cooking and salad dressings.
- **Watch your condiments.** Carbohydrates hide in condiments such as relish and ketchup, which each have 4 grams of carbohydrates per tablespoon, and barbecue sauce, which contains about 8 grams of carbohydrates per tablespoon.
- **Choose lean meats.** If you're switching from a low-fat to a low-carbohydrate diet, you might think you now have license to eat lots of fatty meats. Forget it. Fatty meats are high in saturated fat, which is bad for your heart. Select lean beef, pork, or poultry. Remove any skin and trim visible fat.
- **Fill up on fish.** Seafood is high in protein and contains omega-3 fatty acids, which are polyunsaturated fatty acids that protect against heart attack and are vital to the proper function of brain and nerve cells. Omega-3 fatty acids are particularly abundant in higher-fat, cold-water fish such as mackerel, albacore tuna, salmon, sardines, and lake trout. All seafood, including shellfish and crustaceans such as oysters and shrimp, contain omega-3 fatty acids.
- **Get out and move.** Exercise is a crucial part of any diet. It speeds up metabolism, burns calories, strengthens and tones muscles, increases flexibility, boosts mood, improves circulation, and so much more. Aim for at least 30 minutes of moderate exercise such as walking, biking, or swimming at least five days a week, and more if you can fit it in. Make exercise more enjoyable by working out with friends, giving yourself nonfood rewards when you reach your goals, and trying new sports. Combining moderate exercise with a healthful, low-carbohydrate eating plan will help you lose weight and stay healthy.

Appetizers, Snacks & Beverages

10 g carb

Hot Artichoke Dip

Take this classic to a party and you'll be a hit — it's a tried-and-true favorite. Chopped red sweet pepper gives this version a festive confetti look and a sweet crunch.

1 In a large skillet cook leeks in hot olive oil over medium heat until tender. Place in a 3½- or 4-quart slow cooker. Stir in the artichoke hearts, light mayonnaise, sweet pepper, 1 cup Parmesan cheese, and seasoning.

2 Cover and cook on low-heat setting for 3 to 4 hours until cheese is melted and mixture is heated through.

3 To serve, stir mixture; sprinkle with additional Parmesan cheese. Keep warm on low-heat setting for up to 1 hour. Serve with vegetable dippers.

Nutrition Facts per ¼ cup dip with 1 cup vegetables: 146 cal., 11 g total fat (3 g sat. fat), 14 mg chol., 375 mg sodium, 10 g carbo., 3 g fiber, 4 g pro.

*Note: Do not use regular mayonnaise dressing or cook on high-heat setting or the dip will separate during cooking.

Prep: 20 minutes
Cook: Low 3 to 4 hours
Makes: 5 cups dip
Slow Cooker: 3½- or 4-quart

2 medium leeks, thinly sliced (⅔ cup)
1 tablespoon olive oil
2 14-ounce cans artichoke hearts, drained and coarsely chopped
2 cups light mayonnaise dressing*
1 cup chopped red sweet pepper
1 cup finely shredded Parmesan cheese
1 teaspoon Mediterranean seasoning or lemon-pepper seasoning
Finely shredded Parmesan cheese
Vegetable dippers or toasted whole wheat pita wedges

Picadillo Pita Wedges

Garlic, onion, tomato, and meat are the basic picadillo quartet. This sassy pita dip takes on a new identity with the addition of olives, almonds, and raisins.

1 In a large skillet cook ground beef until brown. Drain off fat. In a 3½- or 4-quart slow cooker stir together the beef, salsa, onion, raisins, olives, vinegar, garlic, cinnamon, and cumin.

2 Cover and cook on low-heat setting for 6 to 8 hours or on high-heat setting for 3 to 4 hours. Stir in the ¼ cup almonds. Sprinkle with additional almonds and serve with toasted pita wedges.

Nutrition Facts per ¼ cup dip with 4 pita wedges: 127 cal., 5 g total fat (1 g sat. fat), 18 mg chol., 257 mg sodium, 13 g carbo., 2 g fiber, 8 g pro.

Prep: 20 minutes
Cook: Low 6 to 8 hours,
    High 3 to 4 hours
Makes: 4 cups dip
Slow Cooker: 3½- or 4-quart

- 1 **pound lean ground beef**
- 1 **16-ounce jar salsa**
- ½ **cup chopped onion (1 medium)**
- ½ **cup raisins**
- ¼ **cup chopped pimiento-stuffed olives**
- 2 **tablespoons red wine vinegar**
- 3 **cloves garlic, minced**
- ½ **teaspoon ground cinnamon**
- ½ **teaspoon ground cumin**
- ¼ **cup toasted slivered almonds**
   Toasted slivered almonds
   Toasted whole wheat pita wedges

10 g
carb

Rio Grande Dip

If you like your snacks on the spicy side, use hot salsa or Monterey Jack cheese with jalapeño peppers.

1 In a large skillet cook the sausage and onion until meat is brown. Drain off fat. In a 3½- or 4-quart slow cooker combine meat mixture, refried black beans, salsa, and undrained chile peppers. Stir in cheese.

2 Cover and cook on low-heat setting for 3 to 4 hours or on high-heat setting for 1½ to 2 hours.

3 Serve immediately or keep covered on low-heat setting for up to 2 hours. Stir just before serving. Serve dip with vegetable dippers.

Nutrition Facts per ¼ cup dip with 1 cup vegetables: 107 cal., 5 g total fat (2 g sat. fat), 13 mg chol., 252 mg sodium, 10 g carbo., 3 g fiber, 6 g pro.

Prep: 15 minutes
Cook: Low 3 to 4 hours,
     High 1½ to 2 hours
Makes: 6 cups dip
Slow Cooker: 3½- or 4-quart

8 ounces bulk Italian sausage
⅓ cup finely chopped onion (1 small)
2 15-ounce cans refried black beans
1½ cups bottled salsa
1 4-ounce can diced green chile
    peppers, undrained
1½ cups shredded Monterey Jack cheese
    (6 ounces)
    Vegetable dippers or toasted whole
    wheat pita wedges

Spicy Sausage and Tomato Dip

Surprise your party guests with their favorite pizza flavors served in a spicy dip. Transfer any leftovers to freezer containers and freeze for up to 3 months. To serve, thaw and reheat in a saucepan.

1 In a large skillet cook sausage, onion, and garlic until meat is brown and onion is tender. Drain fat.

2 In a 3½- or 4-quart slow cooker stir together sausage mixture, tomato sauce, undrained tomatoes, tomato paste, oregano, basil, sugar, and cayenne pepper.

3 Cover and cook on low-heat setting for 5 to 6 hours or on high-heat setting for 2½ to 3 hours. Stir in olives. Serve with vegetable dippers.

Nutrition Facts per ¼ cup dip with 1 cup mixed vegetables: 87 cal., 4 g total fat (2 g sat. fat), 11 mg chol., 275 mg sodium, 8 g carbo., 2 g fiber, 4 g pro.

Prep: 20 minutes
Cook: Low 5 to 6 hours,
 High 2½ to 3 hours
Makes: 7 cups dip
Slow Cooker: 3½- or 4-quart

1 pound bulk Italian sausage
⅔ cup chopped onion
4 cloves garlic, minced
2 15-ounce cans tomato sauce
1 14½-ounce can diced tomatoes,
    undrained
1 6-ounce can tomato paste
4 teaspoons dried oregano, crushed
1 tablespoon dried basil, crushed
2 teaspoons sugar or no-calorie, heat-
    stable, granular sugar substitute
    (Splenda)
¼ teaspoon cayenne pepper
½ cup chopped, pitted ripe olives
    Vegetable dippers or toasted whole
    wheat pita wedges

Supreme Pizza Fondue

Your finicky teens will love this spin on one of their favorite foods. Serve this pizza-flavored fondue for a graduation party or a birthday party.

1 In a large skillet cook the sausage, onion, and garlic until meat is brown. Drain off fat.

2 In a 3½- or 4-quart slow cooker combine spaghetti sauce, mushrooms, pepperoni, and basil. Stir in the sausage mixture.

3 Cover and cook on low-heat setting for 3 hours. If desired, stir in ripe olives and sweet pepper. Cover and cook for 15 minutes more. To serve, spear the dippers with fondue forks and dip into the fondue.

Nutrition Facts per ¼ cup dip with about 1 cup mixed vegetables: 141 cal., 9 g total fat (3 g sat. fat), 15 mg chol., 671 mg sodium, 9 g carbo., 2 g fiber, 6 g pro.

Prep: 20 minutes
Cook: Low 3 hours
Makes: about 5½ cups dip
Slow Cooker: 3½- or 4-quart

4 ounces bulk Italian sausage
⅓ cup finely chopped onion (1 small)
1 clove garlic, minced
1 30-ounce jar meatless spaghetti sauce
1 cup sliced fresh mushrooms
⅔ cup chopped pepperoni or Canadian-style bacon
1 teaspoon dried basil or oregano, crushed
½ cup sliced, pitted ripe olives (optional)
¼ cup chopped green sweet pepper (optional)
    Vegetable dippers, mozzarella or provolone cheese cubes, or whole grain bread cubes

Cheesy Bacon-Horseradish Dip

This dip is for cheese lovers. Cream cheese and cheddar team up with horseradish and bacon for a lively dip that is perfect fare for any party.

1 In a 3½- or 4-quart slow cooker combine cream cheese, cheddar cheese, half-and-half, green onions, horseradish, Worcestershire sauce, garlic, and pepper.

2 Cover and cook on low-heat setting for 4 to 5 hours or on high-heat setting for 2 to 2½ hours, stirring once halfway through cooking. Stir in the bacon. Serve with vegetable dippers, whole wheat pita wedges, or whole grain crackers.

Nutrition Facts per ¼ cup dip with 1 cup mixed vegetables: 245 cal., 21 g total fat (13 g sat. fat), 63 mg chol., 302 mg sodium, 6 g carbo., 1 g fiber, 9 g pro.

Prep: 25 minutes
Cook: Low 4 to 5 hours,
     High 2 to 2½ hours
Makes: 5 cups dip
Slow Cooker: 3½- or 4-quart

3   8-ounce packages cream cheese, softened and cut up
3   cups shredded cheddar cheese (12 ounces)
1   cup half-and-half or light cream
⅓   cup chopped green onions
3   tablespoons prepared horseradish
1   tablespoon Worcestershire sauce
3   cloves garlic, minced
½   teaspoon coarsely ground black pepper
12   slices bacon, crisp-cooked, drained, and finely crumbled (1 cup)
    Vegetable dippers, toasted whole wheat pita wedges, or whole grain crackers

8 g carb

Chipotle Con Queso Dip

Tote this zesty appetizer to a tailgate party or serve it while watching a game on TV. Be sure to whisk before serving to smooth out any lumps.

1 In a 3½- or 4-quart slow cooker combine the cheese spread, undrained tomatoes, chipotle peppers in adobo sauce, and Worcestershire sauce.

2 Cover and cook on low-heat setting for 3 to 3½ hours or on high-heat setting for 1½ to 1¾ hours. Whisk before serving. Serve warm with vegetable dippers. Keep warm on low-heat setting for up to an hour.

Nutrition Facts per 3 tablespoons dip with 1 cup vegetables: 157 cal., 10 g total fat (6 g sat. fat), 31 mg chol., 601 mg sodium, 8 g carbo., 1 g fiber, 9 g pro.

Prep: 10 minutes
Cook: Low 3 to 3½ hours,
High 1½ to 1¾ hours
Makes: 4½ cups dip
Slow Cooker: 3½- or 4-quart

2 pounds packaged process cheese spread, cubed
1 10-ounce can chopped tomatoes and green chile peppers, undrained
1 to 3 chipotle peppers in adobo sauce, chopped
1 tablespoon Worcestershire sauce
   Vegetable dippers or toasted whole wheat pita wedges

Asiago Cheese Dip

8 g carb

Keep this party-perfect dip warm in a slow cooker for up to two hours after cooking. Stir just before serving.

1 In a medium saucepan bring the broth to boiling. Remove from heat and add the dried tomatoes. Cover and let stand for 5 minutes. Drain; discard the liquid. Chop the tomatoes (should have about 1¼ cups).

2 Meanwhile, in a 3½- or 4-quart slow cooker combine the sour cream, mayonnaise, cream cheese, mushrooms, 1 cup green onions, and Asiago cheese. Stir in the chopped tomatoes.

3 Cover and cook on low-heat setting for 3 to 4 hours or on high-heat setting for 1½ to 2 hours. Stir before serving and sprinkle with additional green onion. Keep warm on low-heat setting for 1 to 2 hours. Serve warm with vegetable dippers or pita wedges.

Nutrition Facts per ¼ cup dip with 1 cup vegetables: 212 cal., 19 g total fat (8 g sat. fat), 31 mg chol., 256 mg sodium, 8 g carbo., 2 g fiber, 4 g pro.

Prep: 15 minutes
Cook: Low 3 to 4 hours,
High 1½ to 2 hours
Makes: 7 cups
Slow Cooker: 3½- or 4-quart

1 cup chicken broth or water
4 ounces dried tomatoes (not oil-packed)
4 8-ounce cartons dairy sour cream
1¼ cups mayonnaise
½ of an 8-ounce package cream cheese, cut up
1 cup sliced fresh mushrooms
1 cup thinly sliced green onions (8)
1½ cups shredded Asiago cheese (6 ounces)
Thinly sliced green onion
Vegetable dippers or toasted whole wheat pita wedges

6 g carb

Cheesy Beer-Salsa Dip

Cheese and more cheese—American, Monterey, and cream cheese—makes this a delicious dip. With the addition of salsa and beer, how can this dip not be good?

1 In a 3½- or 4-quart slow cooker combine salsa, cheeses, and beer.

2 Cover and cook on low-heat setting for 3 to 4 hours or on high-heat setting for 1½ to 2 hours.

3 Serve immediately or keep covered on low-heat setting for up to 2 hours. Stir dip just before serving. Serve with vegetable dippers.

Nutrition Facts per ¼ cup dip with 1 cup vegetables: 177 cal., 13 g total fat (8 g sat. fat), 40 mg chol., 485 mg sodium, 6 g carbo., 2 g fiber, 9 g pro.

Prep: 15 minutes
Cook: Low 3 to 4 hours,
High 1½ to 2 hours
Makes: 5½ cups dip
Slow Cooker: 3½- or 4-quart

1 16-ounce jar salsa
4 cups shredded American cheese
   (1 pound)
2 cups shredded Monterey Jack cheese
   (8 ounces)
1 8-ounce package cream cheese,
   cut up
⅔ cup beer or milk
   Vegetable dippers, toasted whole
      whole wheat pita wedges, or whole
      grain crackers

Nacho Cheese Dip

Green chiles, black olives, and cheese make up the best dip for tortilla chips. It's the classic cheese dip everyone loves.

1 Place the undrained tomatoes in a 1½-quart slow cooker; top with the cheese spread, Monterey Jack cheese, cheddar cheese, and cumin.

2 Cover and cook for 3 to 3½ hours* until cheese is melted and mixture is heated through. (Mixture may look slightly curdled.). Stir to combine.

3 To serve, stir in the olives. Serve with vegetable dippers. Keep warm on low for 1 to 2 hours.

Nutrition Facts per ¼ cup dip and 1 cup vegetables: 187 cal., 12 g total fat (7 g sat. fat), 34 mg chol., 586 mg sodium, 11 g carbo., 3 g fiber, 10 g pro.

*Note: Some 1½-quart slow cookers include variable heat settings; others offer only one standard (low) setting. The 1½-quart slow cooker recipes in this book were only tested on the low-heat setting if one was present.

Prep: 10 minutes
Cook: Low 3 to 3½ hours*
Makes: 3 cups dip
Slow Cooker: 1½-quart

1   10-ounce can diced tomatoes and green chiles, undrained
1   8-ounce package process cheese spread, cut into cubes
1   cup shredded Monterey Jack cheese (4 ounces)
1   cup shredded cheddar cheese (4 ounces)
1   teaspoon ground cumin
1   2¼-ounce can sliced pitted ripe olives, drained
    Vegetable dippers or tortilla corn chips

18 g
carb

Ratatouille

Ratatouille (ra-tuh-TOO-ee) is a favorite dish from the French region of Provence. Eggplant, tomatoes, peppers, onions, herbs, and garlic are typically simmered together to create a delicious side dish or an appetizer topper for bread or crackers.

1 In a 3½- or 4-quart slow cooker combine onions, tomato paste, oil, sugar substitute, garlic, dried basil (if using), salt, thyme, and pepper. Add tomatoes, zucchini, and eggplant.

2 Cover and cook on low-heat setting for 7 to 8 hours or on high-heat setting for 3½ to 4 hours. If using, stir in fresh basil. Stir before serving. Serve hot, cold, or at room temperature with bread slices.

Nutrition Facts per ¼ cup spread with 3 bread slices: 99 cal., 2 g total fat (0 g sat. fat), 0 mg chol., 363 mg sodium, 18 g carbo., 2 g fiber, 3 g pro.

Prep: 20 minutes
Cook: Low 7 to 8 hours,
High 3½ to 4 hours
Makes: about 4 cups
(sixteen ¼-cup servings)
Slow Cooker: 3½- or 4-quart

- 1½ cups chopped onions (3 medium)
- 1 6-ounce can tomato paste
- 1 tablespoon olive oil or cooking oil
- 1 tablespoon no-calorie, heat-stable, granular sugar substitute (Splenda)
- 2 cloves garlic, minced
- 1½ teaspoons dried basil, crushed, or 1 tablespoon snipped fresh basil
- 1 teaspoon salt
- 1 teaspoon dried thyme, crushed
- ¼ teaspoon ground black pepper
- 4 medium tomatoes, peeled and coarsely chopped
- 2 medium zucchini, halved lengthwise and sliced
- 1 small eggplant, peeled and cubed (about 3 cups)
- 1 12-ounce loaf baguette-style French bread, cut into ½-inch slices, toasted

Buffalo Wings with Blue Cheese Dip

These wings are saucy, spicy, and delicious. They are great party food, especially when dipped into a cool and creamy dressing.

1 Cut off and discard wing tips. Cut each wing into 2 sections. Place chicken on the unheated rack of a broiler pan. Broil 4 to 5 inches from the heat about 10 minutes or until chicken is brown, turning once. Transfer chicken to a 3½- or 4-quart slow cooker. Combine the chili sauce and hot pepper sauce; pour over chicken wings.

2 Cover and cook on low-heat setting for 4 to 5 hours or on high-heat setting for 2 to 2½ hours. Serve chicken wings warm with Blue Cheese Dip.

Blue Cheese Dip: In a blender container combine one 8-ounce carton dairy sour cream; ½ cup mayonnaise dressing or salad dressing; ½ cup crumbled blue cheese (2 ounces); 1 clove garlic, minced; and 1 tablespoon white vinegar. Cover and blend until smooth. Store dip, covered, in the refrigerator for up to 2 weeks. To serve, transfer dip to a serving bowl. If desired, top dip with additional crumbled blue cheese.

Nutrition Facts per appetizer serving: 192 cal., 14 g total fat (6 g sat. fat), 46 mg chol., 454 mg sodium, 8 g carbo., 2 g fiber, 10 g pro.

Prep: 30 minutes
Cook: Low 4 to 5 hours,
High 2 to 2½ hours
Broil: 10 minutes
Makes: 16 servings
(2 pieces per serving)
Slow Cooker: 3½- or 4-quart

16 chicken wings (about 3 pounds)
1½ cups bottled chili sauce
3 to 4 tablespoons bottled hot pepper sauce
1 recipe Blue Cheese Dip or bottled ranch salad dressing

Thai Chicken Wings with Peanut Sauce

You may have thought these wings could only be enjoyed in a Thai restaurant. The slow cooker makes the hors d'oeuvres a snap to make at home.

1 Place chicken in a 3½- or 4-quart slow cooker. In a small bowl combine salsa, the 2 tablespoons peanut butter, the lime juice, the 2 teaspoons soy sauce, and the ginger. Pour over chicken wings. Toss to coat.

2 Cover and cook on low-heat setting for 5 to 6 hours or on high-heat setting for 2½ to 3 hours.

3 Meanwhile, for the peanut sauce, in a small saucepan use a whisk to combine sugar substitute, the ¼ cup peanut butter, the 3 tablespoons soy sauce, the water, and garlic. Heat over medium-low heat until mixture is smooth, whisking occasionally; set aside (mixture will thicken as it cools).

4 Drain chicken, discard cooking liquid. Return chicken to slow cooker. Gently stir in peanut sauce. Keep warm on low-heat setting for up to 2 hours.

Nutrition Facts per serving: 156 cal., 11 g total fat (3 g sat. fat), 35 mg chol., 376 mg sodium, 3 g carbo., 1 g fiber, 11 g pro.

Prep: 25 minutes
Cook: Low 5 to 6 hours,
　　　High 2½ to 3 hours
Makes: 12 servings
　　　(2 pieces per serving)
Slow Cooker: 3½- or 4-quart

24　chicken wing drummettes (about 2¼ pounds)
½　cup bottled salsa
2　tablespoons creamy peanut butter
1　tablespoon lime juice
2　teaspoons soy sauce
2　teaspoons grated fresh ginger
¼　cup no-calorie, heat-stable, granular sugar substitute (Splenda)
¼　cup creamy peanut butter
3　tablespoons soy sauce
3　tablespoons water
2　cloves garlic, minced

Green Curry Chicken Wings

Add the green curry paste according to your own heat meter. This is a saucy appetizer, so serve with lots of extra napkins.

1 Place onion in a 3½- or 4-quart slow cooker. Use a sharp knife to carefully cut chicken wings into three portions; discard wing tips. Place wing pieces over onions in cooker. Stir together the coconut milk, fish sauce, and curry paste. Pour over chicken wings.

2 Cover and cook on low-heat setting for 5 to 6 hours or on high-heat setting for 2½ to 3 hours. Remove chicken from cooker with a slotted spoon; cover and set aside. Skim fat from cooking liquid.

3 In a medium saucepan stir together the cornstarch and water; stir in cooking liquid. Cook and stir over medium heat until thickened and bubbly. Cook and stir for 2 minutes more. To serve, transfer the chicken to a large serving platter; pour sauce over chicken and sprinkle with basil.

Nutrition Facts per 2-piece serving: 184 cal., 14 g total fat (5 g sat. fat), 47 mg chol., 488 mg sodium, 3 g carbo., 0 g fiber, 12 g pro.

Prep: 20 minutes
Cook: Low 5 to 6 hours,
High 2½ to 3 hours;
plus 10 minutes
Makes: 14 appetizer servings
Slow Cooker: 3½- or 4-quart

⅓ cup finely chopped onion
14 chicken wings (about 3 pounds total)
¾ cup purchased coconut milk
3 tablespoons fish sauce
2 to 3 tablespoons green curry paste
2 tablespoons cornstarch
2 tablespoons cold water
¼ cup shredded fresh basil leaves

13 g
carb

Reuben Spread

They're all here—the intensely-flavored ingredients that make the Reuben sandwich a universal favorite—converted into a party spread to slather on rye bread or crackers.

1 In a 3½- or 4-quart slow cooker combine corned beef, sauerkraut, salad dressing, cheeses, horseradish, and caraway seeds.

2 Cover and cook on low-heat setting for 2½ to 3 hours.

3 Stir just before serving and keep warm on low-heat setting for up to 2 hours. Serve with toasted bread slices.

Nutrition Facts per ¼ cup spread with 2 slices cocktail bread: 210 cal., 14 g total fat (5 g sat. fat), 38 mg chol., 651 mg sodium, 13 g carbo., 2 g fiber, 9 g pro.

Prep: 15 minutes
Cook: Low 2½ to 3 hours
Makes: 5 cups
Slow Cooker: 3½- or 4-quart

- 1 pound cooked corned beef, finely chopped
- 1 16-ounce can sauerkraut, rinsed, drained, and snipped
- 1 cup bottled Thousand Island salad dressing
- 1½ cups shredded Swiss cheese (6 ounces)
- 1 3-ounce package cream cheese, cut up
- 1 tablespoon prepared horseradish
- 1 teaspoon caraway seeds
  Toasted cocktail rye bread slices or rye crackers

Zesty Beef-Filled Tacos

Vegetables, spices, and sweet mango contribute big taste to these steak-filled, appetizer-size tacos.

1 Place onion and carrot in a 3½- or 4-quart slow cooker. Place beef on top of vegetables. Sprinkle with ¼ cup cilantro, the crushed red pepper, and salt; add the undrained tomatoes and water.

2 Cover and cook on low-heat setting for 7 to 9 hours or on high-heat setting for 4 to 5 hours. Remove meat from cooker. Use 2 forks to shred meat. If desired, cut meat to make shorter shreds. Drain vegetable mixture well; discard the liquid. Transfer vegetable mixture to a food processor bowl or blender container. Process or blend with several on/off turns until chopped.

3 Return meat and chopped vegetable mixture to slow cooker. If using low-heat setting, turn to high-heat setting. Cover and cook for 15 to 30 minutes or until heated through. Spoon mixture into miniature taco shells. Top with mango and desired toppings.

Nutrition Facts per appetizer: 53 cal., 2 g total fat (1 g sat. fat), 6 mg chol., 145 mg sodium, 5 g carbo., 1 g fiber, 4 g pro.

Prep: 25 minutes
Cook: Low 7 to 9 hours,
        High 4 to 5 hours;
            plus 15 minutes
Makes: 24 tacos
Slow Cooker: 3½- or 4-quart

- 1 medium onion, cut into wedges
- 1 medium carrot, quartered
- 12 ounces beef flank steak
- ¼ cup snipped fresh cilantro
- ½ to 1 teaspoon crushed red pepper
- ½ teaspoon salt
- 1 14½-ounce can diced tomatoes with roasted garlic, undrained
- ½ cup water
- 24 miniature taco shells
- 1 cup finely chopped, peeled mango (1 medium)
  Toppings (snipped fresh cilantro, sliced green onion, chopped tomato, and/or finely shredded lettuce)

Italian Cocktail Meatballs

These party appetizers make your life easy. Four ingredients and four hours—that's all you need.

1 Place meatballs and roasted sweet peppers in a 1½-quart slow cooker. Sprinkle with crushed red pepper. Pour sauce over mixture in cooker.

2 Cover and cook for 4 to 5 hours.* Skim fat from cocktail sauce. Stir gently before serving.

Nutrition Facts per serving: 99 cal., 8 g total fat (3 g sat. fat), 10 mg chol., 322 mg sodium, 4 g carbo., 1 g fiber, 4 g pro.

*Note: Some 1½-quart slow cookers include variable heat settings; others offer only one standard (low) setting. The 1½-quart slow cooker recipes in this book were only tested on the low-heat setting if one was present.

Prep: 15 minutes
Cook: Low 4 to 5 hours*
Makes: 16 appetizer servings
Slow Cooker: 1½-quart

1 16-ounce package frozen cooked meatballs (32), thawed
½ cup bottled roasted red and/or yellow sweet peppers, cut into 1-inch pieces
⅛ teaspoon crushed red pepper
1½ cups bottled onion-garlic pasta sauce

Hot and Sweet Cocktail Wieners

You'll love the combination of spicy and sweet in this updated version of cocktail wieners. Orange marmalade, chipotle peppers, and tomato sauce make up the sauce. Use cocktail wieners or small, smoked sausage links—or both.

1 In a 1½-quart slow cooker combine cocktail wieners, tomato sauce, orange marmalade spread, and chipotle pepper.

2 Cover and cook for 4 hours. Serve wieners with wooden toothpicks.

Prep: 5 minutes
Cook: Low 4 hours*
Makes: 16 servings
Slow Cooker: 1½-quart

1   16-ounce package cocktail wieners or small, cooked smoked sausage links
1   8-ounce can tomato sauce
¼   cup low-sugar orange marmalade or apricot spread
1   to 2 tablespoons chipotle peppers in adobo sauce, chopped

Nutrition Facts per serving (about 3 wieners): 105 cal., 8 g total fat (3 g sat. fat), 20 mg chol., 343 mg sodium, 3 g carbo., 0 g fiber, 3 g pro.

*Note: Some 1½-quart slow cookers include variable heat settings; others offer only one standard (low) setting. The 1½-quart slow cooker recipes in this book were only tested on the low-heat setting if one was present.

4 g
carb

Asian-Spiced Pecans

Set out bowls of these spirited nuts as part of a party buffet, sprinkle them on a salad, or serve them alongside crunchy pear slices for a light, healthy dessert.

1 Place toasted pecans in a 3½- or 4-quart slow cooker. In a small bowl combine the remaining ingredients. Pour over nuts and stir to coat.

2 Cover and cook on low-heat setting for 2 hours. Stir the nut mixture. Spread in a single layer on waxed paper or foil to cool. (Nuts will appear soft after cooking, but will crisp upon cooling.) Store in a tightly covered container.

Nutrition Facts per ¼ cup: 225 cal., 23 g total fat (4 g sat. fat), 8 mg chol., 146 mg sodium, 4 g carbo., 3 g fiber, 3 g pro.

Prep: 10 minutes
Cook: Low 2 hours
Cool: 1 hour
Makes: 4 cups
Slow Cooker: 3½- or 4-quart

- 1 pound pecan halves, toasted (4 cups)
- ¼ cup butter or margarine, melted
- 2 tablespoons soy sauce
- 1 teaspoon five-spice powder
- ½ teaspoon garlic powder
- ½ teaspoon ground ginger
- ¼ teaspoon cayenne pepper

Sweet-Spiced Nuts

Place toasted nuts, butter, and seasonings in the slow cooker for a couple of hours and you'll have glazed nuts.

1 Place the toasted nuts in a 3½- or 4-quart slow cooker. In a small bowl combine the butter, sugar substitute, apple pie spice, and salt. Pour over nuts and stir to coat.

2 Cover and cook on low-heat setting for 2 hours. Stir nut mixture. Spread in a single layer on waxed paper or foil to cool. (Nuts will appear soft after cooking, but will crisp upon cooling.) Store in a tightly covered container.

Nutrition Facts per serving: 234 cal., 21 g total fat (3 g sat. fat), 6 mg chol., 107 mg sodium, 8 g carbo., 4 g fiber, 8 g pro.

Prep: 20 minutes
Cook: Low 2 hours
Cool: 1 hour
Makes: 4 cups
Slow Cooker: 3½- or 4-quart

- 4 cups whole blanched almonds or walnuts, toasted
- 3 tablespoons butter or margarine, melted
- ⅓ cup no-calorie, heat-stable, granular sugar substitute (Splenda)
- 2 teaspoons apple pie spice or ground cinnamon
- ½ teaspoon salt

13 g
carb

Hot Cocoa

Make a large batch of hot chocolate for the troops. This tasty version is made with heat-stable sugar substitute, reducing your carbohydrate intake.

1 In a 3½- to 5-quart slow cooker combine sugar substitute and cocoa powder. Add milk; use a whisk or rotary beater to combine well. (Cocoa powder may not dissolve completely until the mixture is heated.)

2 Cover and cook on low-heat setting for 3 to 4 hours or on high-heat setting for 1½ to 2 hours.

3 Just before serving, add vanilla. Carefully beat milk mixture with a whisk or rotary beater until well mixed and frothy. Ladle cocoa into mugs.

Spicy Cocoa: Prepare as directed above, except add 1 teaspoon ground cinnamon and ⅛ teaspoon ground nutmeg with the cocoa powder.

Mocha Cocoa: Prepare as directed above, except add 3 tablespoons instant coffee crystals with the cocoa powder.

Nutrition Facts per serving of all versions: 126 cal., 4 g total fat (2 g sat. fat), 15 mg chol., 99 mg sodium, 13 g carbo., 0 g fiber, 8 g pro.

Prep: 10 minutes
Cook: Low 3 to 4 hours,
　　　High 1½ to 2 hours
Makes: 10 (6-ounce) servings
Slow Cooker: 3½- to 5-quart

¾　cup no-calorie, heat-stable, granular
　　sugar substitute (Splenda)
½　cup unsweetened cocoa powder
8　cups milk
1　tablespoon vanilla

Spicy Vegetable Sipper

When it's cold and damp outside, greet guests with the enticing aroma of a spiced cocktail simmering in a slow cooker. On low-heat setting, the hot beverage will stay sipping temperature a couple of hours so guests can help themselves to refills.

1 In a 3½- or 4-quart slow cooker combine vegetable juice, halved celery stalk, sugar substitute, lemon juice, horseradish, Worcestershire sauce, and hot pepper sauce.

2 Cover and cook on low-heat setting for 4 to 5 hours or on high-heat setting for 2 to 2½ hours. Discard celery. Ladle beverage into cups. If desired, garnish each serving with a celery stick. Keep on low for up to 1 to 2 hours.

Nutrition Facts per serving: 34 cal., 0 g total fat (0 g sat. fat), 0 mg chol., 453 mg sodium, 8 g carbo., 1 g fiber, 1 g pro.

Prep: 10 minutes
Cook: Low 4 to 5 hours,
      High 2 to 2½ hours
Makes: 8 (6-ounce) servings
Slow Cooker: 3½- or 4-quart

- 1   46-ounce can vegetable juice
- 1   stalk celery, halved crosswise
- 2   tablespoons no-calorie, heat-stable, granular sugar substitute (Splenda)
- 2   tablespoons lemon juice
- 1½   teaspoons prepared horseradish
- 1   teaspoon Worcestershire sauce
- ½   teaspoon bottled hot pepper sauce
-      Celery sticks (optional)

20 g
carb

Cranberry-Apple Cider

Use processed cider from the grocery shelf; unprocessed cider from the refrigerated section will separate and appear curdled when heated.

1 For spice bag, cut a 6- or 8-inch square from a double thickness of 100-percent-cotton cheesecloth. Place cinnamon and allspice in center of cheesecloth square. Bring corners of cheesecloth together and tie with a clean cotton string.

2 In a 3½- to 4½-quart slow cooker combine apple cider, cranberry juice, and sugar substitute. Add spice bag to cider mixture in cooker.

3 Cover and cook on low-heat setting for 5 to 7 hours or on high-heat setting for 2½ to 3½ hours. Discard the spice bag. Ladle cider into cups. If desired, float a lemon slice in each cup.

Nutrition Facts per serving: 81 cal., 0 g total fat (0 g sat. fat), 0 mg chol., 22 mg sodium, 20 g carbo., 0 g fiber, 0 g pro.

*Note: To break cinnamon stick, place in a heavy plastic bag and gently pound with a meat mallet.

Prep: 10 minutes
Cook: Low 5 to 7 hours,
     High 2½ to 3½ hours
Makes: 8 (8-ounce) servings
Slow Cooker: 3½- to 4½-quart

6 inches stick cinnamon, broken*
1 teaspoon whole allspice
4 cups apple cider or apple juice
4 cups low-calorie cranberry juice
   cocktail (sweetened with Splenda)
¼ cup no-calorie, heat-stable, granular
   sugar substitute (Splenda)
   Lemon slices (optional)

Mulled Cranberry-Raspberry Juice

With a libation like this, your guests may not want to leave the party. It's a great starter for a dinner, a brunch, or a simple evening of appetizers and good cheer.

1 Remove the orange portion of the orange peel using a vegetable peeler. Cut peel into strips. Squeeze juice from orange; discard seeds and pulp. In a 3½- to 5-quart slow cooker combine orange juice, cranberry-raspberry juice, and sugar substitute.

2 For spice bag, cut a 6- or 8-inch square from a double thickness of 100-percent-cotton cheesecloth. Place the orange peel, cinnamon, star anise, and whole cloves in center of cheesecloth square. Bring corners of cheesecloth together and tie with a clean cotton string. Add to slow cooker.

3 Cover and cook on low-heat setting for 5 to 6 hours or on high-heat setting for 2½ to 3 hours. To serve, discard spice bag. Ladle juice into cups. If desired, garnish with additional orange peel.

Nutrition Facts per serving: 38 cal., 0 g total fat (0 g sat. fat), 0 mg chol., 29 mg sodium, 9 g carbo., 0 g fiber, 0 g pro.

*Note: To break cinnamon stick, place in a heavy plastic bag and gently pound with a meat mallet.

Prep: 15 minutes
Cook: Low 5 to 6 hours,
    High 2 ½ to 3 hours
Makes: 10 (6-ounce) servings
Slow Cooker: 3½- to 5-quart

1 small orange
8 cups low-calorie cranberry-raspberry juice cocktail
¼ cup no-calorie, heat-stable, granular sugar substitute (Splenda)
6 inches stick cinnamon, broken*
3 star anise
1 teaspoon whole cloves
    Orange peel strips (optional)

14 g
carb

Spiced Fruit Tea

Your choice of dried fruit flavors this spiced brew. It will satisfy snow bunnies on a wintry day.

1 For spice bag, cut a 6- or 8-inch square from a double thickness of 100-percent-cotton cheesecloth. Place cinnamon and ginger in center of cheesecloth square. Bring corners of cheesecloth together and tie with clean cotton string.

2 In a 3½- to 4½-quart slow cooker combine the tea and juice. Add dried fruit and spice bag to the tea mixture in slow cooker.

3 Cover and cook on low-heat setting for 4 to 6 hours or on high-heat setting for 2 to 3 hours. Discard spice bag and dried fruit. Ladle tea into cups. Float an orange slice in each cup. If desired, sweeten to taste.

Nutrition Facts per serving: 56 cal., 0 g total fat (0 g sat. fat), 0 mg chol., 14 mg sodium, 14 g carbo., 0 g fiber, 0 g pro.

*Note: To break the cinnamon stick, place in a heavy plastic bag and gently pound stick with a meat mallet.

Prep: 15 minutes
Cook: Low 4 to 6 hours,
High 2 to 3 hours
Makes: 8 (6-ounce) servings
Slow Cooker: 3½- to 4½-quart

6 inches stick cinnamon, broken*
1 tablespoon crystallized ginger, chopped
4 cups brewed black tea
4 cups orange-peach-mango juice or orange juice
1 cup dried fruit, such as dried peaches, apricots, and/or pears
Orange slices

Soups & Stews

Beef and Red Bean Chili

Chipotle in adobo is doubly delicious. The smoky flavor of the dried jalapeño is a direct hit of heat, while the adobo sauce is a slow burn. Together, they flavor this chili with a richness that can only be developed during slow cooking.

1 Rinse the beans. Place the beans in a large saucepan or Dutch oven. Add enough water to cover by 2 inches. Bring to boiling; reduce heat. Simmer, uncovered, for 10 minutes. Remove from heat. Cover; let stand for 1 hour.

2 Meanwhile, in a large skillet cook half of the beef and the onion in hot oil over medium-high heat until meat is light brown. Transfer to a 3½- or 4-quart slow cooker. Repeat with remaining beef. Add the broth, chipotle peppers and adobo sauce, oregano, cumin, salt, undrained tomatoes, and tomato sauce to the cooker; stir to combine. Drain and rinse the beans and stir into cooker.

3 Cover and cook on low-heat setting for 10 to 12 hours or on high-heat setting for 5 to 6 hours. Spoon into mugs or bowls. Top with cilantro and sweet pepper.

Nutrition Facts per serving: 276 cal., 6 g total fat (2 g sat. fat), 67 mg chol., 873 mg sodium, 22 g carbo., 8 g fiber, 31 g pro.

Prep: 20 minutes
Stand: 1 hour
Cook: Low 10 to 12 **hours,**
     High 5 to 6 **hours**
Makes: 8 **servings**
Slow Cooker: 3½- or 4-**quart**

1   **cup dry red beans or dry kidney beans**
1   **tablespoon olive oil**
2   **pounds boneless beef chuck roast, cut into 1-inch cubes**
1   **cup coarsely chopped onion (1 large)**
1   **14-ounce can beef broth**
1   **or 2 chipotle peppers in adobo sauce, finely chopped, plus 2 teaspoons adobo sauce**
2   **teaspoons dried oregano, crushed**
1   **teaspoon ground cumin**
½   **teaspoon salt**
1   **14½-ounce can diced tomatoes with mild chiles, undrained**
1   **15-ounce can tomato sauce**
¼   **cup snipped fresh cilantro**
1   **medium red sweet pepper, chopped**

Hearty Beef Chili

Serve this meat-filled chili for a fall open house. Offer several toppers, such as black olives, tortilla chips, or sour cream, so guests can personalize their chili.

1 In a 6-quart slow cooker combine both cans of undrained tomatoes, vegetable juice, chili powder, cumin, oregano, and garlic. Stir in the meat, onions, celery, and sweet pepper.

2 Cover and cook on low-heat setting for 8 to 10 hours or on high-heat setting for 4 to 5 hours.

3 If using low-heat setting, turn to high-heat setting. Stir in the beans. Cover and cook 15 minutes more. Spoon into bowls. If desired, serve with toppers.

Nutrition Facts per serving: 224 cal., 6 g total fat (2 g sat. fat), 49 mg chol., 807 mg sodium, 24 g carbo., 6 g fiber, 24 g pro.

Prep: 20 minutes
Cook: Low 8 to 10 hours,
High 4 to 5 hours;
plus 15 minutes
Makes: 10 servings
Slow Cooker: 6-quart

1   28-ounce can diced tomatoes, undrained
1   10-ounce can chopped tomatoes and green chile peppers, undrained
2   cups vegetable juice or tomato juice
1   to 2 tablespoons chili powder
1   teaspoon ground cumin
1   teaspoon dried oregano, crushed
3   cloves garlic, minced
1½ pounds beef or pork stew meat, cut into 1-inch cubes
2   cups chopped onions (2 large)
1½ cups chopped celery (3 stalks)
1   cup chopped green sweet pepper (1 large)
2   15-ounce cans black beans, kidney beans, and/or garbanzo beans (chickpeas), rinsed and drained
    Toppers such as shredded cheddar cheese, dairy sour cream, snipped fresh cilantro, and/or sliced, pitted ripe olives (optional)

Texas Chili

Red alert! In addition to pure heat, the most incendiary of the chile options also offers well-blended taste.

1 In a 4- to 6-quart slow cooker combine meat, onion, garlic, the 3 dried peppers, cumin, red pepper, undrained tomatoes, beans, broth, and oregano.

2 Cover and cook on low-heat setting for 8 to 10 hours or on high-heat setting for 4 to 5 hours. Serve in bowls. If desired, top with sliced chile peppers.

Nutrition Facts per serving: 318 cal., 7 g total fat (2 g sat. fat), 57 mg chol., 717 mg sodium, 29 g carbo., 8 g fiber, 36 g pro.

Prep: 20 minutes
Cook: Low 8 to 10 hours,
　　　High 4 to 5 hours
Makes: 8 servings
Slow Cooker: 4- to 6-quart

2½　pounds beef round steak, cut into
　　　½-inch cubes
1　cup chopped onion (1 large)
4　cloves garlic, minced
3　dried ancho or Anaheim chile peppers,
　　　seeded and crumbled
2　teaspoons ground cumin
1　to 1½ teaspoons crushed red pepper
2　14½-ounce cans diced tomatoes,
　　　undrained
2　15-ounce cans pinto beans or red
　　　kidney beans, rinsed and drained
1　14-ounce can beef broth
½　teaspoon dried oregano, crushed
　　　Sliced fresh or pickled chile peppers
　　　(optional)

Southwest Chili

If you have a small family and have leftovers, enjoy a second round of chili spooned over baked potatoes or make chili dogs with your favorite frankfurters.

1 In a very large skillet cook ground beef, onion, sweet pepper, and garlic until meat is brown. Drain off fat. Transfer to a 4½- to 6-quart slow cooker. Stir together the water and tomato paste. Add to slow cooker along with undrained tomatoes, mustard, chili powder, black pepper, salt, cayenne pepper, cumin, and beans. Stir to combine.

2 Cover and cook on low-heat setting for 8 to 10 hours or on high-heat setting for 4 to 5 hours.

Nutrition Facts per serving: 414 cal., 18 g total fat (7 g sat. fat), 75 mg chol., 772 mg sodium, 36 g carbo., 9 g fiber, 32 g pro.

Prep: 20 minutes
Cook: Low 8 to 10 **hours,**
      High 4 to 5 **hours**
Makes: 8 **servings**
Slow Cooker: 4½- to 6-quart

- 2 pounds lean ground beef
- 2 cups chopped onion (2 large)
- ½ cup chopped green or red sweet peppers
- 6 cloves garlic, minced
- 3½ cups water
- 1 12-ounce can tomato paste
- 1 14½-ounce can diced tomatoes, undrained
- 1 tablespoon prepared mustard
- 1 teaspoon chili powder
- 1 teaspoon black pepper
- ½ teaspoon salt
- ½ to 1 teaspoon cayenne pepper
- ½ teaspoon ground cumin
- 1 15-ounce can dark red kidney beans, rinsed and drained
- 1 15-ounce can Great Northern beans, rinsed and drained

28 g
carb

Chili with Refried Beans

This warming chili really is full of beans—refried and chili beans! Top it with a spoonful of sour cream to cool the heat.

1 In a large skillet cook beef and onion until meat is brown and onion is tender, stirring occasionally and leaving a few large pieces of beef. Drain off fat.

2 In a 5- to 6-quart slow cooker place the beef mixture, chili beans with gravy, salsa, refried beans, beer, chili powder, and cumin.

3 Cover and cook on low-heat setting for 6 to 8 hours or on high-heat setting for 3 to 4 hours. Just before serving, stir lime juice into chili. Ladle chili into bowls. If desired, garnish with sour cream.

Nutrition Facts per serving: 339 cal., 12 g total fat (4 g sat. fat), 57 mg chol., 856 mg sodium, 28 g carbo., 8 g fiber, 25 g pro.

Prep: 20 minutes
Cook: Low 6 to 8 hours,
       High 3 to 4 hours
Makes: 10 servings
Slow Cooker: 5- to 6-quart

2 pounds lean ground beef
1 cup chopped onion (1 large)
2 15¾-ounce cans chili beans with
      chili gravy
1 16-ounce jar thick and chunky salsa
1 16-ounce can refried beans
1 12-ounce can beer or one 14-ounce
      can beef broth
2 tablespoons chili powder
1 tablespoon ground cumin
2 tablespoons lime juice
   Dairy sour cream (optional)

Fireside Beef Stew

This is the kind of stew that makes you want to stay inside and curl up next to the fireplace. Chunks of beef, potatoes, squash, and green beans make this a hearty, yet healthful stew.

1 Place flour in a plastic bag. Add meat pieces, a few at time, shaking to coat. In a large skillet brown meat in hot oil; drain off fat. In a 3½- to 4½-quart slow cooker combine meat, potatoes, squash, onions, and garlic. In a large bowl combine the broth, vegetable juice, Worcestershire sauce, lemon juice, paprika, pepper, and allspice. Pour over meat.

2 Cover and cook on low-heat setting for 10 to 12 hours or on high-heat setting for 5 to 6 hours.

3 If using low-heat setting, turn to high-heat setting. Add green beans to slow cooker. Cover and cook for 15 minutes more or until beans are crisp-tender.

Nutrition Facts per serving: 260 cal., 8 g total fat (2 g sat. fat), 45 mg chol., 460 mg sodium, 28 g carbo., 4 g fiber, 21 g pro.

Prep: 25 minutes
Cook: Low 10 to 12 hours,
High 5 to 6 hours;
plus 15 minutes
Makes: 6 servings
Slow Cooker: 3½- to 4½-quart

2   tablespoons all-purpose flour
1   pound boneless beef chuck roast, cut
      into 1-inch pieces
2   tablespoons cooking oil
1   pound tiny new potatoes, quartered
1   pound butternut squash, peeled,
      seeded, and cut into 1-inch pieces
      (about 2½ cups)
2   small onions, cut in wedges
2   cloves garlic, minced
1   14-ounce can beef broth
1   cup vegetable juice
2   tablespoons Worcestershire sauce
1   tablespoon lemon juice
½   teaspoon paprika
¼   teaspoon black pepper
⅛   teaspoon ground allspice
1   9-ounce package frozen Italian-style
      green beans or 2 cups frozen peas

Beef Stew with a Kick

When jalapeño pinto beans are unavailable, add one finely chopped jalapeño chile pepper—seeded if you want less heat.

1 In a 4- to 6-quart slow cooker combine undrained tomatoes, broth, tomato paste, chili powder, Italian seasoning, crushed red pepper, cloves, allspice, and cinnamon. Add meat, onions, and beans.

2 Cover and cook on low-heat setting for 10 to 12 hours or on high-heat setting for 5 to 6 hours.

3 If using low-heat setting, turn to high-heat setting. Add zucchini and sweet pepper. Cover and cook for 30 minutes.

Nutrition Facts per serving: 272 cal., 5 g total fat (2 g sat. fat), 48 mg chol., 1,201 mg sodium, 34 g carbo., 8 g fiber, 25 g pro.

Prep: 20 minutes
Cook: Low 10 to 12 hours,
High 5 to 6 hours;
plus 30 minutes
Makes: 6 servings
Slow Cooker: 4- to 6-quart

2 14½-ounce cans Mexican-style stewed tomatoes, undrained
3½ cups beef broth
1 6-ounce can tomato paste
4 teaspoons chili powder
1 tablespoon dried Italian seasoning, crushed
¼ teaspoon crushed red pepper
⅛ teaspoon ground cloves
⅛ teaspoon ground allspice
⅛ teaspoon ground cinnamon
1 pound boneless beef chuck roast, cut into 1-inch cubes
1½ cups coarsely chopped onions
1 15-ounce can pinto beans or jalapeño pinto beans, rinsed and drained
1 medium zucchini, halved lengthwise and cut into ½-inch pieces
1 medium yellow or green sweet pepper, cut into 1-inch pieces

34 g carb

Salsa Verde Beef Stew

Purchased salsa adds to the heat and spice in this beef stew. It's a spicy twist on a classic favorite.

1 In a large skillet brown half of the meat at a time in hot oil over medium-high heat. Drain off fat.

2 In a 3½- to 5-quart slow cooker combine meat, potatoes, onion, sweet pepper, undrained tomatoes, beans, salsa, garlic, and cumin.

3 Cover and cook on low-heat setting for 8 to 9 hours or on high-heat setting for 5 to 6 hours.

Nutrition Facts per serving: 325 cal., 7 g total fat (2 g sat. fat), 67 mg chol., 638 mg sodium, 34 g carbo., 6 g fiber, 32 g pro.

Prep: 30 minutes
Cook: Low 8 to 9 hours,
     High 5 to 6 hours
Makes: 6 main-dish servings
Slow Cooker: 3½- to 5-quart

1½ pounds boneless beef chuck pot
     roast, cut into 1-inch cubes
1   tablespoon cooking oil
4   medium unpeeled potatoes, cut into
     1-inch pieces
1   cup coarsely chopped onion (1 large)
1   green sweet pepper, cut into
     ½-inch pieces
1   14½-ounce can Mexican-style stewed
     tomatoes, undrained
1   15- or 16-ounce can pinto beans,
     rinsed and drained
1   cup bottled mild or medium
     green salsa
2   cloves garlic, minced
1   teaspoon ground cumin

42 g
carb

New Mexico Beef Stew

Chipotle peppers are dried, smoked jalapeño peppers, so they pack considerable heat. Canned in piquant adobo sauce, they're convenient for seasoning stews. You'll find them in the ethnic foods aisle of supermarkets or in Hispanic food markets.

1 In a 4- to 5½-quart slow cooker place corn, garbanzo beans, celery root, onion, garlic, and chipotle peppers. Add meat. Sprinkle with salt, black pepper, and thyme. Pour undrained tomatoes over meat.

2 Cover and cook on low-heat setting for 12 to 14 hours or on high-heat setting for 6 to 7 hours. Stir before serving. Season to taste.

Nutrition Facts per serving: 367 cal., 8 g total fat (2 g sat. fat), 54 mg chol., 1,078 mg sodium, 42 g carbo., 7 g fiber, 33 g pro.

Prep: 30 minutes
Cook: Low 12 to 14 hours,
    High 6 to 7 hours
Makes: 6 servings
Slow Cooker: 4- to 5½-quart

- 2 cups fresh corn kernels or one 10-ounce package frozen whole kernel corn, thawed
- 1 15-ounce can garbanzo beans (chickpeas), rinsed and drained
- 2 cups chopped, peeled celery root or 1 cup sliced celery
- 1 cup chopped onion (1 large)
- 3 cloves garlic, minced
- 2 to 3 canned chipotle peppers in adobo sauce, chopped
- 1½ pounds boneless beef chuck roast, cut into ¾-inch pieces
- 1 teaspoon salt
- ½ teaspoon black pepper
- 1 teaspoon dried thyme, crushed
- 1 28-ounce can whole tomatoes, cut up and undrained

Provençal Beef Stew

Perfect for a cozy dinner with friends, all this stew needs to round out the meal are some cheese, olives, and a hearty red wine to quaff.

1 Peel a strip from around the center of each potato. In a 4-quart slow cooker combine potatoes, carrots, shallots, and olives. Top with meat. In a small bowl combine beef broth, garlic, tapioca, herbes de Provence, salt, and pepper. Pour over meat.

2 Cover and cook on low-heat setting for 10 to 12 hours or on high-heat setting for 4 to 5 hours. Stir in wine during last 30 minutes of cooking.

3 If desired, sprinkle each serving with parsley and capers.

Nutrition Facts per serving: 198 cal., 5 g total fat (2 g sat. fat), 54 mg chol., 308 mg sodium, 16 g carbo., 3 g fiber, 20 g pro.

Prep: 20 minutes
Cook: Low 10 to 12 hours,
    High 4 to 5 hours
Makes: 6 servings
Slow Cooker: 4-quart

8   small tiny new potatoes
1   pound small carrots with tops, peeled
    and trimmed, or one 16-ounce
    package peeled baby carrots
1   cup coarsely chopped shallots
    or onion
½   cup pitted green or ripe olives
1½ pounds boneless beef chuck roast, cut
    into 2-inch pieces
1   cup beef broth
4   to 6 cloves garlic, minced
1   tablespoon quick-cooking tapioca
1   teaspoon dried herbes de Provence,
    crushed
¼   teaspoon salt
¼   teaspoon cracked black pepper
¼   cup dry red wine
    Snipped fresh parsley (optional)
    Capers (optional)

Beef and Borscht Stew

When peeling fresh beets, wear latex gloves to prevent your hands from being stained. Don't forget to pass the sour cream, a creamy note to this traditional Russian dish.

1 In a large skillet brown beef, half at a time, in hot oil. Drain off fat.

2 Meanwhile, in a 4- to 5-quart slow cooker combine beets, tomatoes, potatoes, carrots, onion, and garlic. Add meat. In a large bowl combine broth, tomato paste, vinegar, brown sugar (if desired), salt, dill, pepper, and bay leaf. Add to cooker.

3 Cover and cook on low-heat setting for 8 to 10 hours or on high-heat setting for 4 to 4½ hours.

4 If using low-heat setting, turn to high-heat setting. Stir in cabbage. Cover and cook 30 minutes more. Discard bay leaf. Ladle into bowls. If desired, garnish each serving with sour cream.

Nutrition Facts per serving: 260 cal., 6 g total fat (2 g sat. fat), 45 mg chol., 46 mg sodium, 30 g carbo., 5 g fiber, 23 g pro.

Prep: 40 minutes
Cook: Low 8 to 10 hours,
High 4 to 4½ hours;
plus 30 minutes
Makes: 6 to 8 servings
Slow Cooker: 4- to 5-quart

1   pound beef stew meat, cut into
      ¾-inch pieces
1   tablespoon cooking oil
4   medium beets, peeled and cut into
      ½-inch pieces, or one 16-ounce
      can diced beets, drained
2   medium tomatoes, coarsely chopped
2   medium potatoes, peeled and cut into
      ½-inch pieces
2   medium carrots, shredded
½   cup chopped onion (1 medium)
3   cloves garlic, minced
4   cups beef broth
1   6-ounce can tomato paste
2   tablespoons red wine vinegar
1   tablespoon brown sugar (optional)
1   teaspoon salt
½   teaspoon dried dill
¼   teaspoon black pepper
1   bay leaf
3   cups shredded cabbage
      Dairy sour cream or plain yogurt
      (optional)

Spiced Beef Stew with Jerusalem Artichokes

Look for Jerusalem artichokes, also called sunchokes, from fall through winter in the supermarket's produce section. These tubers resemble fresh ginger but are a variety of sunflower, not artichoke. The crunchy white flesh tastes nutty and sweet.

1 In a large skillet brown meat, half at a time, in hot oil. Drain off fat.

2 For spice bag, cut a 6- or 8-inch square from a double-thickness of 100-percent-cotton cheesecloth. Place allspice, dill seeds, and bay leaf in the center of the cheesecloth square. Bring up the corners and tie together with clean cotton string. Set aside.

3 In a bowl stir together undrained tomatoes, tomato sauce, vinegar, garlic, celery salt, and pepper.

4 In a 3½- or 4-quart slow cooker place Jerusalem artichokes, onions, and mushrooms. Add meat and spice bag. Pour tomato mixture over all.

5 Cover and cook on low-heat setting for 9 to 10 hours or on high-heat setting for 4 to 5 hours. Discard spice bag.

Nutrition Facts per serving: 296 cal., 12 g total fat (3 g sat. fat), 60 mg chol., 574 mg sodium, 23 g carbo., 3 g fiber, 26 g pro.

Prep: 30 minutes
Cook: Low 9 to 10 hours,
High 4 to 5 hours
Makes: 5 servings
Slow Cooker: 3½- or 4-quart

1¼ pounds boneless beef chuck steak, cut into ¾-inch cubes
1 tablespoon olive oil or cooking oil
8 whole allspice
½ teaspoon dill seeds
1 bay leaf
1 14½-ounce can diced tomatoes, undrained
1 8-ounce can tomato sauce
2 tablespoons cider vinegar
2 cloves garlic, minced
¼ teaspoon celery salt
¼ teaspoon black pepper
1 pound Jerusalem artichokes, red-skin potatoes, or new potatoes; cut into ¼-inch slices
2 cups frozen pearl onions or 1 medium onion, cut into thin wedges
8 ounces fresh mushrooms, halved

Beef and Garden Vegetable Soup

This rich and satisfying chili-flavored soup has chunks of beef and a basketful of vegetables. Stewing the bones adds beefy flavor and body to the broth.

1 Cut meat into 1-inch cubes, reserving bones and trimming off fat.

2 In a 3½- to 6-quart slow cooker place the carrots, celery, potato, cabbage, onion, beef, and reserved bones. Add the water, tomato juice, bouillon, Worcestershire sauce, chili powder, and bay leaves.

3 Cover and cook on low-heat setting for 8 to 10 hours or on high-heat setting for 4 to 5 hours. Discard bones and bay leaves. Skim off fat.

Nutrition Facts per serving: 305 cal., 13 g total fat (4 g sat. fat), 64 mg chol., 1,463 mg sodium, 14 g carbo., 2 g fiber, 33 g pro.

Prep: 30 minutes
Cook: Low 8 to 10 hours,
High 4 to 5 hours
Makes: 6 to 8 servings
Slow Cooker: 3½- to 6-quart

2 to 2½ pounds meaty beef shank crosscuts
2 medium carrots, bias-sliced
2 medium stalks celery, sliced
1 large potato, peeled and cubed
1 cup coarsely chopped cabbage
⅓ cup coarsely chopped onion (1 small)
3 cups water
2 cups tomato juice
2 tablespoons instant beef bouillon granules
1 tablespoon Worcestershire sauce
1 teaspoon chili powder
2 bay leaves

Vegetable-Beef Soup

If you like classic beef soup, this is it. Convenience products make it easy to put together.

1 In a large skillet brown the meat, half at a time, in hot oil. Drain off fat. In a 3½- or 4-quart slow cooker combine meat and remaining ingredients.

2 Cover and cook on low-heat setting for 8 to 10 hours or on high-heat setting for 4 to 5 hours.

Nutrition Facts per serving: 289 cal., 12 g total fat (4 g sat. fat), 48 mg chol., 519 mg sodium, 26 g carbo., 3 g fiber, 19 g pro.

Prep: 25 minutes
Cook: Low 4 to 5 hours,
        High 8 to 10 hours
Makes: 6 servings
Slow Cooker: 3½- or 4-quart

- 1 pound boneless beef chuck roast, cut into ¾-inch pieces
- 1 tablespoon cooking oil
- 4 cups water
- 1 14½-ounce can diced tomatoes, undrained
- 2 cups frozen mixed vegetables
- 2 cups frozen loose-pack hash brown potatoes or 2 medium potatoes, peeled and chopped
- 1 1-ounce envelope onion soup mix (½ of a 2-ounce package)
- 1 teaspoon instant beef bouillon granules
- 1 clove garlic, minced, or ⅛ teaspoon garlic powder
- ⅛ teaspoon black pepper

Easy Vegetable-Beef Soup

This full-flavored soup calls for surprisingly few ingredients. If desired, you could substitute ground turkey for the ground beef.

1 In a large skillet cook beef until brown. Drain off fat. Transfer meat to a 3½- or 4-quart slow cooker. Add the broth, water frozen vegetables, undrained tomatoes, soup, onion, seasoning, and garlic powder.

2 Cover and cook on low-heat setting for 7 to 8 hours or on high-heat setting for 3½ to 4 hours.

Nutrition Facts per serving: 314 cal., 12 g total fat (4 g sat. fat), 71 mg chol., 1,011 mg sodium, 26 g carbo., 5 g fiber, 27 g pro.

Prep: 20 minutes
Cook: Low 7 to 8 hours,
  High 3½ to 4 hours
Makes: 4 to 6 servings
Slow Cooker: 3½- or 4-quart

- 1 pound lean ground beef
- 1 14-ounce can beef broth
- 1¼ cups water
- 1 10-ounce package frozen mixed vegetables
- 1 14½-ounce can diced tomatoes, undrained
- 1 10¾-ounce can condensed tomato soup
- 1 tablespoon dried minced onion
- 1 teaspoon dried Italian seasoning, crushed
- ¼ teaspoon garlic powder

Beef and Pumpkin Soup

Pumpkin, plus a dash of nutmeg, lends a harvest flair to this pasta-filled soup. If fresh pumpkin isn't available, use butternut squash instead.

1 In a 3½- to 5-quart slow cooker combine meat, corn, pumpkin, water, tomato sauce, onion, sweet pepper, garlic, salt, black pepper, and nutmeg.

2 Cover and cook on low-heat setting for 10 to 12 hours or on high-heat setting for 5 to 6 hours.

3 Cook pasta according to package directions; drain. Stir pasta into the soup. Ladle soup into bowls; sprinkle each serving with parsley.

Nutrition Facts per serving: 244 cal., 5 g total fat (2 g sat. fat), 67 mg chol., 450 mg sodium, 24 g carbo., 3 g fiber, 28 g pro.

Prep: 20 minutes
Cook: Low 10 to 12 hours,
      High 5 to 6 hours
Makes: 6 servings
Slow Cooker: 3½- to 5-quart

1½ pounds beef stew meat, cut into
       1-inch cubes
1   10-ounce package frozen whole
       kernel corn
1½ cups ½-inch pieces peeled and
       seeded pumpkin or butternut
       squash
1½ cups water
1   8-ounce can tomato sauce
¾   cup chopped onion
½   cup chopped green sweet pepper
1   clove garlic, minced
½   teaspoon salt
¼   teaspoon black pepper
⅛   teaspoon ground nutmeg
2   ounces dried whole wheat macaroni
       or other small pasta
¼   cup snipped fresh parsley

Zesty Beef and Slaw Soup

Soup lovers can't resist this combination of spicy tomato, beef, and vegetables.

1 In a large skillet cook ground beef, onion, and garlic until meat is brown and onion is tender. Drain off fat.

2 In a 3½- to 5-quart slow cooker combine meat mixture, cabbage, corn, green beans, vegetable juice, undrained tomatoes, Worcestershire sauce, basil, and pepper.

3 Cover and cook on low-heat setting for 8 to 10 hours or on high-heat setting for 4 to 5 hours.

Nutrition Facts per serving: 324 cal., 16 g total fat (6 g sat. fat), 56 mg chol., 750 mg sodium, 28 g carbo., 4 g fiber, 18 g pro.

Prep: 15 minutes
Cook: Low 8 to 10 hours,
    High 4 to 5 hours
Makes: 6 servings
Slow Cooker: 3½- to 5-quart

1 pound lean ground beef
½ cup chopped onion (1 medium)
2 cloves garlic, minced
2 cups packaged shredded cabbage
    with carrot (coleslaw mix)
1 10-ounce package frozen whole
    kernel corn
1 9-ounce package frozen cut
    green beans
4 cups hot-style vegetable juice
1 14½-ounce can Italian-style stewed
    tomatoes, undrained
1 tablespoon Worcestershire sauce
1 teaspoon dried basil, crushed
¼ teaspoon black pepper

Pork Cider Stew

Pork and apples are perfect complements in this hearty dish that you'll want to enjoy time and again. The deep, nutty kick comes from a sprinkling of caraway.

1 Trim fat from meat. Cut meat into 1-inch cubes. In a 3½- to 6-quart slow cooker combine meat, potatoes, carrots, onions, apple, celery, and tapioca. Stir in apple cider, salt, caraway seeds, and pepper.

2 Cover and cook on low-heat setting for 10 to 12 hours or high-heat setting for 5 to 6 hours.

Nutrition Facts per serving: 273 cal., 8 g total fat (3 g sat. fat), 76 mg chol., 395 mg sodium, 26 g carbo., 3 g fiber, 24 g pro.

Prep: 20 minutes
Cook: Low 10 to 12 hours,
    High 5 to 6 hours
Makes: 8 servings
Slow Cooker: 3½- to 6-quart

- 2 pounds pork shoulder roast
- 3 medium potatoes, cubed (2½ cups)
- 3 medium carrots, cut into ½-inch pieces (1½ cups)
- 2 medium onions, sliced
- 1 medium apple, cored and coarsely chopped (1 cup)
- ½ cup coarsely chopped celery
- 3 tablespoons quick-cooking tapioca
- 2 cups apple cider or apple juice
- 1 teaspoon salt
- 1 teaspoon caraway seeds
- ¼ teaspoon black pepper

36 g
carb

Italian Pork Stew

Sausage, pork, and red wine make this hearty stew flavorful. For extra herb flavor, garnish the stew with snipped fresh thyme or oregano.

1 Rinse beans; drain. In a large saucepan combine beans and the 6 cups water. Bring to boiling; reduce heat. Simmer, uncovered, for 10 minutes. Remove from heat. Cover and let stand for 1 hour. Drain and rinse beans. Transfer beans to a 4- to 5-quart slow cooker.

2 In a large skillet cook sausage over medium heat until sausage is no longer pink, breaking up sausage as it cooks. Drain off fat. Transfer sausage to slow cooker. In the same skillet cook the pork, half at a time, until pork is no longer pink. Drain off fat. Transfer to cooker. Add onions, carrots, and garlic. Stir in the 3 cups water, bouillon, thyme, and oregano.

3 Cover and cook on low-heat setting for 7 to 8 hours or on high-heat setting for 3½ to 4 hours.

4 If using low-heat setting, turn to high-heat setting. Stir wine into tomato paste; add to mixture in cooker along with parsley. Cover and cook for 15 minutes more.

Nutrition Facts per serving: 357 cal., 10 g total fat (4 g sat. fat), 50 mg chol., 372 mg sodium, 36 g carbo., 11 g fiber, 28 g pro.

Prep: 30 minutes
Stand: 1 hour
Cook: Low 7 to 8 **hours,**
          High 3½ to 4 **hours;**
          plus 15 **minutes**
Makes: 8 **servings**
Slow Cooker: 4- to 5-**quart**

2	cups dry Great Northern beans
6	cups cold water
8	ounces bulk Italian sausage
1	pound lean boneless pork, cut into ¾-inch cubes
1½	cups coarsely chopped onions
1½	cups carrots cut into ½-inch pieces
3	cloves garlic, minced
3	cups water
1	teaspoon instant beef bouillon granules
½	teaspoon dried thyme, crushed
½	teaspoon dried oregano, crushed
¼	cup dry red wine
½	of a 6-ounce can (⅓ cup) tomato paste
¼	cup snipped fresh parsley

Green Chile Stew

The few extra minutes it takes to brown the pork are well spent. Browning brings out the flavor of the meat as well as adding appealing color.

1 Trim fat from pork. Cut pork into ½-inch cubes. In a large skillet brown half of the pork in hot oil. Transfer meat to a 3½- to 4½-quart slow cooker. Brown remaining meat with onion. Drain off the fat; transfer meat and onion to the slow cooker.

2 Add water, potatoes, hominy, chile peppers, tapioca, garlic salt, salt, black pepper, cumin, and oregano.

3 Cover and cook on low-heat setting for 7 to 8 hours or on high-heat setting for 4 to 5 hours. If desired, garnish with snipped cilantro.

Nutrition Facts per serving: 346 cal., 9 g total fat (2 g sat. fat), 85 mg chol., 816 mg sodium, 33 g carbo., 4 g fiber, 32 g pro.

Prep: 25 minutes
Cook: Low 7 to 8 hours,
       High 4 to 5 hours
Makes: 6 servings
Slow Cooker: 3½- to 4½-quart

2 pounds boneless pork sirloin or
   shoulder roast
1 tablespoon cooking oil
½ cup chopped onion (1 medium)
3 cups water
4 medium potatoes, peeled and cut into
   ½-inch cubes
1 15-ounce can hominy or whole kernel
   corn, drained
2 4-ounce cans chopped green chile
   peppers
2 tablespoons quick-cooking tapioca
1 teaspoon garlic salt
½ teaspoon salt
½ teaspoon black pepper
½ teaspoon ground cumin
⅛ teaspoon dried oregano, crushed
   Snipped fresh cilantro (optional)

Spicy Pork and Potato Stew

Poblano peppers are mild to medium-hot. They're long and deep green with an irregular bell-pepper shape. Remove the membranes and seeds for the mildest flavor.

1 In a large skillet brown meat, half at a time, in hot oil. Drain off fat.

2 In a 3½- or 4-quart slow cooker place potatoes, onion, poblano peppers, jalapeño pepper, garlic, and stick cinnamon. Add meat. In a bowl combine broth, undrained tomatoes, chili powder, oregano, and black pepper; pour over all.

3 Cover and cook on low-heat setting for 8 to 10 hours or on high-heat setting for 4 to 5 hours. Discard stick cinnamon. Stir in cilantro.

Nutrition Facts per serving: 285 cal., 11 g total fat (3 g sat. fat), 50 mg chol., 753 mg sodium, 28 g carbo., 3 g fiber, 19 g pro.

*Note: Because hot chile peppers, such as jalapeños, contain volatile oils that can burn your skin and eyes, avoid direct contact with chiles as much as possible. When working with chile peppers, wear plastic or rubber gloves. If your bare hands do come into contact with the peppers, wash your hands well with soap and water.

Prep: 30 minutes
Cook: Low 8 to 10 hours,
       High 4 to 5 hours
Makes: 6 servings
Slow Cooker: 3½- or 4-quart

1 pound boneless pork shoulder roast, cut into 1-inch cubes
1 tablespoon cooking oil
1 pound whole, tiny new potatoes, quartered
1 cup chopped onion (1 large)
2 fresh poblano chile peppers, seeded and cut into 1-inch pieces
1 fresh jalapeño chile pepper, seeded and chopped*
4 cloves garlic, minced
2 inches stick cinnamon
3 cups chicken broth
1 14½-ounce can diced tomatoes, undrained
1 tablespoon chili powder
1 teaspoon dried oregano, crushed
¼ teaspoon black pepper
¼ cup snipped fresh cilantro or parsley

Sancocho Pork Stew

This hearty stew, believed to originate in Panama, is mildly spiced with chili powder and chile peppers. The yams or sweet potatoes lend a complementary sweetness.

1 In a 3½- to 5-quart slow cooker place yams, sweet pepper, corn, onion, and garlic. Add meat, chili powder, coriander, and salt. Pour the water and undrained tomatoes over all.

2 Cover and cook on low-heat setting for 7 to 8 hours or on high-heat setting for 3½ to 4 hours, adding the frozen green beans the last 15 minutes.

Nutrition Facts per serving: 256 cal., 6 g total fat (2 g sat. fat), 55 mg chol., 388 mg sodium, 32 g carbo., 5 g fiber, 20 g pro.

Prep: 20 minutes
Cook: Low 7 to 8 hours,
 High 3½ to 4 hours
Makes: 8 servings
Slow Cooker: 3½- to 5-quart

3 medium yams or sweet potatoes, peeled and cut into 2-inch pieces
1 large green sweet pepper, cut into strips
1 cup frozen whole kernel corn
1 medium onion, sliced and separated into rings
3 cloves garlic, minced
1½ pounds boneless pork shoulder, cut into ¾-inch cubes
1 teaspoon chili powder
¾ teaspoon ground coriander
½ teaspoon salt
2 cups water
1 10-ounce can chopped tomatoes with green chile peppers, undrained
1 9-ounce package frozen cut green beans

Southern Ham Stew

Want to dish up down-home cooking? Try this hearty stew featuring Southern standbys—collard greens, black-eyed peas, okra, and hominy.

1 Rinse black-eyed peas; drain. In a large saucepan combine peas and the 4 cups water. Bring to boiling; reduce heat. Simmer, uncovered, for 10 minutes. Drain and rinse peas.

2 In a 3½- to 6-quart slow cooker combine peas, ham, hominy, frozen okra, onion, garlic, Cajun seasoning, and pepper. Stir in the 4½ cups fresh water.

3 Cover and cook on low-heat setting for 8 to 10 hours or on high-heat setting for 4 to 5 hours.

4 If using low-heat setting, turn to high-heat setting. Stir in collard greens and undrained tomatoes. Cover and cook for 10 minutes more. Ladle into bowls.

Nutrition Facts per serving: 245 cal., 5 g total fat (1 g sat. fat), 20 mg chol., 673 mg sodium, 35 g carbo., 7 g fiber, 16 g pro.

Prep: 20 minutes
Cook: Low 8 to 10 hours,
High 4 to 5 hours;
plus 10 minutes
Makes: 8 servings
Slow Cooker: 3½- to 6-quart

1½ cups dry black-eyed peas (about 9½ ounces)
4 cups water
2 cups cubed cooked ham
1 15-ounce can white hominy, rinsed and drained
1 10-ounce package frozen cut okra
1 cup chopped onion (1 large)
4 cloves garlic, minced
1 to 2 teaspoons Cajun or Creole seasoning
¼ teaspoon black pepper
4½ cups water
4 cups chopped collard greens or fresh spinach
1 14½-ounce can stewed tomatoes, undrained

Ham and Bean Soup

Every slow cooker cookbook needs a ham and bean soup recipe! This version is as classic as you can get.

1 Rinse beans; place in a large saucepan. Add the 4 cups cold water. Bring to boiling; reduce heat. Simmer, uncovered, for 10 minutes. Remove from heat. Cover; let stand for 1 hour. Drain and rinse beans.

2 In a 4- to 6-quart slow cooker combine beans, ham, the 5 cups water, celery, carrots, onion, thyme, and, if desired, liquid smoke.

3 Cover and cook on low-heat setting for 8 to 10 hours or on high-heat setting for 4 to 5 hours. Stir in parsley.

Nutrition Facts per serving: 393 cal., 11 g total fat (4 g sat. fat), 67 mg chol., 1,751 mg sodium, 36 g carbo., 14 g fiber, 38 g pro.

Prep: 15 minutes
Stand: 1 hour
Cook: Low 8 to 10 hours,
         High 4 to 5 hours
Makes: 8 servings
Slow Cooker: 4- to 6-quart

2	cups dry navy beans
4	cups cold water
2	pounds cooked ham, cut into ½-inch cubes
5	cups water
2	cups sliced celery (4 stalks)
2	cups sliced carrots (4)
½	cup chopped onion (1 medium)
½	teaspoon dried thyme, crushed
½	teaspoon liquid smoke (optional)
¼	cup snipped fresh parsley

33 g
carb

Ham and Lentil Soup

Unlike dry beans, lentils simmer to perfection in your crockery cooker without precooking. In this soup, lemon peel and spinach freshen the mild nutty taste of lentils.

1 Rinse and drain lentils. In a 3½- or 4-quart slow cooker combine lentils, water, celery, carrots, onion, bouillon granules, garlic, lemon peel, and cayenne pepper.

2 Cover and cook on low-heat setting for 7 to 8 hours or on high-heat setting for 3½ to 4 hours.

3 If using low-heat setting, turn to high-heat setting. Add ham. Cover and cook for 10 minutes more. Stir in spinach; serve immediately.

For a 5- to 6-quart cooker: Recipe may be doubled. Makes 8 to 12 servings.

Nutrition Facts per serving: 235 cal., 4 g total fat (1 g sat. fat), 21 mg chol., 815 mg sodium, 33 g carbo., 6 g fiber, 18 g pro.

Prep: 15 minutes
Cook: Low 7 to 8 hours,
        High 3½ to 4 hours;
        plus 10 minutes
Makes: 4 to 6 servings
Slow Cooker: 3½- or 4-quart

1 cup dry lentils
4 cups water
1 cup chopped celery (2 stalks)
1 cup sliced carrots (2 medium)
½ cup chopped onion (1 medium)
2 teaspoons instant chicken bouillon
    granules
1 teaspoon bottled minced garlic or
    2 cloves garlic, minced
½ teaspoon finely shredded lemon peel
⅛ to ¼ teaspoon cayenne pepper
1 cup cubed cooked ham
2 cups chopped fresh spinach

Spicy Pork and Vegetable Soup

This sophisticated and tasty soup is packed full of winter vegetables. Fresh spinach added just before serving adds a touch of color and a boost of nutrition.

1 In a large skillet brown half of the meat in hot oil. Drain meat; place in a 3½- or 4-quart slow cooker. Brown remaining meat with onion, garlic, and paprika; drain and place in slow cooker.

2 Add water, parsnips, squash, sweet potato, undrained corn, bouillon granules, salt, and cayenne pepper to slow cooker. Stir mixture to combine.

3 Cover and cook on low-heat setting for 10 to 11 hours or on high-heat setting for 5 to 5½ hours. Add spinach; stir until slightly wilted. Serve immediately.

Nutrition Facts per serving: 243 cal., 9 g total fat (2 g sat. fat), 51 mg chol., 907 mg sodium, 25 g carbo., 5 g fiber, 18 g pro.

Prep: 30 minutes
Cook: Low 10 to 11 hours,
 High 5 to 5½ hours
Makes: 6 servings
Slow Cooker: 3½- or 4-quart

- 1 pound boneless pork, cut into ½-inch cubes, or beef stew meat
- 1 tablespoon cooking oil
- ½ cup chopped onion (1 medium)
- 2 cloves garlic, minced
- 1 teaspoon paprika
- 3 cups water
- 2 medium parsnips or 3 medium carrots, cut into ¼-inch pieces (1½ cups)
- ½ pound winter squash, peeled and cut into ½-inch pieces (1½ cups)
- 1 medium sweet potato, peeled and cut into ½-inch pieces (1⅓ cups)
- 1 8¾-ounce can whole kernel corn, undrained
- 4 teaspoons instant beef bouillon granules
- ½ teaspoon salt
- ¼ teaspoon cayenne pepper
- 2 cups torn fresh spinach

26 g
carb

Pork and Hominy Soup

Combine pork, hominy, and chili powder to make a flavorful rendition of pozole. Hominy, dried corn that has had the hulls removed, is found in the canned vegetable section of the supermarket.

1 In a large skillet brown meat, half at a time, in hot oil. Drain off fat.

2 Transfer meat to a 3½- or 4-quart slow cooker. Add sweet pepper, tomato, onion, garlic, hominy, chile peppers, chili powder, and oregano. Pour broth over all.

3 Cover and cook on low-heat setting for 8 to 10 hours or on high-heat setting for 4 to 5 hours. If desired, serve with sour cream.

Nutrition Facts per serving: 277 cal., 11 g total fat (3 g sat. fat), 51 mg chol., 1,015 mg sodium, 26 g carbo., 5 g fiber, 19 g pro.

Prep: 30 minutes
Cook: Low 8 to 10 hours,
High 4 to 5 hours
Makes: 6 servings
Slow Cooker: 3½- or 4-quart

- 1 pound boneless pork shoulder, trimmed and cut into 1-inch cubes
- 1 tablespoon cooking oil
- 1 medium red or green sweet pepper, cut into ½-inch pieces
- 1 medium tomato, chopped
- ½ cup chopped onion (1 medium)
- 4 cloves garlic, minced
- 2 14½-ounce cans golden hominy, drained
- 1 4-ounce can diced green chile peppers, undrained
- 1 tablespoon chili powder
- ½ teaspoon dried oregano, crushed
- 2 14-ounce cans chicken broth
  Dairy sour cream (optional)

Tuscan Sausage and Bean Soup

Savor the flavors of sun-drenched Tuscany with this hearty vegetable soup.

1 Rinse beans. In a large saucepan combine the beans and the 4 cups cold water. Bring to boiling; reduce heat. Simmer for 10 minutes. Remove from heat. Cover and let stand 1 hour. Drain and rinse beans.

2 Meanwhile, in a medium skillet cook sausage until brown. Drain on paper towels.

3 In a 3½- to 5-quart slow cooker combine the drained beans, the 2¼ cups water, broth, onion, garlic, Italian seasoning, sausage, squash, and wine.

4 Cover and cook on low-heat setting for 9 to 10 hours or on high-heat setting for 5 to 6 hours or until beans are tender.

5 If using low-heat setting, turn to high-heat setting. Stir spinach and undrained tomatoes into soup. Cover and cook for 10 to 15 minutes more or until heated through. Serve in bowls. If desired, sprinkle each serving with Parmesan cheese.

Nutrition Facts per serving: 329 cal., 14 g total fat (5 g sat. fat), 31 mg chol., 841 mg sodium, 33 g carbo., 10 g fiber, 17 g pro.

Prep: 20 minutes
Stand: 1 hour
Cook: Low 9 to 10 hours,
      High 5 to 6 hours;
           plus 10 minutes
Makes: 6 servings
Slow Cooker: 3½- to 5-quart

1¼ cups dry Great Northern beans
 4 cups cold water
 8 ounces uncooked Italian sausage
      links, cut into ½- to ¾-inch slices
2¼ cups water
 2 14-ounce cans beef broth
 1 cup chopped onion (1 large)
 2 cloves garlic, minced
 1 teaspoon dried Italian seasoning,
      crushed
 1 medium yellow summer squash or
      zucchini, sliced (about 1½ cups)
⅓ cup dry red wine or water
½ of a 10-ounce package frozen
      chopped spinach, thawed and well
      drained
 1 14½-ounce can low-sodium diced
      tomatoes, undrained
    Grated Parmesan cheese (optional)

19 g
carb

Lamb and Barley Stew with Mint

Pearl barley adds a slightly chewy texture to this stew. "Pearl" refers to the polishing process of the hulled grain. It is sold in regular and quick-cooking forms.

1 In a large skillet brown half of the meat in hot oil; remove meat from skillet. Drain off fat; place in a 3½- to 5-quart slow cooker. Cook remaining meat, the onion, and garlic until meat is brown and onion is tender. Drain fat and add to slow cooker.

2 Add the broth, undrained tomatoes, barley, wine (if desired), dried dill (if using), salt, and black pepper to slow cooker. Stir to combine.

3 Cover and cook on low-heat setting for 8 to 10 hours or on high-heat setting for 4 to 5 hours. To serve, stir in roasted peppers and mint. If using, stir in the fresh dill.

Nutrition Facts per serving: 266 cal., 11 g total fat (3 g sat. fat), 58 mg chol., 709 mg sodium, 19 g carbo., 4 g fiber, 23 g pro.

Prep: 20 minutes
Cook: Low 8 to 10 hours,
High 4 to 5 hours
Makes: 6 servings
Slow Cooker: 3½- to 5-quart

1½ pounds lamb stew meat, cut into
    1-inch cubes
2 tablespoons cooking oil
½ cup chopped onion (1 medium)
4 cloves garlic, minced
2½ cups chicken broth
1 14½-ounce can diced tomatoes,
    undrained
½ cup regular barley
¼ cup dry white wine (optional)
2 tablespoons snipped fresh dill or
    1½ teaspoons dried dill
½ teaspoon salt
¼ teaspoon black pepper
1½ 7-ounce jars roasted red sweet
    peppers, drained and thinly sliced
    (about 1½ cups)
¼ cup snipped fresh mint

Irish Stew

Lamb, potatoes, and onions are the standard components of Irish stew. The lamb benefits from the long, slow cooking time, which produces tender morsels of flavorful meat.

1 In a large skillet brown lamb, half at a time, in hot oil. Drain off fat. In a 3½- or 4-quart slow cooker combine turnips, carrots, potatoes, onions, tapioca, salt, pepper, and thyme. Stir in lamb and broth.

2 Cover and cook on low-heat setting for 10 to 12 hours or on high-heat setting for 5 to 6 hours.

Nutrition Facts per serving: 255 cal., 6 g total fat (2 g sat. fat), 57 mg chol., 837 mg sodium, 27 g carbo., 4 g fiber, 22 g pro.

Prep: 30 minutes
Cook: Low 10 to 12 hours,
High 5 to 6 hours
Makes: 5 servings
Slow Cooker: 3½- or 4-quart

1 pound lean boneless lamb, cut into
1-inch pieces
1 tablespoon cooking oil
2½ cups ½-inch pieces peeled turnips
(2 medium)
1½ cups ½-inch pieces carrots
(3 medium)
1½ cups ½-inch pieces peeled potatoes
(2 medium)
2 medium onions, cut into wedges
¼ cup quick-cooking tapioca
½ teaspoon salt
¼ teaspoon black pepper
¼ teaspoon dried thyme, crushed
3 cups beef broth

Scotch Broth

Scotch broth is one of the more familiar uses of barley in America. Traditionally made with lamb, this stew is equally good with beef.

1 In a 3½- or 4-quart slow cooker place the meat, leek, turnip, and carrots. Stir in the broth, beer, barley, and pepper.

2 Cover and cook on low-heat setting for 8 to 10 hours or on high-heat setting for 4 to 5 hours. Stir in parsley before serving.

Nutrition Facts per serving: 226 cal., 3 g total fat (1 g sat. fat), 43 mg chol., 347 mg sodium, 27 g carbo., 6 g fiber, 19 g pro.

Prep: 25 minutes
Cook: Low 8 to 10 hours,
High 4 to 5 hours
Makes: 5 servings
Slow Cooker: 3½- or 4-quart

12	ounces lamb or beef stew meat, cut into 1-inch cubes
1	large leek, halved lengthwise and sliced (about ½ cup)
1	large turnip, peeled and cut into ½-inch pieces (1 cup)
2	medium carrots, cut into ½-inch slices (about 1 cup)
3	14-ounce cans beef broth
1	12-ounce bottle dark beer
⅔	cup regular barley
½	teaspoon freshly ground black pepper
2	tablespoons snipped fresh parsley

Persian-Style Stew

In Persian stews like this one, yellow split peas are a classic ingredient. During cooking, the peas soften and fall apart, giving the stew a thick consistency.

1 In a large skillet brown meat, half at a time, in hot oil. Drain off fat. Transfer meat to a 3½- to 5-quart slow cooker. Stir in leeks, onion, split peas, garlic, bay leaves, dried oregano (if using), cumin, and pepper. Pour broth over all.

2 Cover and cook on low-heat setting for 8 to 10 hours or on high-heat setting for 4 to 5 hours.

3 If using low-heat setting, turn to high-heat setting. Stir raisins into stew. Cover; cook for 10 minutes more. Discard bay leaves. Stir in lemon juice and, if using, the fresh oregano. If desired, serve with hot cooked bulgur.

Nutrition Facts per serving: 203 cal., 5 g total fat (1 g sat. fat), 54 mg chol., 433 mg sodium, 17 g carbo., 4 g fiber, 22 g pro.

Prep: 25 minutes
Cook: Low 8 to 10 hours,
High 4 to 5 hours;
plus 10 minutes
Makes: 8 servings
Slow Cooker: 3½- to 5-quart

- 1½ to 2 pounds lamb or beef stew meat, cut into 1-inch cubes
- 1 tablespoon cooking oil
- 3 leeks, cut into 1-inch pieces
- 1 cup chopped onion (1 large)
- ½ cup dry yellow split peas
- 4 cloves garlic, sliced
- 2 bay leaves
- 1 tablespoon snipped fresh oregano or 1 teaspoon dried oregano, crushed
- 1½ teaspoons ground cumin
- ¼ teaspoon black pepper
- 3 cups chicken broth
- ⅓ cup raisins
- 2 tablespoons lemon juice
  Hot cooked bulgur or brown rice (optional)

31 g
carb

Lamb-Lentil Soup

Lentils make this dish extra easy because they don't require presoaking or precooking—just rinse them and add to the slow cooker with the rest of the ingredients.

1 In a large skillet brown meat in hot oil. Drain fat. Meanwhile, in a 3½- or 4-quart slow cooker place celery, carrots, and lentils. Top with meat. Stir in soup, thyme, salt, and pepper. Gradually stir in water.

2 Cover and cook on low-heat setting for 7 to 8 hours or on high-heat setting for 3½ to 4 hours.

Nutrition Facts per serving: 303 cal., 8 g total fat (2 g sat. fat), 46 mg chol., 791 mg sodium, 31 g carbo., 14 g fiber, 26 g pro.

Prep: 20 minutes
Cook: Low 7 to 8 hours,
         High 3½ to 4 hours
Makes: 5 servings
Slow Cooker: 3½- or 4-quart

12 ounces lean boneless lamb or beef, cut into ½-inch cubes
1   tablespoon cooking oil
1   cup thinly sliced celery (2 stalks)
1   cup coarsely chopped carrots (2 medium)
1   cup dry lentils, rinsed and drained
1   10½-ounce can condensed French onion soup
1½ teaspoons dried thyme, crushed
½   teaspoon salt
½   teaspoon black pepper
3¼ cups water

Lamb and Barley Vegetable Soup

Look for lean lamb at the supermarket or buy extra (2½ pounds) and trim it yourself. Beef and pork make delicious substitutes.

1 In a 3½- to 6-quart slow cooker place meat, mushrooms, barley, onion, carrot, parsnip, undrained tomatoes, garlic, marjoram, salt, pepper, and bay leaf. Pour broth over all.

2 Cover and cook on low-heat setting for 6 to 8 hours or on high-heat setting for 3 to 4 hours. Discard bay leaf.

Nutrition Facts per serving: 212 cal., 4 g total fat (1 g sat. fat), 53 mg chol., 643 mg sodium, 20 g carbo., 4 g fiber, 23 g pro.

Prep: 25 minutes
Cook: Low 6 to 8 hours,
High 3 to 4 hours
Makes: 8 servings
Slow Cooker: 3½- to 6-quart

1½ pounds lamb stew meat, cut into
    1-inch cubes
2 cups sliced fresh mushrooms
½ cup regular barley
1 cup chopped onion (1 large)
1 medium carrot, cut into ½-inch pieces
1 large parsnip, peeled and cut into
    ½-inch pieces
1 14½-ounce can Italian-style stewed
    tomatoes, undrained
2 cloves garlic, minced
1 teaspoon dried marjoram, crushed
½ teaspoon salt
¼ teaspoon black pepper
1 bay leaf
4 cups beef broth

Chicken and Rice Stew

Mushrooms, wild rice, brown rice, leeks, and rosemary give a fragrant, earthy quality to this classic hearty fare.

1 In a 3½- to 6-quart slow cooker place mushrooms, carrots, leeks, brown rice, and wild rice. Add chicken. Top with thyme, rosemary, and pepper. Pour broth over all.

2 Cover and cook on low-heat setting for 7 to 8 hours or on high-heat setting for 3½ to 4 hours. Stir in cream of mushroom soup. Cook 10 minutes more.

Nutrition Facts per serving: 264 cal., 6 g total fat (2 g sat. fat), 33 mg chol., 908 mg sodium, 32 g carbo., 3 g fiber, 22 g pro.

Prep: 20 minutes
Cook: Low 7 to 8 hours,
High 3½ to 4 hours;
plus 10 minutes
Makes: 6 servings
Slow Cooker: 3½- to 6-quart

- 3 cups quartered button mushrooms (8 ounces)
- 2 medium carrots, sliced (1 cup)
- 2 medium leeks, sliced (⅔ cup)
- ½ cup uncooked brown rice
- ½ cup uncooked wild rice, rinsed and drained
- 12 ounces skinless, boneless chicken breasts, cut into ¾-inch pieces
- 1 teaspoon dried thyme, crushed
- ½ teaspoon dried rosemary, crushed
- ¼ teaspoon coarsely ground black pepper
- 3 14-ounce cans reduced-sodium chicken broth (5¼ cups)
- 1 10¾-ounce can condensed cream of mushroom soup

Creamy Chicken Chowder

If desired for this recipe, substitute soups and broths that are lower sodium. The Mexican flavors will still wake up your taste buds.

1 In a 3½- or 4-quart slow cooker combine chicken, corn, soup, undrained chile peppers, cilantro, and taco seasoning mix. Stir in broth.

2 Cover and cook on low-heat setting for 4 to 6 hours or on high-heat setting for 2 to 3 hours.

3 Stir about 1 cup of the hot soup into the sour cream. Stir sour cream mixture and cheese into the mixture in cooker; cover and let stand 5 minutes. Whisk until combined.

Nutrition Facts per serving: 327 cal., 15 g total fat (8 g sat. fat), 74 mg chol., 1,906 mg sodium, 23 g carbo., 2 g fiber, 25 g pro.

Prep: 20 minutes
Cook: Low 4 to 6 hours,
      High 2 to 3 hours
Stand: 5 minutes
Makes: 6 servings
Slow Cooker: 3½- or 4-quart

1 pound skinless, boneless chicken breasts, cut into ½-inch pieces
1 11-ounce can whole kernel corn with sweet peppers, drained
1 10¾-ounce can condensed cream of potato soup
1 4-ounce can diced green chile peppers, undrained
2 tablespoons snipped fresh cilantro
1 1¼-ounce envelope taco seasoning mix
3 cups chicken broth
1 8-ounce carton dairy sour cream
½ of an 8-ounce package cheese spread with jalapeño peppers, cubed

White Chili Soup

Although beans contain a high amount of carbohydrate, they also are high in protein and fiber. This helps slow digestion time, preventing blood sugars from increasing rapidly.

1 In a 3½- or 4-quart slow cooker combine the drained beans, chicken, onion, sweet peppers, jalapeño peppers, garlic, cumin, salt, and oregano. Stir in broth.

2 Cover and cook on low-heat setting for 8 to 10 hours or on high-heat setting for 4 to 5 hours. Ladle soup into bowls. If desired, top with cheese.

Nutrition Facts per serving: 422 cal., 6 g total fat (2 g sat. fat), 52 mg chol., 709 mg sodium, 54 g carbo., 13 g fiber, 38 g pro.

Prep: 25 minutes
Cook: Low 8 to 10 hours,
       High 4 to 5 hours
Makes: 6 servings
Slow Cooker: 3½- or 4-quart

3   15- to 15½-ounce cans white kidney
      (cannellini) beans, Great Northern,
      pinto, or rinsed and drained
2½ cups chopped, cooked chicken
1   cup chopped onion (1 large)
1½ cups chopped red, green, and/or
      yellow sweet peppers (2 medium)
2   fresh jalapeño chile peppers, seeded
      and chopped (see note, page 62)
2   cloves garlic, minced
2   teaspoons ground cumin
½   teaspoon salt
½   teaspoon dried oregano, crushed
3½ cups chicken broth
      Shredded Monterey Jack cheese
      (optional)

Tex-Mex Chicken Soup

Already-flavored, frozen chicken makes this soup convenient to make—no messy chicken to cut up! When you're preparing the soup, remember to put the chicken in the refrigerator to thaw. It is added to the soup and cooks in just 15 minutes.

1 In a 3½- or 4-quart slow cooker combine undrained tomatoes, broth, water, tomato sauce, onion, chile peppers, cumin, chili powder, Worcestershire sauce, and garlic powder.

2 Cover and cook on low-heat setting for 8 to 10 hours or on high-heat setting for 4 to 5 hours.

3 If using low-heat setting, turn to high-heat setting. Stir in chicken strips. Cover and cook for 15 minutes more. Stir in tortillas and serve immediately. Garnish each serving with shredded cheese.

Nutrition Facts per serving: 189 cal., 6 g total fat (3 g sat. fat), 26 mg chol., 615 mg sodium, 22 g carbo., 2 g fiber, 13 g pro.

Prep: 20 minutes
Cook: Low 8 to 10 hours,
High 4 to 5 hours;
plus 15 minutes
Makes: 8 servings
Slow Cooker: 3½- or 4-quart

- 1 14½-ounce can diced tomatoes, undrained
- 1 14-ounce can beef broth
- 2 cups water
- 1 8-ounce can tomato sauce
- ½ cup chopped onion (1 medium)
- 1 4-ounce can chopped green chile peppers, undrained
- 1 teaspoon ground cumin
- 1 teaspoon chili powder
- 1 teaspoon Worcestershire sauce
- ½ teaspoon garlic powder
- 1 9-ounce package frozen cooked Southwestern-flavor chicken breast strips, thawed
- 8 corn tortillas, torn into 1- to 2-inch pieces
- ¾ cup shredded cheddar cheese or Monterey Jack cheese with jalapeño peppers (3 ounces)

Bean Soup with Chicken and Vegetables

Fennel adds a subtle licorice flavor to the soup. This good, hearty soup makes a complete meal.

1 Rinse beans; drain. In a large saucepan combine beans and the 6 cups water. Bring to boiling; reduce heat. Simmer, uncovered, for 10 minutes. Remove from heat. Cover and let stand for 1 hour. Drain and rinse beans.

2 Meanwhile, in a 4- to 5-quart slow cooker combine onion, fennel, carrots, garlic, thyme, marjoram, and pepper. Place beans over vegetables. Pour broth over all.

3 Cover and cook on low-heat setting for 8 to 10 hours or on high-heat setting for 4 to 5 hours.

4 If using low-heat setting, turn to high-heat setting. Stir in chicken and tomatoes. Cover and cook 30 minutes more. Stir in parsley.

Nutrition Facts per serving: 214 cal., 5 g total fat (1 g sat. fat), 39 mg chol., 763 mg sodium, 22 g carbo., 9 g fiber, 20 g pro.

Prep: 30 minutes
Stand: 1 hour
Cook: Low 8 to 10 hours,
High 4 to 5 hours;
plus 30 minutes
Makes: 8 servings
Slow Cooker: 4- to 5-quart

1 cup dry Great Northern beans
6 cups water
1 cup chopped onion (1 large)
1 medium fennel bulb, trimmed and cut into ½-inch pieces
2 medium carrots, chopped (1 cup)
2 cloves garlic, minced
1 teaspoon dried thyme, crushed
1 teaspoon dried marjoram, crushed
¼ teaspoon black pepper
3 14-ounce cans chicken broth
2½ cups chopped cooked chicken
1 14½-ounce can diced tomatoes, undrained
2 tablespoons snipped fresh parsley

Chicken and Garbanzo Bean Soup

Shredded spinach adds freshness and color to this vegetable soup. Add it just before serving the soup to keep the spinach from wilting too much.

1 Rinse the garbanzo beans; place in a large saucepan. Add enough water to cover the beans by 2 inches. Bring to boiling; reduce heat. Simmer, uncovered, for 10 minutes. Remove from heat. Cover and let stand for 1 hour. Drain and rinse beans.

2 Place chicken and beans in a 3½- to 5-quart slow cooker. Add carrots, celery, onion, dried marjoram and thyme (if using), bouillon granules, salt, and pepper. Pour water over all.

3 Cover and cook on low-heat setting for 8 to 10 hours or on high-heat setting for 4 to 5 hours. Remove the chicken; cool slightly. Cut meat into bite-size pieces. Return to cooker. Add the spinach and, if using, the fresh marjoram and thyme. Let stand 5 minutes before serving.

Nutrition Facts per serving: 205 cal., 4 g total fat (1 g sat. fat), 40 mg chol., 625 mg sodium, 23 g carbo., 9 g fiber, 20 g pro.

Prep: 20 minutes
Stand: 1 hour plus 5 minutes
Cook: Low 8 to 10 hours,
    High 4 to 5 hours
Makes: 6 servings
Slow Cooker: 3½- to 5-quart

1 cup dry garbanzo beans (chickpeas)
1 pound skinless, boneless chicken breasts or thighs
2½ cups sliced carrots (5 medium)
1½ cups sliced celery (3 stalks)
1 cup chopped onion (1 large)
1 tablespoon snipped fresh marjoram or 1 teaspoon dried marjoram, crushed
1 tablespoon snipped fresh thyme or 1 teaspoon dried thyme, crushed
1 tablespoon instant chicken bouillon granules
¼ teaspoon salt
¼ teaspoon black pepper
4 cups water
1 cup shredded fresh spinach or escarole

Easy Cassoulet Soup

Cooked on the stove, this soup could take hours of your attention. That's the beauty of the slow cooker! Enjoy this hearty soup without having to watch it cook all day long.

1 In a 3½- to 5-quart slow cooker place chicken, sausage, carrots, sweet pepper, onion, garlic, beans, and undrained tomatoes. Add broth, wine, parsley, thyme, cayenne pepper, and bay leaf.

2 Cover and cook on low-heat setting for 7 to 8 hours or on high-heat setting for 3½ to 4 hours. Discard bay leaf.

Nutrition Facts per serving: 186 cal., 4 g total fat (1 g sat. fat), 41 mg chol., 727 mg sodium, 23 g carbo., 6 g fiber, 17 g pro.

Prep: 20 minutes
Cook: Low 7 to 8 hours,
      High 3½ to 4 hours
Makes: 8 servings
Slow Cooker: 3½- to 5-quart

8 ounces skinless, boneless chicken thighs, cut into 1-inch pieces
8 ounces cooked smoked turkey sausage, halved lengthwise and cut into ½-inch slices
2 medium carrots, cut into ½-inch pieces
1 medium red or green sweet pepper, cut into ½-inch pieces
1 cup chopped onion (1 large)
3 cloves garlic, minced
2 15-ounce cans cannellini beans or Great Northern beans, rinsed and drained
1 14½-ounce can Italian-style stewed tomatoes, undrained
1½ cups chicken broth
½ cup dry white wine or chicken broth
1 tablespoon snipped fresh parsley
1 teaspoon dried thyme, crushed
⅛ to ¼ teaspoon cayenne pepper
1 bay leaf

Deviled Chicken Soup

Deviled refers to a food that is seasoned with piquant ingredients such as red pepper, hot pepper sauce, or, as in this dish, mustard. Add more or less to your liking.

1 In a 3½- or 4-quart slow cooker combine the chicken, potato, corn, onion, celery, mustard, pepper, and garlic powder. Pour vegetable juice and broth over all.

2 Cover and cook on low-heat setting for 8 to 10 hours or on high-heat setting for 4 to 5 hours.

Nutrition Facts per serving: 192 cal., 5 g total fat (1 g sat. fat), 36 mg chol., 800 mg sodium, 23 g carbo., 1 g fiber, 15 g pro.

Prep: 20 minutes
Cook: Low 8 to 10 hours,
       High 4 to 5 hours
Makes: 6 servings
Slow Cooker: 3½- or 4-quart

- 1 pound skinless, boneless chicken thighs, cut into bite-size pieces
- 1 large red potato, chopped
- ½ of a 16-ounce package (1½ cups) frozen whole kernel corn
- ½ cup chopped onion (1 medium)
- ½ cup chopped celery (1 stalk)
- 3 tablespoons Dijon-style mustard
- ¼ teaspoon black pepper
- ⅛ teaspoon garlic powder
- 2½ cups vegetable juice
- 1 14-ounce can reduced-sodium chicken broth

15 g carb

Thai Chicken Soup

Lemongrass is a popular herb used in Thai cooking. It resembles a very large green onion. Use only the fibrous white bulb to impart a lemon fragrance and flavor.

1 In a 3½- to 5-quart slow cooker combine the chicken, broth, carrots, onion, ginger, garlic, lemongrass, and crushed red pepper.

2 Cover and cook on low-heat setting for 6 to 7 hours or on high-heat setting for 3 to 3½ hours. If necessary, skim off fat. Stir coconut milk, sweet pepper, mushrooms, and cilantro into chicken mixture. Cover; let stand 5 to 10 minutes. Discard lemongrass (if using). Ladle soup into bowls. Sprinkle peanuts over each serving.

Nutrition Facts per serving: 328 cal., 20 g total fat (13 g sat. fat), 40 mg chol., 764 mg sodium, 15 g carbo., 4 g fiber, 23 g pro.

Prep: 20 minutes
Cook: Low 6 to 7 hours,
High 3 to 3½ hours
Stand: 5 minutes
Makes: 6 servings
Slow Cooker: 3½- to 5-quart

1 pound skinless, boneless chicken breasts or thighs, cut into ¾-inch pieces
4 cups chicken broth
2 cups bias-sliced carrots (4 medium)
1 cup chopped onion (1 large)
2 tablespoons grated fresh ginger
3 cloves garlic, minced
2 stalks lemongrass, cut into 1-inch pieces, or 1 teaspoon finely shredded lemon peel
½ teaspoon crushed red pepper
1 15-ounce can unsweetened coconut milk
1 medium red, yellow, and/or green sweet pepper, cut into ½-inch pieces
2 4-ounce cans straw or button mushrooms, drained
¼ cup snipped fresh cilantro
⅓ cup chopped roasted peanuts

Hearty Turkey Soup

Dried herbs and herb blends are preferred for slow cooking because they release their flavor gradually. Dried Italian seasoning is a fragrant blend of basil, oregano, rosemary, fennel seeds, and sometimes garlic powder and cayenne pepper.

1 In a large skillet cook the turkey, celery, carrot, and onion until turkey is no longer pink; drain fat. Transfer mixture to a 3½- or 4-quart slow cooker. Stir in tomato juice, frozen green beans, mushrooms, tomato, Italian seasoning, Worcestershire sauce, garlic salt, pepper, and bay leaf.

2 Cover and cook on low-heat setting for 5 to 6 hours or on high-heat setting for 2½ to 3 hours. Discard bay leaf.

Nutrition Facts per serving: 253 cal., 10 g total fat (3 g sat. fat), 90 mg chol., 970 mg sodium, 19 g carbo., 4 g fiber, 24 g pro.

Prep: 30 minutes
Cook: Low 5 to 6 hours,
High 2½ to 3 hours
Makes: 4 or 5 servings
Slow Cooker: 3½- or 4-quart

- 1 pound ground turkey or chicken
- 1 cup chopped celery (2 stalks)
- ½ cup thinly sliced carrot (1 medium)
- ½ cup chopped onion (1 medium)
- 3 cups tomato juice
- 2 cups frozen French-cut green beans
- 1 cup sliced fresh mushrooms
- ½ cup chopped tomato
- 2 teaspoons dried Italian seasoning, crushed
- 1½ teaspoons Worcestershire sauce
- ¾ teaspoon garlic salt
- ¼ teaspoon black pepper
- 1 bay leaf

34 g
carb

Split Pea and Smoked Turkey Soup

Cooked smoked turkey products are available at the supermarket deli. No need for anything fussy, however. This soup is full of many flavorful ingredients.

1 Rinse split peas; drain. In a 3½- or 4-quart slow cooker combine the split peas, smoked turkey, carrots, chives, garlic, and dried basil and oregano (if using). Pour broth and water over all.

2 Cover and cook on low-heat setting for 6 to 8 hours or on high-heat setting for 3 to 4 hours. Stir in dried tomatoes; cover and let stand for 10 minutes. If using, stir in fresh basil and oregano.

Nutrition Facts per serving: 243 cal., 3 g total fat (1 g sat. fat), 19 mg chol., 1,089 mg sodium, 34 g carbo., 13 g fiber, 21 g pro.

Prep: 20 minutes
Cook: Low 6 to 8 hours,
　　　　High 3 to 4 hours
Stand: 10 minutes
Makes: 8 servings
Slow Cooker: 3½- or 4-quart

- 2　cups dry yellow split peas (1 pound)
- 2　cups chopped cooked smoked turkey
　　　or sliced cooked turkey sausage
- 1½　cups coarsely shredded carrots
　　　(3 medium)
- 1　cup chopped chives
- 1　clove garlic, minced
- 1　tablespoon snipped fresh basil or
　　　1 teaspoon dried basil, crushed
- 1　tablespoon snipped fresh oregano or
　　　1 teaspoon dried oregano, crushed
- 5　cups chicken broth
- 2　cups water
- ½　cup snipped dried tomatoes (not
　　　oil-packed)

Manhattan-Style Clam Chowder

To save time and retain fiber, don't peel the potatoes. Just scrub and cube them.

1 Drain clams, reserving liquid (should have about ⅔ cup liquid). Place clams in a small bowl; cover and chill.

2 In a 3½- or 4-quart slow cooker combine reserved clam liquid, potatoes, onion, celery, sweet pepper, undrained tomatoes, tomato juice, thyme, and bay leaf.

3 Cover and cook on low-heat setting for 8 to 10 hours or on high-heat setting for 4 to 5 hours.

4 If using low-heat setting, turn to high-heat setting. Stir in clams. Cover and cook for 5 minutes more. Discard bay leaf. Ladle soup into bowls. Sprinkle each serving with crumbled bacon.

Nutrition Facts per serving: 238 cal., 5 g total fat (1 g sat. fat), 34 mg chol., 719 mg sodium, 30 g carbo., 4 g fiber, 17 g pro.

Prep: 20 minutes
Cook: Low 8 to 10 hours,
       High 4 to 5 hours;
           plus 5 minutes
Makes: 4 servings
Slow Cooker: 3½- or 4-quart

2   6½-ounce cans minced clams or one 10-ounce can baby clams
2   medium potatoes, peeled and cut into ½-inch cubes
1   cup chopped onion (1 large)
1   cup chopped celery with leaves (2 stalks)
½   cup chopped green sweet pepper (1 small)
1   14½-ounce can Italian-style stewed tomatoes, undrained
1½ cups hot-style tomato juice or hot-style vegetable juice
½   teaspoon dried thyme, crushed
1   bay leaf
4   slices bacon, crisp-cooked, drained, and crumbled, or ¼ cup cooked bacon pieces

Black Bean Soup

Set out an assortment of toppings such as sour cream, chopped avocado, sliced green onions, and chopped tomatoes to serve with this bean soup.

1 Rinse beans. In a large saucepan combine beans and 6 cups of the water. Bring to boiling; reduce heat. Simmer, uncovered, for 10 minutes. Remove from heat. Cover; let stand for 1 hour. Drain and rinse beans; set aside.

2 In a 4- to 5½-quart slow cooker combine beans, the remaining 6 cups water, carrots, onion, celery, bouillon cubes, cumin, coriander, savory, garlic, chili powder, and pepper.

3 Cover and cook on low-heat setting for 12 to 14 hours or on high-heat setting for 6 to 7 hours. Mash beans slightly just before serving. Stir in half-and-half.

Nutrition Facts per serving: 259 cal., 5 g total fat (2 g sat. fat), 11 mg chol., 530 mg sodium, 42 g carbo., 10 g fiber, 14 g pro.

*Note: Each cube makes 2 cups broth.

Prep: 25 minutes
Stand: 1 hour
Cook: Low 12 to 14 hours,
      High 6 to 7 hours
Makes: 8 servings
Slow Cooker: 4- to 5½-quart

1	pound dry black beans
12	cups water
1	cup coarsely chopped carrots (2 medium)
1	cup coarsely chopped onion (1 large)
1	cup coarsely chopped celery (2 stalks)
2	large vegetable bouillon cubes*
2	teaspoons ground cumin
2	teaspoons ground coriander
2	teaspoons dried savory, crushed
2	cloves garlic, minced
1	teaspoon chili powder
½	teaspoon black pepper
1	cup half-and-half or light cream

Cheesy Mexican-Style Vegetable Soup

Two soup favorites—cheese and vegetable—team up for a Mexican-style variation.

1 In a 3½- or 4-quart slow cooker place zucchini, sweet pepper, onion, beans, and corn. Pour undrained tomatoes over vegetables and beans. Combine cheese sauce and broth; pour over all.

2 Cover and cook on low-heat setting for 6 to 8 hours or on high-heat setting for 3 to 4 hours.

Nutrition Facts per serving: 239 cal., 11 g total fat (4 g sat. fat), 30 mg chol., 1,160 mg sodium, 30 g carbo., 6 g fiber, 10 g pro.

Prep: 15 minutes
Cook: Low 6 to 8 hours,
High 3 to 4 hours
Makes: 6 servings
Slow Cooker: 3½- or 4-quart

2 cups chopped zucchini (1 large)
¾ cup chopped red or green sweet pepper (1 medium)
½ cup chopped onion (1 medium)
1 15-ounce can black beans, rinsed and drained
1 10-ounce package frozen whole kernel corn, thawed
1 14½-ounce can diced tomatoes with green chiles, undrained
1 16-ounce jar cheddar cheese pasta sauce
1 cup reduced-sodium chicken broth or vegetable broth

Mexican Minestrone

Salsa and stewed tomatoes spice up minestrone, a popular Italian soup.

1 In a 3½- or 4-quart slow cooker combine all the ingredients, except sour cream.

2 Cover and cook on high-heat setting for 7 to 9 hours or until vegetables are tender. Top each serving with a spoonful of sour cream.

Nutrition Facts per serving: 193 cal., 3 g total fat (2 g sat. fat), 5 mg chol., 901 mg sodium, 37 g carbo., 7 g fiber, 11 g pro.

*Note: The Test Kitchen recommends cooking this recipe on a high-heat setting only.

Prep: 10 minutes
Cook: High 7 to 9 hours*
Makes: 8 servings
Slow Cooker: 3½- or 4-quart

- 2 15-ounce cans black beans, rinsed and drained
- 2 14½-ounce cans Mexican-style stewed tomatoes, undrained
- 1 15¼-ounce can whole kernel corn, rinsed and drained
- 1 14-ounce can reduced-sodium chicken broth
- 2 medium red-skin potatoes, coarsely chopped (2 cups)
- 1 cup bottled salsa
- 1 cup frozen cut green beans
  Dairy sour cream

Indian Vegetable Soup

Chock-full of nutty garbanzo beans, red-skinned potatoes, and chunks of eggplant, this curried soup makes a hearty meal.

1 In a 4- to 6-quart slow cooker combine eggplant, potatoes, undrained tomatoes, and garbanzo beans. Sprinkle vegetables with the ginger, mustard seeds, coriander, curry powder, and pepper. Pour broth over all.

2 Cover and cook on low-heat setting for 8 to 10 hours or on high-heat setting for 4 to 5 hours. Ladle into bowls and sprinkle with cilantro.

Nutrition Facts per serving: 162 cal., 2 g total fat (0 g sat. fat), 0 mg chol., 889 mg sodium, 30 g carbo., 7 g fiber, 8 g pro.

Prep: 30 minutes
Cook: Low 8 to 10 hours,
       High 4 to 5 hours
Makes: 6 to 8 servings
Slow Cooker: 4- to 6-quart

- 1 medium eggplant, cut into ½-inch cubes (5 to 6 cups)
- 1 pound red-skin potatoes, cut into 1-inch pieces (3 cups)
- 2 cups chopped tomatoes or one 14½-ounce can low-sodium tomatoes, cut up and undrained
- 1 15-ounce can garbanzo beans (chickpeas), rinsed and drained
- 1 tablespoon grated fresh ginger
- 1½ teaspoons mustard seeds
- 1½ teaspoons ground coriander
- 1 teaspoon curry powder
- ¼ teaspoon black pepper
- 4 cups vegetable broth or chicken broth
- 2 tablespoons snipped fresh cilantro

30 g carb

Lentil-Veggie Soup

Combine lentils with vegetables to make a thick and satisfying soup that is perfect for a cold-weather meal.

1 Rinse lentils. In a 3½- or 4-quart slow cooker place lentils, carrots, celery, onion, garlic, basil, oregano, thyme, and bay leaf. Stir in broth, water, and undrained tomatoes.

2 Cover and cook on low-heat setting for 12 hours or on high-heat setting for 5 to 6 hours. Discard bay leaf. Stir in parsley.

Nutrition Facts per serving: 165 cal., 1 g total fat (0 g sat. fat), 0 mg chol., 713 mg sodium, 30 g carbo., 12 g fiber, 11 g pro.

Prep: 20 minutes
Cook: Low 12 hours,
High 5 to 6 hours
Makes: 6 servings
Slow Cooker: 3½- or 4-quart

1   cup dry lentils
1   cup chopped carrots (2 medium)
1   cup chopped celery (2 stalks)
1   cup chopped onion (1 large)
2   cloves garlic, minced
½   teaspoon dried basil, crushed
½   teaspoon dried oregano, crushed
¼   teaspoon dried thyme, crushed
1   bay leaf
2   14-ounce cans vegetable broth or
     chicken broth
1½   cups water
1   14½-ounce can Italian-style stewed
     tomatoes, undrained
¼   cup snipped fresh parsley

Spiced Butternut Squash and Lentil Soup

The magic of this soup is garam masala. Find it with the spices in your supermarket or in an Indian market. The North Indian blend of ground spices can include cinnamon, nutmeg, cloves, coriander, cumin, cardamom, pepper, chiles, fennel, and mace.

1 Rinse and drain lentils. In a 3½- or 4-quart slow cooker place lentils, squash, onion, carrot, and celery. Sprinkle garlic and garam masala over vegetables. Pour chicken broth over all.

2 Cover and cook on low-heat setting for 8 to 9 hours or on high-heat setting for 4 to 4½ hours. Ladle into bowls.

Nutrition Facts per serving: 199 cal., 2 g total fat (0 g sat. fat), 0 mg chol., 639 mg sodium, 31 g carbo., 13 g fiber, 16 g pro.

Prep: 25 minutes
Cook: Low 8 to 9 hours,
      High 4 to 4½ hours
Makes: 5 to 6 servings
Slow Cooker: 3½- or 4-quart

1   cup dry lentils
2½ cups peeled butternut squash, cut into ¾-inch pieces
½   cup chopped onion (1 medium)
½   cup chopped carrot (1 medium)
½   cup chopped celery (1 stalk)
2   cloves garlic, minced
1   teaspoon garam masala
4   cups chicken broth or vegetable broth

Eggplant-Tomato Stew with Garbanzos

Garbanzo beans and chickpeas are one and the same. Usually they are stocked along with canned beans or in the Mexican foods section of the supermarket.

1 In a 5- to 6-quart slow cooker combine eggplant, tomatoes, carrots, beans, onion, celery, garlic, broth, tomato paste, oregano, basil, salt, black pepper, cayenne pepper, and bay leaf.

2 Cover and cook on low-heat setting for 8 to 9 hours or on high-heat setting for 4 to 4½ hours. Discard bay leaf.

Nutrition Facts per serving: 170 cal., 2 g total fat (0 g sat. fat), 0 mg chol., 923 mg sodium, 33 g carbo., 9 g fiber, 9 g pro.

Prep: 25 minutes
Cook: Low 8 to 9 hours,
   High 4 to 4½ hours
Makes: 8 servings
Slow Cooker: 5- to 6-quart

1 medium eggplant, peeled, if desired, and cut into ½-inch cubes
2 cups chopped tomatoes (4 medium)
1½ cups sliced carrots (3 medium)
1 15-ounce can garbanzo beans (chickpeas), rinsed and drained
1 15-ounce can red kidney beans, rinsed and drained
1 cup chopped onion (1 large)
1 cup sliced celery (2 stalks)
3 cloves garlic, minced
3 cups vegetable broth or chicken broth
1 6-ounce can Italian-style tomato paste
½ teaspoon dried oregano, crushed
½ teaspoon dried basil, crushed
¼ teaspoon salt
¼ teaspoon black pepper
¼ teaspoon crushed red pepper
1 bay leaf

French Onion Soup

Fit this classic French dish into your schedule by cooking it as little as 2½ hours on high or as long as 5 (or even up to 10) hours on low. Precooking the onions can be done on the stove top with very little attention required.

1 In a large skillet cook the onions and garlic in hot butter, covered, over medium-low heat about 20 minutes or until tender, stirring occasionally.

2 Transfer onion mixture to a 3½- or 4-quart slow cooker. Add beef broth, Worcestershire sauce, and pepper. Cover; cook on low-heat setting for 5 hours or on high-heat setting for 2½ hours.

3 Ladle soup into bowls. If desired, top each serving with a bread slice. Sprinkle each serving with cheese.

Nutrition Facts per serving: 126 cal., 9 g total fat (6 g sat. fat), 25 mg chol., 719 mg sodium, 6 g carbo., 1 g fiber, 5 g pro.

Prep: 30 minutes
Cook: Low 5 hours,
    High 2½ hours
Makes: 6 appetizer servings
Slow Cooker: 3½- or 4-quart

- 4 to 6 onions, thinly sliced (4 to 6 cups)
- 1 clove garlic, minced
- 3 tablespoons butter or margarine
- 4½ cups beef broth
- 1½ teaspoons Worcestershire sauce
- ⅛ teaspoon black pepper
- 6 1-inch slices baguette-style French bread (optional)
- ½ cup shredded Swiss or Gruyère cheese

31 g
carb

Creamy Curried Vegetable Soup

Indian cuisine has a lovely way with vegetables, slightly hot, slightly sweet, saucy, and fresh. It's sublime in this soup. Stretch leftovers with scoops of hot rice.

1 In a 3½- to 6-quart slow cooker combine potatoes, cauliflower, carrots, sweet pepper, onion, and beans. Sprinkle curry powder, ginger, salt, and red pepper over vegetables and beans. Pour broth over all.

2 Cover and cook on low-heat setting for 8 to 10 hours or on high-heat setting for 4 to 5 hours. Stir in coconut milk. Ladle into bowls and sprinkle with cilantro.

Nutrition Facts per serving: 293 cal., 16 g total fat (13 g sat. fat), 0 mg chol., 1,030 mg sodium, 31 g carbo., 7 g fiber, 9 g pro.

Prep: 25 minutes
Cook: Low 8 to 10 hours, High 4 to 5 hours
Makes: 6 to 8 servings
Slow Cooker: 3½- to 6-quart

1 pound potatoes, peeled and cut into 1-inch pieces (3 cups)
3 cups cauliflower florets
1½ cups sliced carrots (3 medium)
¾ cup coarsely chopped red sweet pepper (1 medium)
½ cup chopped onion (1 medium)
1 15-ounce can garbanzo beans, rinsed and drained
2 to 3 teaspoons curry powder
2 teaspoons grated fresh ginger
½ teaspoon salt
⅛ teaspoon crushed red pepper
2 14-ounce cans chicken broth or vegetable broth (3½ cups total)
1 14-ounce can unsweetened coconut milk
2 tablespoons snipped fresh cilantro

Beef

28 g
carb

Beef Roast and Vegetables

Leave the peels on the potatoes; you'll save time as well as valuable nutrients and fiber.

1 Trim fat from meat. If necessary, cut roast to fit into a 5- to 6-quart slow cooker. In the cooker place potatoes, carrots, and onion. Add bay leaf and pepper. Place meat on top of vegetables. Pour broth over all.

2 Cover and cook on low-heat setting for 12 to 14 hours or on high-heat setting for 6 to 7 hours.

3 In a small bowl combine flour and butter. Remove meat from cooker and set aside. Stir flour mixture and green beans into cooker. Return meat to cooker; cover and cook an additional 1 hour.

4 To serve, discard bay leaf. Arrange roast and vegetables on a warm serving platter. Skim fat from gravy. Spoon some of the gravy over roast; pass remaining gravy with roast and vegetables.

Nutrition Facts per serving: 447 cal., 21 g total fat (9 g sat. fat), 112 mg chol., 521 mg sodium, 28 g carbo., 4 g fiber, 35 g pro.

Prep: 20 minutes
Cook: Low 13 to 15 hours,
High 7 to 8 hours
Makes: 6 servings
Slow Cooker: 5- to 6-quart

1 2- to 2½-pound beef round tip roast
1½ pounds small potatoes (about 10), halved, or medium potatoes (about 4), quartered
2 medium carrots, cut into 1-inch pieces (1 cup)
1 large onion, sliced
1 bay leaf
¼ teaspoon black pepper
1 10-ounce can condensed beef broth
3 tablespoons all-purpose flour
3 tablespoons butter or margarine, melted
1 10-ounce package frozen cut green beans

Beef Roast with Sweet Potatoes

This old-fashioned dinner favorite is seasoned with cinnamon. Top the fork-tender meat with a quick stove-top gravy made from the cooking juices.

1 Trim fat from meat. If necessary, cut roast to fit into a 3½- or 4-quart slow cooker. In a large skillet brown meat on all sides in hot oil. Drain fat.

2 In the cooker place the onion, then the potatoes. Place meat on top of vegetables. In a small bowl combine water, bouillon granules, celery seeds, cinnamon, and pepper. Pour over meat and vegetables.

3 Cover and cook on low-heat setting for 8 to 10 hours or on high-heat setting for 4 to 5 hours.

4 Remove meat and vegetables from cooker and place on platter; if desired, reserve juices for gravy.

5 For gravy, pour juices into a large measuring cup. Skim fat. If necessary, add water to equal 2 cups liquid. In a saucepan stir cornstarch into 2 tablespoons cold water; add cooking juices. Cook and stir until thickened and bubbly. Cook and stir 2 minutes more. Serve gravy with roast and vegetables.

Nutrition Facts per serving: 328 cal., 8 g total fat (2 g sat. fat), 89 mg chol., 306 mg sodium, 28 g carbo., 4 g fiber, 34 g pro.

Prep: 15 minutes
Cook: Low 8 to 10 hours,
High 4 to 5 hours
Makes: 6 servings
Slow Cooker: 3½- or 4-quart

1   2-pound boneless beef chuck pot roast
1   tablespoon cooking oil
1   medium onion, sliced
2   pounds sweet potatoes or regular baking potatoes, peeled and quartered
¾   cup water
1½   teaspoons instant beef bouillon granules
¼   teaspoon celery seeds
¼   teaspoon ground cinnamon
¼   teaspoon black pepper
2   tablespoons cornstarch (optional)
2   tablespoons cold water (optional)

17 g
carb

Beef Roast with Tomato-Wine Sauce

Sure to become an autumn favorite, this recipe highlights some of the produce you'll find at farmers' markets during that time of year.

1 Trim fat from meat. If necessary, cut roast to fit into a 3½- to 6-quart slow cooker. In a large skillet brown meat on all sides in hot oil. Drain fat.

2 Meanwhile, in the cooker place turnips, carrots, tomato sauce, wine, tapioca, salt, allspice, and pepper; stir. Place roast on top of vegetables. Place squash on roast.

3 Cover and cook on low-heat setting for 10 to 12 hours or high-heat setting for 5 to 6 hours. Transfer meat and vegetables to a warm serving platter. Skim fat from sauce. Pass sauce with roast.

Nutrition Facts per serving: 404 cal., 24 g total fat (9 g sat. fat), 87 mg chol., 537 mg sodium, 17 g carbo., 3 g fiber, 26 g pro.

Prep: 30 minutes
Cook: Low 10 to 12 hours,
      High 5 to 6 hours
Makes: 6 servings
Slow Cooker: 3½- to 6-quart

1 2- to 2½-pound beef chuck pot roast
1 tablespoon cooking oil
2 medium turnips, peeled and cut into
    1-inch pieces (2 cups)
3 medium carrots, cut into ½-inch
    pieces (1½ cups)
1 15-ounce can tomato sauce
¼ cup dry red wine or beef broth
3 tablespoons quick-cooking tapioca
¼ teaspoon salt
⅛ teaspoon ground allspice
⅛ teaspoon black pepper
1 pound winter squash, peeled, seeded,
    and cut into thin wedges or 1½- to
    2-inch pieces (2 cups)

Herbed-Port Pot Roast

Port wine is the flavor star here. No need to buy expensive port, which is aged for several years. The less expensive ruby port is sufficient.

1 Trim fat from meat. If necessary, cut roast to fit into a 3½- or 4-quart slow cooker. Place meat in the cooker.

2 In a bowl combine onion, port wine, tomato sauce, tapioca, Worcestershire sauce, thyme, oregano, and garlic. Pour over meat.

3 Cover and cook on low-heat setting for 8 to 10 hours or on high-heat setting for 4 to 5 hours. Transfer meat to a serving platter. Skim fat from gravy. Pass gravy with roast. If desired, serve with hot cooked pasta.

Nutrition Facts per serving: 230 cal., 5 g total fat (2 g sat. fat), 84 mg chol., 247 mg sodium, 9 g carbo., 1 g fiber, 31 g pro.

Prep: 15 minutes
Cook: Low 8 to 10 hours,
High 4 to 5 hours
Makes: 8 to 10 servings
Slow Cooker: 3½- or 4-quart

1 2½- to 3-pound beef chuck pot roast
½ cup chopped onion (1 medium)
½ cup port wine or apple juice
1 8-ounce can tomato sauce
3 tablespoons quick-cooking tapioca
1 tablespoon Worcestershire sauce
1 teaspoon dried thyme, crushed
1 teaspoon dried oregano, crushed
2 cloves garlic, minced
   Hot cooked whole wheat pasta
      (optional)

31 g
carb

Pot Roast with Mushroom Sauce

Luscious mushroom sauce turns a budget beef roast into a silver-spoon standout.

1 Trim fat from meat. If necessary, cut roast to fit into a 3½- to 4½-quart slow cooker. In the cooker combine potatoes, frozen carrots, mushroom pieces, tarragon, and salt. Place meat on top of the vegetables. Pour soup over all.

2 Cover and cook on low-heat setting for 10 to 12 hours or on high-heat setting for 5 to 6 hours.

Nutrition Facts per serving: 338 cal., 8 g total fat (3 g sat. fat), 62 mg chol., 817 mg sodium, 31 g carbo., 5 g fiber, 35 g pro.

Prep: 20 minutes
Cook: Low 10 to 12 hours,
High 5 to 6 hours
Makes: 5 to 6 servings
Slow Cooker: 3½- to 4½-quart

1 1½-pound boneless beef chuck eye roast, eye of round roast, or round rump roast
4 medium unpeeled potatoes, quartered (about 1½ pounds)
1 16-ounce package frozen tiny whole carrots
1 4-ounce can mushroom stems and pieces, drained
½ teaspoon dried tarragon or basil, crushed
¼ teaspoon salt
1 10¾-ounce can condensed golden mushroom soup

Pot Roast with Dried Tomatoes

Dried tomatoes, lima beans, peas, carrots, turnip, and herbs unite for a roast that's blessed with a full, robust flavor.

1 Trim fat from meat. If necessary, cut roast to fit into a 3½- or 4-quart slow cooker. In the cooker combine the carrots, turnip, dried tomatoes, onion, garlic, bouillon granules, basil, oregano, and pepper. Place meat on top of vegetables. Pour water over all.

2 Cover and cook on low-heat setting for 8 to 10 hours or on high-heat setting for 4 to 5 hours. Stir in lima beans and peas. Let stand, covered, for 10 minutes.

3 Transfer meat and vegetables to a serving platter using a slotted spoon. If desired, serve cooking juices over meat.

Nutrition Facts per serving: 252 cal., 5 g total fat (1 g sat. fat), 67 mg chol., 368 mg sodium, 22 g carbo., 6 g fiber, 30 g pro.

Prep: 25 minutes
Cook: Low 8 to 10 hours,
High 4 to 5 hours
Stand: 10 minutes
Makes: 6 servings
Slow Cooker: 3½- or 4-quart

- 1 1½- to 2-pound boneless beef chuck pot roast
- 2 carrots, cut into ½-inch pieces
- 1 medium turnip, peeled and cubed (1 cup)
- ½ cup snipped dried tomatoes (not oil-packed)
- ⅓ cup chopped onion (1 small)
- 1 clove garlic, minced
- 1 teaspoon instant beef bouillon granules
- ½ teaspoon dried basil, crushed
- ½ teaspoon dried oregano, crushed
- ⅛ teaspoon black pepper
- 1 cup water
- 1 10-ounce package frozen lima beans or whole kernel corn
- 1 cup frozen peas

Pot Roast with Dill

To season meat, some cooks prefer the taste and texture of kosher salt, which is coarsely ground and additive-free.

1 Trim fat from meat. If necessary, cut roast to fit into a 3½- or 4-quart slow cooker. In a large skillet brown the meat on all sides in hot oil. Drain fat. Transfer meat to cooker; add the water. Sprinkle roast with 2 teaspoons of fresh dill or ¾ teaspoon of dried dill, the salt, and black pepper.

2 Cover and cook on low-heat setting for 10 to 12 hours or on high-heat setting for 5 to 6 hours. Transfer meat to a serving platter, reserving juices; cover roast with foil to keep warm. Pour cooking juices into a large measuring cup; skim fat. Measure 1 cup juices.

3 For sauce, in a small saucepan stir together yogurt and flour. Stir in 1 cup reserved cooking juices and remaining dill. Cook and stir until thickened and bubbly. Cook and stir for 1 minute more. Pour some of the sauce over meat; pass remaining sauce. If desired, serve with pasta.

Nutrition Facts per serving: 275 cal., 10 g total fat (3 g sat. fat), 113 mg chol., 302 mg sodium, 3 g carbo., 0 g fiber, 42 g pro.

Prep: 20 minutes
Cook: Low 10 to 12 hours,
High 5 to 6 hours;
plus 10 minutes
Makes: 6 servings
Slow Cooker: 3½- or 4-quart

1	2½- to 3-pound boneless beef chuck pot roast
1	tablespoon cooking oil
½	cup water
1	tablespoon snipped fresh dill or 1 teaspoon dried dill
½	teaspoon coarse salt or ¼ teaspoon regular salt
½	teaspoon black pepper
½	cup plain yogurt
2	tablespoons all-purpose flour Hot cooked whole wheat pasta (optional)

Pantry Pot Roast

Subtle allspice and mixed fruit create an interesting flavor for this pot roast. Choose packages of dried fruit that contain larger pieces rather than diced fruit, which will disintegrate during the long cooking time.

1 Trim fat from meat. If necessary, cut roast to fit into a 3½- or 4-quart slow cooker. In a Dutch oven brown meat on all sides in hot oil. Drain fat. Sprinkle meat with salt and pepper. Cut up any extra-large pieces of dried fruit. In the cooker place dried fruit and onion wedges. Place meat on top of the fruit and onions. Sprinkle with allspice. Add apple juice.

2 Cover and cook on low-heat setting for 8 to 10 hours or on high-heat setting for 4 to 5 hours.

Nutrition Facts per serving: 452 cal., 26 g total fat (9 g sat. fat), 98 mg chol., 194 mg sodium, 27 g carbo., 2 g fiber, 29 g pro.

Prep: 15 minutes
Cook: Low 8 to 10 hours,
High 4 to 5 hours
Makes: 6 servings
Slow Cooker: 3½- or 4-quart

1   2-pound boneless beef chuck pot roast
1   tablespoon cooking oil
    Salt
    Black pepper
1   7- to 8-ounce package mixed dried fruit
2   cups thin onion wedges
¼   teaspoon ground allspice
1   5½-ounce can apple juice

Saucy Pot Roast

This recipe is the epitome of comfort food and will have your family asking for seconds.

1 Trim fat from meat. If necessary, cut roast to fit into a 3½- or 4-quart slow cooker. In a large skillet brown meat on all sides in hot oil. In the cooker place carrots, celery, onion, and garlic. Sprinkle tapioca over vegetables. Place meat on top of vegetables.

2 In a medium bowl combine undrained tomatoes, tomato paste, brown sugar (if desired), salt, pepper, and bay leaf; pour over the meat.

3 Cover and cook on low-heat setting for 10 to 12 hours or on high-setting for 4 to 5 hours. Discard bay leaf. Transfer roast to a warm serving platter. Skim fat from gravy; drizzle some of the sauce over the meat. Pass remaining sauce. If desired, serve with hot cooked pasta.

Nutrition Facts per serving: 289 cal., 9 g total fat (2 g sat. fat), 89 mg chol., 710 mg sodium, 16 g carbo., 3 g fiber, 34 g pro.

Prep: 25 minutes
Cook: Low 10 to 12 hours,
  High 4 to 5 hours
Makes: 6 to 8 servings
Slow Cooker: 3½- or 4-quart

1 2- to 2½-pound beef chuck pot roast
1 tablespoon cooking oil
2 medium carrots, coarsely chopped
    (1 cup)
2 stalks celery, sliced (1 cup)
1 medium onion, sliced
2 cloves garlic, minced
1 tablespoon quick-cooking tapioca
1 14½-ounce can Italian-style stewed
    tomatoes, undrained
1 6-ounce can Italian-style tomato
    paste
1 tablespoon brown sugar (optional)
½ teaspoon salt
¼ teaspoon black pepper
1 bay leaf
    Hot cooked whole wheat pasta
    (optional)

German-Style Beef Roast

Many versions of German pot roast feature tangy, spicy flavors. Red wine, chopped dill pickles, and hearty mustard set this one apart.

1 Trim fat from meat. If necessary, cut roast to fit into a 3½- or 4-quart slow cooker. In a large skillet brown the meat on all sides in hot oil. Drain fat.

2 In the cooker place the carrots, onions, celery, and pickles. Place the meat on top of vegetables. In a small bowl combine the ½ cup red wine, the mustard, pepper, cloves, and bay leaves. Pour over meat.

3 Cover and cook on low-heat setting for 8 to 10 hours or on high-heat setting for 4 to 5 hours. Remove the meat from the cooker and place on a serving platter; cover with foil to keep warm.

4 For gravy, transfer vegetables and cooking liquid to a 2-quart saucepan. Skim fat. Discard bay leaves. Stir together flour and the 2 tablespoons wine. Stir into the mixture in saucepan. Cook and stir over medium heat until thickened and bubbly. Cook and stir for 1 minute more. Serve meat and vegetables with gravy. If desired, serve with hot cooked pasta and garnish with bacon.

Nutrition Facts per serving: 256 cal., 7 g total fat (2 g sat. fat), 84 mg chol., 467 mg sodium, 10 g carbo., 2 g fiber, 31 g pro.

Prep: 25 minutes
Cook: Low 8 to 10 hours,
High 4 to 5 hours,
plus 10 minutes
Makes: 8 servings
Slow Cooker: 3½- or 4-quart

1 2½- to 3-pound boneless beef chuck pot roast
1 tablespoon cooking oil
2 cups sliced carrots (2)
2 cups chopped onions (2 large)
1 cup sliced celery (2 stalks)
¾ cup chopped kosher-style dill pickles
½ cup dry red wine or beef broth
⅓ cup German-style mustard
½ teaspoon coarse ground black pepper
¼ teaspoon ground cloves
2 bay leaves
2 tablespoons all-purpose flour
2 tablespoons dry red wine or beef broth
Hot cooked whole wheat pasta (optional)
Crumbled cooked bacon (optional)

17 g
carb

Pot Roast with Chipotle-Fruit Sauce

Vary the amount of chipotle peppers to provide the level of heat you can tolerate.

1 Sprinkle both sides of the meat with garlic-pepper seasoning. If necessary, cut the roast to fit into a 3½- or 4-quart slow cooker. Place meat in the cooker. Add fruit and chipotle peppers. Pour water over all.

2 Cover and cook on low-heat setting for 10 to 11 hours or on high-heat setting for 5 to 5½ hours. Transfer meat and fruit to a serving platter. Cover with foil to keep warm.

3 Transfer cooking liquid to a large measuring cup; skim fat. In a medium saucepan combine cornstarch and the 1 tablespoon water; add cooking liquid. Cook and stir until thickened and bubbly; cook and stir for 2 minutes more. Thinly slice meat. To serve, spoon sauce over sliced meat and fruit.

Nutrition Facts per serving: 275 cal., 6 g total fat (2 g sat. fat), 101 mg chol., 378 mg sodium, 17 g carbo., 1 g fiber, 37 g pro.

Prep: 15 minutes
Cook: Low 10 to 11 hours,
    High 5 to 5½ hours;
        plus 10 minutes
Makes: 8 servings
Slow Cooker: 3½- or 4-quart

- 1 3-pound boneless beef chuck pot roast
- 2 teaspoons garlic-pepper seasoning
- 1 7-ounce package dried mixed fruit
- 1 tablespoon finely chopped chipotle peppers in adobo sauce
- ½ cup water
- 2 teaspoons cornstarch
- 1 tablespoon water

Asian-Style Pot Roast

Black bean garlic sauce, a staple in Chinese cuisine, gives a rich, exotic flavor to pot roast. Look for the sauce in the Asian foods section of the supermarket or in Asian grocery stores.

1 Trim fat from meat. If necessary, cut roast to fit into a 4- to 5½-quart slow cooker. In a large skillet brown meat on all sides in hot oil. Drain off fat.

2 In the cooker stir together the 1½ cups water, garlic sauce, bouillon granules, and, if desired, sugar. Add sweet pepper, onion, and green beans. Place meat on top of the vegetables.

3 Cover and cook on low-heat setting for 10 to 12 hours or on high-heat setting for 5 to 6 hours.

4 Transfer meat and vegetables to a serving platter, reserving juices; cover meat with foil to keep warm.

5 If using low-heat setting, turn to high-heat setting. For the sauce, in a small bowl combine cornstarch and the 3 tablespoons cold water; stir into cooking juices in cooker. Cover and cook about 15 minutes more or until sauce is slightly thickened.

6 Use two forks to separate beef into serving pieces. Serve meat with the sauce, vegetables, and, if desired, hot cooked rice.

Prep: 30 minutes
Cook: Low 10 to 12 hours,
High 5 to 6 hours;
plus 15 minutes
Makes: 6 servings
Slow Cooker: 4- to 5½-quart

- 1 2-pound boneless beef chuck pot roast
- 1 tablespoon cooking oil
- 1½ cups hot water
- ¼ cup black bean garlic sauce
- 1 teaspoon instant beef bouillon granules
- 1 tablespoon sugar (optional)
- 1 medium red sweet pepper, cut into thin strips
- ½ medium white onion, sliced into thin strips
- 8 ounces green beans, trimmed
- 3 tablespoons cornstarch
- 3 tablespoons cold water
   Hot cooked brown rice (optional)

Nutrition Facts per serving: 261 cal., 9 g total fat (2 g sat. fat), 89 mg chol., 470 mg sodium, 10 g carbo., 2 g fiber, 34 g pro.

19 g
carb

Curried Pot Roast

A combination of ginger, curry, and turmeric takes this spicy roast beyond the ordinary. Savor every drop of flavor by serving with a gravy made from the cooking juices.

1 Trim fat from meat. If necessary, cut roast to fit into a 3½- or 4-quart slow cooker. In a small bowl stir together the ginger, curry powder, turmeric, salt, and pepper. Rub spice mixture over surface of meat. In the cooker place the onions, carrots, and garlic. Place the meat on top of the vegetables. Sprinkle with thyme; add undrained tomatoes, beef broth, and bay leaf.

2 Cover and cook on low-heat setting for 8 to 10 hours or on high-heat setting for 4 to 5 hours. Remove bay leaf. Transfer meat and vegetables to a serving platter, reserving juices. Keep meat and vegetables warm.

3 For gravy, pour juices into a large measuring cup. Skim fat and discard bay leaf; measure juices. If necessary, add enough water to the juices to equal 1½ cups. Place juices in a small saucepan. Combine flour and the water. Stir water mixture into juices in saucepan. Cook and stir until thickened and bubbly. Cook and stir for 1 minute more. Serve gravy with meat and vegetables.

Nutrition Facts per serving: 348 cal., 10 g total fat (4 g sat. fat), 120 mg chol., 477 mg sodium, 19 g carbo., 4 g fiber, 42 g pro.

Prep: 35 minutes
Cook: Low 8 to 10 hours,
High 4 to 5 hours;
plus 10 minutes
Makes: 6 servings
Slow Cooker: 3½- or 4-quart

1 2½-pound boneless beef chuck pot roast
1 teaspoon ground ginger
1 teaspoon curry powder
1 teaspoon ground turmeric
½ teaspoon salt
¼ teaspoon black pepper
2 cups chopped onions (2 large)
6 medium carrots, cut into 1-inch pieces
2 cloves garlic, minced
½ teaspoon dried thyme, crushed
1 14½-ounce can diced tomatoes, undrained
½ cup beef broth
1 bay leaf
¼ cup all-purpose flour
½ cup cold water

Jerk Beef Roast

Jamaican jerk seasoning is the must-have ingredient for this roast. You'll enjoy the combination of spicy-sweet flavors, such as chiles, thyme, cinnamon, ginger, allspice, and cloves, this seasoning contributes.

1 Trim fat from meat. If necessary, cut roast to fit into a 3½- or 4-quart slow cooker. Place meat in the cooker. In a bowl combine water, raisins, steak sauce, balsamic vinegar, sugar (if desired), tapioca, pepper, Jamaican jerk seasoning, and garlic. Pour mixture over roast.

2 Cover and cook on low-heat setting for 8 to 10 hours or on high-heat setting for 4 to 5 hours. Skim fat from the cooking liquid. Serve beef with the cooking liquid and, if desired, hot cooked rice.

Nutrition Facts per serving: 237 cal., 6 g total fat (2 g sat. fat), 89 mg chol., 310 mg sodium, 12 g carbo., 1 g fiber, 33 g pro.

Prep: 30 minutes
Cook: Low 8 to 10 hours,
     High 4 to 5 hours
Makes: 6 servings
Slow Cooker: 3½- or 4-quart

1 2- to 2½-pound boneless beef chuck
     pot roast
¾ cup water
¼ cup raisins
¼ cup steak sauce
3 tablespoons balsamic vinegar
2 tablespoons sugar (optional)
2 tablespoons quick-cooking tapioca
1 teaspoon cracked black pepper
1 teaspoon Jamaican jerk seasoning
2 cloves garlic, minced
   Hot cooked brown rice (optional)

11 g
carb

Easy Beef Steak with Mushrooms

A few everyday ingredients transform a beef steak into a savory dinner. You can put it in the slow cooker while your morning coffee brews.

1 Trim any fat from meat. Cut meat into 4 serving-size pieces. Place onion slices in a 3½- or 4-quart slow cooker. Arrange mushrooms over onions; add meat. Stir together gravy and wine; pour over meat.

2 Cover and cook on low-heat setting for 8 to 10 hours or on high-heat setting for 4 to 5 hours.

For a 5- to 6-quart cooker: Recipe can be doubled. Makes 8 servings.

Nutrition Facts per serving: 220 cal., 4 g total fat (2 g sat. fat), 51 mg chol., 814 mg sodium, 11 g carbo., 3 g fiber, 31 g pro.

Prep: 10 minutes
Cook: Low 8 to 10 hours,
     High 4 to 5 hours
Makes: 4 servings
Slow Cooker: 3½- or 4-quart

1 pound boneless beef round steak, cut 1 inch thick
2 medium onions, sliced
2 4½-ounce jars whole mushrooms, drained
1 12-ounce jar beef gravy
¼ cup dry red wine or apple juice

Round Steak with Herbs

Cream of celery soup is the flavor base in this beef recipe. If you like, try other soup flavors such as cream of mushroom or onion.

1 Trim fat from meat. Cut steak into serving-size portions. Place onion in a 3½- or 4-quart slow cooker; place meat on top of onion. In a small bowl combine soup, oregano, thyme, and pepper; pour over meat.

2 Cover and cook on low-heat setting for 10 to 12 hours or on high-heat setting for 5 to 6 hours. If desired, serve with hot cooked pasta.

Nutrition Facts per serving: 249 cal., 9 g total fat (3 g sat. fat), 78 mg chol., 475 mg sodium, 5 g carbo., 1 g fiber, 34 g pro.

Prep: 10 minutes
Cook: Low 10 to 12 hours,
    High 5 to 6 hours
Makes: 6 servings
Slow Cooker: 3½- or 4-quart

- 2 pounds beef round steak, cut ¾ inch thick
- 1 medium onion, sliced
- 1 10¾-ounce can condensed cream of celery soup
- ½ teaspoon dried oregano, crushed
- ¼ teaspoon dried thyme, crushed
- ¼ teaspoon black pepper
  Hot cooked whole wheat pasta (optional)

24 g
carb

Round Steak with Garden Vegetables

Be sure to wait to add the zucchini until the last 30 minutes of the cooking time so it doesn't turn to mush.

1 Trim fat from meat. Cut steak into 4 serving-size pieces; sprinkle lightly with salt and pepper. Place meat in a 3½- or 4-quart slow cooker. Top meat with carrots, onion, and mushrooms.

2 In a medium bowl stir together undrained tomatoes, tomato paste, and Worcestershire sauce. Pour tomato mixture over meat and vegetables.

3 Cover and cook on low-heat setting for 8 to 9 hours or on high-heat setting for 4 to 4½ hours, adding zucchini during the last 30 minutes of cooking.

Nutrition Facts per serving: 336 cal., 8 g total fat (2 g sat. fat), 98 mg chol., 1,008 mg sodium, 24 g carbo., 5 g fiber, 41 g pro.

Prep: 15 minutes
Cook: Low 8 to 9 hours,
      High 4 to 4½ hours
Makes: 4 servings
Slow Cooker: 3½- or 4-quart

1½   pounds boneless beef round steak, cut
     ¾ to 1 inch thick
    Salt
    Black pepper
2   cups packaged, peeled baby carrots
1   large onion, cut into wedges
1   4½-ounce jar sliced mushrooms,
    drained
1   14½-ounce can diced tomatoes with
    basil, oregano, and garlic,
    undrained
3   tablespoons Italian-style tomato paste
1   tablespoon Worcestershire sauce
1   small zucchini, halved lengthwise and
    sliced (1 cup)

Italian-Style Steak

You can use red wine for a hearty dish and white wine or beef broth for a mild dish. All choices are delicious.

1 Place meat in a 3½- or 4-quart slow cooker. Add carrots, celery, mushrooms, green onions, undrained tomatoes, broth, wine, tapioca, Italian seasoning, salt, pepper, and bay leaf.

2 Cover and cook on low-heat setting for 9 to 10 hours or on high-heat setting for 4½ to 5 hours. Discard bay leaf. If desired, serve with hot cooked pasta.

Nutrition Facts per serving: 233 cal., 6 g total fat (2 g sat. fat), 54 mg chol., 551 mg sodium, 13 g carbo., 2 g fiber, 27 g pro.

Prep: 20 minutes
Cook: Low 9 to 10 hours,
        High 4½ to 5 hours
Makes: 6 servings
Slow Cooker: 3½- or 4-quart

1½ pounds boneless beef bottom round steak, trimmed and cut into 1-inch cubes
2 medium carrots, cut into ½-inch pieces
2 stalks celery, cut into ½-inch pieces
1 cup quartered fresh mushrooms
½ cup sliced green onions (4)
1 14½-ounce can Italian-style stewed tomatoes, undrained
1 cup beef broth
½ cup dry red wine, white wine, or beef broth
3 tablespoons quick-cooking tapioca
1 teaspoon dried Italian seasoning, crushed
½ teaspoon salt
¼ teaspoon black pepper
1 bay leaf
   Hot cooked whole wheat pasta (optional)

6 g
carb

Herbed Steak and Mushrooms

Bottom round steak, less expensive than tip round steak, is a good choice for the slow cooker because the moist heat tenderizes the meat.

1 Trim fat from meat. Cut steak into serving-size portions. In a 3½- or 4-quart slow cooker place the onion and mushrooms. Place beef steak on the vegetables. In a bowl combine soup, wine, basil, marjoram, and pepper; pour over meat.

2 Cover and cook on low-heat setting for 8 to 10 hours or on high-heat setting for 4 to 5 hours. If desired, serve with hot cooked pasta.

Nutrition Facts per serving: 274 cal., 11 g total fat (3 g sat. fat), 73 mg chol., 461 mg sodium, 6 g carbo., 1 g fiber, 36 g pro.

Prep: 15 minutes
Cook: Low 8 to 10 hours,
   High 4 to 5 hours
Makes: 6 servings
Slow Cooker: 3½- or 4-quart

2   pounds beef round steak, cut
      ¾ inch thick
1   medium onion, sliced
2   cups sliced fresh mushrooms or two
      4-ounce jars sliced mushrooms,
      drained
1   10¾-ounce can condensed cream of
      mushroom soup
¼   cup dry white wine or beef broth
½   teaspoon dried basil, crushed
¼   teaspoon dried marjoram, crushed
¼   teaspoon black pepper
      Hot cooked whole wheat pasta
      (optional)

So-Easy Pepper Steak

Give this pepper steak Cajun, Mexican, or Italian flavor by changing the style of stewed tomatoes.

1 Trim fat from meat. Cut meat into serving-size pieces. Sprinkle meat lightly with salt and black pepper. Place meat in a 3½- or 4-quart slow cooker. In a medium bowl combine undrained tomatoes, tomato paste, and hot pepper sauce. Pour tomato mixture over meat. Top with frozen vegetables.

2 Cover and cook on low-heat setting for 10 to 12 hours or on high-heat setting for 5 to 6 hours. If desired, serve with hot cooked pasta.

Nutrition Facts per serving: 196 cal., 5 g total fat (2 g sat. fat), 54 mg chol., 411 mg sodium, 9 g carbo.,1 g fiber, 27 g pro.

Prep: 15 minutes
Cook: Low 10 to 12 hours, High 5 to 6 hours
Makes: 8 servings
Slow Cooker: 3½- or 4-quart

2   pounds boneless beef round steak, cut ¾ to 1 inch thick
    Salt
    Black pepper
1   14½-ounce can Cajun-, Mexican-, or Italian-style stewed tomatoes, undrained
⅓   cup tomato paste with Italian seasoning
½   teaspoon bottled hot pepper sauce
1   16-ounce package frozen pepper stir-fry vegetables (yellow, green, and red sweet peppers with onion)
    Hot cooked whole wheat pasta (optional)

Italian Steak Rolls

These delicious steak rolls take on an Italian flair from Parmesan cheese and spaghetti sauce.

1 For the vegetable filling, in a small bowl combine carrot, zucchini, sweet pepper, green onions, Parmesan cheese, parsley, garlic, and black pepper. Spoon ¼ cup of the vegetable filling on each piece of meat. Roll up meat around the filling and tie each roll with string or secure with wooden toothpicks.

2 Place the meat rolls in a 3½- or 4-quart slow cooker. Pour spaghetti sauce over the meat rolls.

3 Cover and cook on low-heat setting for 8 to 10 hours or on high-heat setting for to 4 to 5 hours. Discard string or toothpicks. If desired, serve meat rolls and sauce with hot cooked pasta.

Nutrition Facts per serving: 261 cal., 9 g total fat (3 g sat. fat), 73 mg chol., 523 mg sodium, 7 g carbo., 2 g fiber, 36 g pro.

*Note: If you can't find tenderized round steak, have the butcher tenderize 2 pounds boneless beef round steak and cut it into 6 pieces. Or cut 2 pounds boneless beef round steak into 6 serving-size pieces; place meat between 2 pieces of plastic wrap and, using a meat mallet, pound the steak to ¼- to ½-inch thickness.

Prep: 30 minutes
Cook: Low 8 to 10 hours,
        High 4 to 5 hours
Makes: 6 servings
Slow Cooker: 3½- or 4-quart

½ cup shredded carrot
⅓ cup chopped zucchini
⅓ cup chopped red or green sweet
    pepper
¼ cup sliced green onions
2 tablespoons grated Parmesan cheese
1 tablespoon snipped fresh parsley
1 clove garlic, minced
¼ teaspoon black pepper
6 tenderized beef round steaks*
    (about 2 pounds total)
2 cups meatless spaghetti sauce
    Hot cooked whole wheat pasta
    (optional)

Swiss Steak Café

If you like coffee, you'll enjoy this recipe. Strong brewed coffee contributes to the flavor notes in this steak dish.

1 Trim fat from meat. Cut steak into serving-size pieces. In a 12-inch skillet brown meat on all sides in hot oil (add more oil, if necessary). Drain off fat.

2 Place onion in a 3½- or 4-quart slow cooker. Add meat. Sprinkle meat with tapioca. Add soy sauce, garlic, bay leaves, and oregano. Pour coffee over all.

3 Cover and cook on low-heat setting for 8 to 10 hours or on high-heat setting for 4 to 5 hours.

4 Transfer meat and onions to a serving platter. Discard bay leaves. Spoon some of the cooking juices over meat and onions before serving.

Nutrition Facts per serving: 256 cal., 9 g total fat (3 g sat. fat), 72 mg chol., 399 mg sodium, 6 g carbo., 1 g fiber, 35 g pro.

Prep: 20 minutes
Cook: Low 8 to 10 hours,
High 4 to 5 hours
Makes: 6 servings
Slow Cooker: 3½- or 4-quart

2 pounds boneless beef round steak, cut ¾ inch thick
1 tablespoon cooking oil
3 medium onions, cut into wedges
4 teaspoons quick-cooking tapioca
2 tablespoons soy sauce
1 teaspoon bottled minced garlic or 2 cloves garlic, minced
2 bay leaves
½ teaspoon dried oregano, crushed
1 cup strong brewed coffee

6 g
carb

Brisket in Ale

The flavorful gravy—made from the beer-spiked cooking liquid—is the finishing touch to this tender meat dish.

1 Trim fat from meat. If necessary, cut brisket to fit into a 3½- to 6-quart slow cooker. In the cooker place onions, bay leaf, and brisket. In a medium bowl combine beer, chili sauce, sugar substitute, thyme, salt, pepper, and garlic; pour over meat.

2 Cover and cook on low-heat setting for 10 to 12 hours or on high-heat setting for 5 to 6 hours.

3 Transfer brisket and onions to a serving platter using a slotted spoon; cover with foil to keep warm. Discard bay leaf.

4 For gravy, pour juices into a large measuring cup; skim fat. Measure 2½ cups liquid; discard remaining liquid. In a medium saucepan stir together the cornstarch and water; stir in the reserved liquid. Cook and stir until thickened and bubbly; cook and stir for 2 minutes more. Pass gravy with meat.

Nutrition Facts per serving: 170 cal., 6 g total fat (2 g sat. fat), 46 mg chol., 216 mg sodium, 6 g carbo., 1 g fiber, 20 g pro.

Prep: 25 minutes
Cook: Low 10 to 12 **hours,**
High 5 to 6 **hours;**
plus 10 **minutes**
Makes: 10 **servings**
Slow Cooker: 3½- to 6-**quart**

- 1 3- to 4-pound fresh beef brisket
- 2 medium onions, thinly sliced and separated into rings
- 1 bay leaf
- 1 12-ounce can beer
- ¼ cup chili sauce
- 2 tablespoons no-calorie, heat-stable, granular sugar substitute (Splenda)
- ½ teaspoon dried thyme, crushed
- ¼ teaspoon salt
- ¼ teaspoon black pepper
- 1 clove garlic, minced
- 2 tablespoons cornstarch
- 2 tablespoons water

Tangy Barbecue Beef

Brisket benefits from a long cooking time, so simmer it on low heat if your crockery cooker has a high/low option. Top this open-face, knife-and-fork sandwich with colorful mango slices.

1 In a small bowl combine chili powder, celery seeds, salt, and pepper. Rub spice mixture onto all sides of the brisket. Scatter half of the onions in the bottom of a 3½- to 6-quart slow cooker. Place brisket on the onions, cutting meat to fit cooker, if necessary. Scatter remaining onions on top of brisket. In a small bowl stir together barbecue sauce and beer. Pour over brisket and onions.

2 Cover and cook on low-heat setting for 10 to 12 hours or until meat is fork-tender. Transfer meat to a cutting board; let stand for 15 minutes. Halve meat crosswise. Use two forks to shred meat. Return meat to sauce mixture in cooker. Heat through using the high-heat setting.

3 To serve, use a slotted spoon to divide the meat mixture among each of 8 bun halves. If desired, season to taste with hot pepper sauce. Top with mango slices. (Freeze any remaining meat mixture in a freezer container for up to 3 months.)

Nutrition Facts per serving: 303 cal., 9 g total fat (3 g sat. fat), 72 mg chol., 780 mg sodium, 27 g carbo., 2 g fiber, 27 g pro.

Prep: 25 minutes
Cook: Low 10 to 12 hours
Stand: 15 minutes
Makes: 8 servings
Slow Cooker: 3½- to 6-quart

- 2 tablespoons chili powder
- 1 teaspoon celery seeds
- ½ teaspoon salt
- ½ teaspoon freshly ground pepper
- 1 3-pound fresh beef brisket, trimmed
- 2 onions, thinly sliced
- 1 cup bottled smoke-flavored barbecue sauce
- ½ cup beer
- 4 whole wheat buns, split and toasted
  Bottled hot pepper sauce (optional)
  Mango slices

7 g
carb

Beef Brisket with Barbecue Sauce

When you feel like having a barbecue without the use of a grill, here's the answer. A classic homemade barbecue sauce is made from some of the cooking liquid and passed with the juicy, tender meat.

1 For cooking liquid, in a bowl combine water, Worcestershire sauce, vinegar, bouillon granules, mustard, chili powder, cayenne pepper, and garlic. Reserve ½ cup liquid for sauce; set aside in refrigerator. Trim fat from meat. If necessary, cut brisket to fit into a 3½- or 4-quart slow cooker. Place meat in cooker. Pour remaining liquid over brisket.

2 Cover and cook on low-heat setting for 10 to 12 hours or on high-heat setting for 5 to 6 hours.

3 For sauce, in a small saucepan combine the ½ cup reserved liquid, catsup, sugar substitute, and butter. Heat through. Pass sauce with meat.

Nutrition Facts per serving: 194 cal., 9 g total fat (4 g sat. fat), 56 mg chol., 482 mg sodium, 7 g carbo., 0 g fiber, 21 g pro.

Prep: 25 minutes
Cook: Low 10 to 12 hours,
High 5 to 6 hours;
plus 10 minutes
Makes: 8 servings
Slow Cooker: 3½- or 4-quart

- ¾ cup water
- ¼ cup Worcestershire sauce
- 1 tablespoon vinegar
- 1 teaspoon instant beef bouillon granules
- ½ teaspoon dry mustard
- ½ teaspoon chili powder
- ¼ teaspoon cayenne pepper
- 2 cloves garlic, minced
- 1 2½-pound fresh beef brisket
- ½ cup catsup
- 2 tablespoons no-calorie, heat-stable, granular sugar substitute (Splenda)
- 2 tablespoons butter or margarine

Beef Brisket with Spicy Gravy

For a real timesaver, separately freeze half of the meat and half of the cooking liquid. Simply reheat the meat and finish the sauce for a quick dinner.

1 Trim fat from meat. If necessary, cut brisket to fit into a 3½- or 4-quart slow cooker. In a medium bowl combine the 2 cups water, catsup, soup mix, Worcestershire sauce, cinnamon, garlic, and pepper. Pour over brisket.

2 Cover and cook on low-heat setting for 10 to 11 hours or on high-heat setting for 5 to 5½ hours. Remove meat; keep warm. Pour cooking liquid into a glass measuring cup. Skim fat. Measure 1½ cups cooking liquid; set aside (discard remaining liquid).

3 For gravy, in a small saucepan stir the ¼ cup cold water into the flour. Stir in the 1½ cups cooking liquid. Cook and stir until thickened and bubbly. Cook and stir for 1 minute more.

4 Slice meat thinly across the grain. Serve with the hot gravy.

Nutrition Facts per serving: 247 cal., 9 g total fat (3 g sat. fat), 76 mg chol., 338 mg sodium, 5 g carbo., 0 g fiber, 33 g pro.

Note: To freeze, transfer ¾ cup of the liquid to a moisture and vapor-proof container. Cool slightly. Seal, label, and freeze up to 6 months. Transfer half of the beef to a moisture- and vapor-proof container. Seal, label, and freeze for up to 6 months. To serve, thaw meat and cooking liquid. Warm meat in a covered baking dish in a 350° oven for 20 minutes. For gravy, in a small saucepan stir together the ¾ cup cooking liquid, ¼ cup cold water, and 4 teaspoons all-purpose flour. Cook and stir until thickened and bubbly. Cook and stir 1 minute more. Serve as directed.

Prep: 15 minutes
Cook: Low 10 to 11 hours, High 5 to 5½ hours; plus 10 minutes
Makes: 10 to 12 servings
Slow Cooker: 3½- or 4-quart

- 1   3½- to 4-pound fresh beef brisket
- 2   cups water
- ¼   cup catsup
- 1   envelope (½ of an 2.2 ounce package) onion soup mix
- 2   tablespoons Worcestershire sauce
- ½   teaspoon ground cinnamon
- ½   teaspoon bottled minced garlic
- ¼   teaspoon black pepper
- ¼   cup cold water
- 3   tablespoons all-purpose flour

New England Boiled Dinner

On a chilly day, this slow-cooker version of the traditional one-pot meal will warm you through and through. And it's perfect for a St. Patrick's Day celebration.

1 If desired, prepare Sour Cream Sauce; cover and chill.

2 In a 5- to 6-quart slow cooker combine potatoes, carrots, onion, and garlic. Trim fat from the brisket. (Discard seasoning packet if present.) If necessary, cut brisket to fit into the cooker. Place brisket on top of vegetables. Sprinkle with dill seeds, rosemary, and salt. Pour broth over brisket. Cover and cook on low-heat setting for 11 to 12 hours or on high-heat setting for 5½ to 6 hours.

3 If using low-heat setting, turn to high-heat setting. Add cabbage wedges. Cover and cook for 30 to 60 minutes more or until cabbage is tender. Transfer meat to a cutting board. Thinly slice meat across the grain. Place meat slices on a serving platter. Using a slotted spoon, transfer vegetables to serving platter. If desired, serve with Sour Cream Sauce.

Sour Cream Sauce: In a small bowl stir together ½ cup mayonnaise or salad dressing, ½ cup dairy sour cream, 2 tablespoons horseradish mustard, and 2 teaspoons snipped fresh chives. Cover and chill for up to 24 hours.

Nutrition Facts per serving: 408 cal., 21 g total fat (6 g sat. fat), 85 mg chol., 647 mg sodium, 26 g carbo., 5 g fiber, 29 g pro.

Prep: 20 minutes
Chill: 5 to 24 hours
Cook: Low 11 to 12 hours,
High 5½ to 6 hours;
plus 30 minutes
Makes: 8 servings
Slow Cooker: 5- to 6-quart

1 recipe Sour Cream Sauce (optional)
6 medium potatoes, peeled and quartered (about 2 pounds)
6 medium carrots, cut into 2-inch lengths
1 large onion, quartered
3 cloves garlic, minced
1 3- to 3½-pound corned beef brisket
2 teaspoons dried dill seeds
1 teaspoon dried rosemary, crushed
½ teaspoon salt
2 14-ounce cans beef broth
1 small head cabbage, cut into 8 wedges

Short Ribs with Leeks

Lemon peel brightens the flavors of this succulent dish. Try it when you have a house full of guests and want to spend time with them instead of in the kitchen.

1 Place mushrooms, carrots, and leeks in a 3½- or 4-quart slow cooker. Place beef over vegetables. Sprinkle with lemon peel, pepper, rosemary, thyme, and salt. Add broth.

2 Cover and cook on low-heat setting for 7 to 8 hours or on high-heat setting for 3½ to 4 hours.

3 Transfer meat and vegetables to serving dish using a slotted spoon. Cover with foil to keep warm. Skim fat from remaining cooking liquid. Measure 1 cup cooking liquid. Place in a small saucepan. In a small bowl stir together sour cream and flour. Stir into cooking liquid using a whisk. Cook and stir over medium heat until slightly thickened and bubbly; cook and stir for 1 minute more. Ladle sauce over meat and vegetables.

Nutrition Facts per serving: 173 cal., 8 g total fat (4 g sat. fat), 33 mg chol., 252 mg sodium, 10 g carbo., 2 g fiber, 15 g pro.

Prep: 30 minutes
Cook: Low 7 to 8 hours, High 3½ to 4 hours; plus 10 minutes
Makes: 6 servings
Slow Cooker: 3½- or 4-quart

- 8 ounces fresh mushrooms, halved
- 4 medium carrots, cut into 1-inch pieces
- 4 medium leeks, cut into 1-inch slices
- 2 pounds boneless beef short ribs
- 2 teaspoons finely shredded lemon peel
- ½ teaspoon black pepper
- ½ teaspoon dried rosemary, crushed
- ½ teaspoon dried thyme, crushed
- ¼ teaspoon salt
- ¾ cup beef broth
- ⅓ cup dairy sour cream
- 1 tablespoon all-purpose flour

Cholent

Pronounced CHAW-lent, this hearty Jewish dish traditionally simmers on the stove top or bakes for many hours. The slow cooker gives similar flavorful results.

1 Rinse beans. In a large saucepan combine beans and water. Bring to boiling; reduce heat. Simmer, uncovered, for 10 minutes. Remove from heat. Cover; let stand for 1 hour. Drain and rinse beans; set aside.

2 Trim fat from ribs. Season meat with salt and pepper. In a 4-quart Dutch oven brown the ribs on both sides, half at a time, in the hot oil over medium-high heat. Drain fat. Remove from heat; set ribs aside.

3 In a 5- to 6-quart slow cooker combine drained beans, carrots, onions, potatoes, barley, garlic, the ½ teaspoon salt, the ½ teaspoon pepper, and paprika. Top with ribs. Pour broth over all.

4 Cover and cook on low-heat setting for 11 to 12 hours or on high-heat setting for 5½ to 6 hours. Sprinkle each serving with parsley just before serving.

Nutrition Facts per serving: 276 cal., 7 g total fat (2 g sat. fat), 27 mg chol., 484 mg sodium, 34 g carbo., 8 g fiber, 19 g pro.

Prep: 30 minutes
Stand: 1 hour
Cook: Low 11 to 12 hours,
High 5½ to 6 hours
Makes: 8 servings
Slow Cooker: 5- to 6-quart

¾   cup dry baby lima beans or dry Great
    Northern beans
6   cups water
2½   pounds beef short ribs, cut into
    serving-size pieces
    Salt
    Black pepper
1   tablespoon cooking oil
5   medium carrots, cut into 1-inch
    pieces
2   medium onions, cut into ¼-inch slices
2   medium red-skin potatoes, cut into
    1½-inch cubes
½   cup regular barley
4   cloves garlic, minced
½   teaspoon salt
½   teaspoon black pepper
¼   teaspoon paprika
2½   cups beef broth
    Snipped fresh parsley

Short Ribs with Horseradish Sauce

A sour cream and horseradish sauce complements these ribs perfectly.

1 Place carrots and onions in a 4- to 5-quart slow cooker. Place beef on top of vegetables. In a small bowl stir together wine, broth, mustard, garlic, salt, thyme, and pepper. Add broth mixture and bay leaf to cooker.

2 Cover and cook on low-heat setting for 9 to 10 hours or on high-heat setting for 4½ to 5 hours.

3 Transfer ribs and vegetables to a serving dish using a slotted spoon; reserve cooking liquid. Discard the bay leaf. Skim fat from liquid. Pour some of the cooking liquid over ribs to moisten. Serve ribs with Horseradish Sauce.

Horseradish Sauce: In a small bowl, combine one 8-ounce container light dairy sour cream, 2 to 3 tablespoons prepared horseradish, and ⅛ teaspoon salt. Cover and chill.

Nutrition Facts per serving: 499 cal., 27 g total fat (13 g sat. fat), 120 mg chol., 617 mg sodium, 10 g carbo., 2 g fiber, 47 g pro.

Prep: 25 minutes
Cook: Low 9 to 10 hours, High 4½ to 5 hours
Makes: 6 servings
Slow Cooker: 4- to 5-quart

- 3 large carrots, cut into 1-inch pieces
- 2 medium onions, cut into wedges
- 3 pounds boneless beef short ribs, trimmed and cut into 2-inch pieces
- ½ cup dry red wine
- ¼ cup beef broth
- 2 tablespoons Dijon-style mustard
- 1 tablespoon minced garlic
- ½ teaspoon salt
- ½ teaspoon dried thyme, crushed
- ¼ teaspoon black pepper
- 1 bay leaf
- 1 recipe Horseradish Sauce

10 g carb

Classic Beef Stroganoff

Some recipes should not be changed and this is one. It is delicious served over whole wheat pasta.

1 Cut up any large pieces of stew meat. In a large skillet brown meat, half at a time, in hot oil. Drain off fat.

2 In a 3½- or 4-quart slow cooker place mushrooms, onions, garlic, oregano, salt, thyme, pepper, and bay leaf. Add stew meat. Pour beef broth and sherry over all.

3 Cover and cook on low-heat setting for 8 to 10 hours or on high-heat setting for 4 to 5 hours. Discard bay leaf.

4 If using low-heat setting, turn to high-heat setting. In a bowl whisk together sour cream, flour, and water until smooth. Stir about 1 cup of the hot liquid into sour cream mixture. Return all to cooker; stir to combine. Cover and cook about 30 minutes more or until thickened and bubbly. If desired, serve over hot cooked pasta; sprinkle with parsley.

Nutrition Facts per serving: 302 cal., 15 g total fat (7 g sat. fat), 84 mg chol., 402 mg sodium, 10 g carbo., 1 g fiber, 28 g pro.

Prep: 30 minutes
Cook: Low 8 to 10 hours,
High 4 to 5 hours;
plus 30 minutes
Makes: 6 servings
Slow Cooker: 3½- or 4-quart

1½	pounds beef stew meat
1	tablespoon cooking oil
2	cups sliced fresh mushrooms
½	cup sliced green onions or ½ cup chopped onion
2	cloves garlic, minced
½	teaspoon dried oregano, crushed
¼	teaspoon salt
¼	teaspoon dried thyme, crushed
¼	teaspoon black pepper
1	bay leaf
1½	cups beef broth
⅓	cup dry sherry
1	8-ounce carton dairy sour cream
⅓	cup all-purpose flour
¼	cup water
	Hot cooked whole wheat pasta (optional)
	Snipped fresh parsley (optional)

Easy Beef Burgundy

This beef burgundy is easy because of the canned soup and onion soup mix. The hardest part is cutting up the meat and mushrooms.

1 In a large skillet brown the meat, half at a time, in hot oil. Drain off fat. In a 3½- to 5-quart slow cooker combine celery soup, mushroom soup, Burgundy, and onion soup mix. Stir in meat and mushrooms.

2 Cover and cook on low-heat setting for 8 to 10 hours or on high-heat setting for 4 to 5 hours. If desired, serve over hot cooked pasta.

Nutrition Facts per serving: 333 cal., 18 g total fat (4 g sat. fat), 60 mg chol., 984 mg sodium, 11 g carbo., 1 g fiber, 28 g pro.

Prep: 20 minutes
Cook: Low 8 to 10 hours,
High 4 to 5 hours
Makes: 6 servings
Slow Cooker: 3½- to 5-quart

1½ pounds beef stew meat, trimmed and
   cut into 1-inch cubes
2 tablespoons cooking oil
1 10¾-ounce can condensed cream of
   celery soup
1 10¾-ounce can condensed cream of
   mushroom soup
¾ cup Burgundy wine
1 envelope (½ of a 2.2-ounce package)
   onion soup mix
8 ounces fresh mushrooms, sliced
   (3 cups)
   Hot cooked whole wheat pasta or
   brown rice (optional)

Beef in Red Wine

Dry red wine is the major flavor contributor in this dish, so don't use a cheap cooking wine. Choose a wine that is reasonably priced and drinkable, such as Cabernet Sauvignon, Merlot, or Pinot Noir.

1 Place the beef and onions in a 3½- or 4-quart slow cooker. Add bouillon cubes. Sprinkle with cornstarch, salt, and pepper. Pour wine over all.

2 Cover and cook on low-heat setting for 10 to 12 hours or on high-heat setting for 5 to 6 hours. If desired, serve over pasta.

Nutrition Facts per serving: 215 cal., 4 g total fat (1 g sat. fat), 64 mg chol., 405 mg sodium, 7 g carbo., 1 g fiber, 26 g pro.

Prep: 15 minutes
Cook: Low 10 to 12 hours,
High 5 to 6 hours
Makes: 6 servings
Slow Cooker: 3½- or 4-quart

1½ pounds beef stew meat, trimmed and cut into 1-inch cubes
2 medium onions, cut up
2 beef bouillon cubes or 1 envelope (½ of a 2.2-ounce package) onion soup mix
3 tablespoons cornstarch
Salt
Black pepper
1½ cups dry red wine
Hot cooked whole wheat pasta (optional)

Mediterranean Beef Ragout

Gremolata—a garnish consisting of parsley, lemon, and garlic—is typically served on osso buco, a classic Italian veal stew. Here it dresses up a beef stew.

1 In a large skillet brown meat, half at a time, in hot oil. Drain off fat. Transfer meat to a 3½- or 4-quart slow cooker. Add onions and carrots. In a bowl stir together the undrained tomatoes, broth, garlic, thyme, salt, and pepper. Pour over meat and vegetables.

2 Cover and cook on low-heat setting for 7 to 9 hours or on high-heat setting for 3½ to 4½ hours.

3 If using low-heat setting, turn to high-heat setting. Stir in zucchini and green beans. Cover and cook for 30 minutes more. If desired, serve over hot couscous. Top each serving with Gremolata.

Gremolata: Stir together ¼ cup snipped fresh parsley, 1 tablespoon finely shredded lemon peel, and 2 cloves garlic, minced.

Nutrition Facts per serving: 221 cal., 7 g total fat (2 g sat. fat), 67 mg chol., 369 mg sodium, 13 g carbo., 3 g fiber, 26 g pro.

Prep: 25 minutes
Cook: Low 7 to 9 hours,
High 3½ to 4½ hours;
plus 30 minutes
Makes: 6 servings
Slow Cooker: 3½- or 4-quart

1½ pounds beef stew meat, trimmed and cut into 1-inch cubes
1 tablespoon olive oil
2 medium onions, cut into wedges
3 medium carrots, cut into ½-inch slices
1 14½-ounce can diced tomatoes, undrained
½ cup beef broth
2 cloves garlic, minced
1½ teaspoons dried thyme, crushed
¼ teaspoon salt
¼ teaspoon black pepper
1 medium zucchini, halved lengthwise and cut into ¼-inch slices
6 ounces fresh green beans, cut into 2-inch pieces (1¾ cups)
Hot cooked whole wheat couscous or brown rice (optional)
1 recipe Gremolata

33 g
carb

Beef Goulash with Artichokes

Hungarian paprika is lighter in color and more pungent in flavor than other paprikas. The Hungarian type is labeled as either sweet (mild) or hot. The hot variety is used here. Look for it in specialty markets.

1. In a 3½- to 5-quart slow cooker place potatoes, onion, and garlic. Add beef. In a bowl combine broth, undrained tomatoes, tomato paste, paprika, fennel seeds, and salt. Pour over meat and vegetables.

2. Cover and cook on low-heat setting for 10 to 12 hours or on high-heat setting for 5 to 6 hours.

3. Stir thawed artichoke hearts into cooker. Cover and let stand for 10 minutes. If desired, serve over hot cooked pasta. Top each serving with a spoonful of sour cream.

Nutrition Facts per serving: 321 cal., 8 g total fat (3 g sat. fat), 72 mg chol., 834 mg sodium, 33 g carbo., 7 g fiber, 31 g pro.

Prep: 15 minutes
Cook: Low 10 to 12 hours,
    High 5 to 6 hours
Stand: 10 minutes
Makes: 6 servings
Slow Cooker: 3½- to 5-quart

3   medium potatoes, cut into 1-inch cubes
1   cup chopped onion (1 large)
2   cloves garlic, minced
1½ pounds beef stew meat, trimmed and cut into 1-inch cubes
1   14-ounce can beef broth
1   14-ounce can chunky tomatoes with garlic and spices, undrained
1   6-ounce can tomato paste
2   tablespoons hot-style Hungarian paprika or paprika
1   teaspoon fennel seeds
½ teaspoon salt
1   9-ounce package frozen artichoke hearts, thawed
   Hot cooked whole wheat pasta (optional)
⅓ cup dairy sour cream

Hungarian Beef Goulash

Here's a dish to soothe your soul with its comfort-food quality. Serve it over whole wheat noodles, if you like.

1 In a 3½- or 4-quart slow cooker combine stew meat, carrots, onions, and garlic. In a small bowl combine beef broth, tomato paste, paprika, lemon peel, salt, caraway seeds, black pepper, and bay leaf. Stir broth mixture into meat mixture.

2 Cover and cook on low-heat setting for 8 to 9 hours or on high-heat setting for 3½ to 4½ hours.

3 If using low-heat setting, turn to high-heat setting. Stir in sweet pepper strips. Cover and cook for 30 minutes more. Discard bay leaf. If desired, serve with hot cooked pasta. Top each serving with about 1 tablespoon sour cream.

Nutrition Facts per serving: 320 cal., 8 g total fat (3 g sat. fat), 72 mg chol., 834 mg sodium, 33 g carbo., 7 g fiber, 31 g pro.

Prep: 25 minutes
Cook: Low 8 to 9 hours,
High 3½ to 4½ hours;
plus 30 minutes
Makes: 6 servings
Slow Cooker: 3½- or 4-quart

1½ pounds beef stew meat
2 medium carrots, bias-sliced into ½-inch pieces
2 medium onions, thinly sliced
3 cloves garlic, minced
1¼ cups beef broth
1 6-ounce can tomato paste
1 tablespoon sweet or hot Hungarian paprika
1 teaspoon finely shredded lemon peel
½ teaspoon salt
½ teaspoon caraway seeds
¼ teaspoon black pepper
1 bay leaf
1 red or green sweet pepper, cut into bite-size strips
Hot cooked whole wheat noodles (optional)
⅓ cup dairy sour cream or plain yogurt

17 g
carb

South-of-the-Border Steak and Beans

Queso fresco (KAY-so FRESK-O), meaning "fresh cheese" in Spanish, is optional for this dish. If you choose to use it, look for it in stores specializing in Mexican food products or in larger supermarkets.

1 Trim fat from meat. Place meat in a 3½- or 4-quart slow cooker. In a bowl stir together undrained tomatoes, onion, garlic, dried oregano (if using), chili powder, cumin, salt, and black pepper. Pour over meat.

2 Cover and cook on low-heat setting for 7 to 9 hours or on high-heat setting for 3½ to 4½ hours.

3 If using low-heat setting, turn to high-heat setting. Stir in sweet pepper strips and pinto beans. Cover and cook for 30 minutes. Remove meat; cool slightly. Shred or thinly slice meat across the grain. Stir fresh oregano (if using) into bean mixture.

4 If desired, spoon rice into soup bowls. Arrange meat on top of rice. Spoon bean mixture over meat. If desired, sprinkle with cheese and additional fresh oregano.

Nutrition Facts per serving: 262 cal., 8 g total fat (3 g sat. fat), 45 mg chol., 452 mg sodium, 17 g carbo., 4 g fiber, 29 g pro.

Prep: 25 minutes
Cook: Low 7 to 9 hours,
High 3½ to 4½ hours;
plus 30 minutes
Makes: 6 servings
Slow Cooker: 3½- or 4-quart

1½ pounds beef flank steak
1 10-ounce can chopped tomatoes with green chile peppers, undrained
½ cup chopped onion (1 medium)
2 cloves garlic, minced
1 tablespoon snipped fresh oregano or 1 teaspoon dried oregano, crushed
1 teaspoon chili powder
1 teaspoon ground cumin
¼ teaspoon salt
¼ teaspoon black pepper
2 small green, red, and/or yellow sweet peppers, cut into strips
1 15-ounce can pinto beans, rinsed and drained
Hot cooked brown rice (optional)
Crumbled queso fresco or feta cheese (optional)
Snipped fresh oregano (optional)

Gingered Beef and Vegetables

If you like the flavor of ginger, this beef dish will please you. Serve it over brown rice instead of white rice to add fiber, more nutrients, and a nutty flavor.

1 In a 3½- or 4-quart slow cooker combine beef, carrots, green onions, and garlic. In a bowl combine water, soy sauce, ginger, bouillon granules, and crushed red pepper. Pour over meat mixture.

2 Cover and cook on low-heat setting for 9 to 10 hours or on high-heat setting for 4½ to 5 hours.

3 If using low-heat setting, turn to high-heat setting. In a small bowl stir together cornstarch and water. Stir cornstarch mixture and sweet pepper into meat mixture. Cover and cook for 20 to 30 minutes or until thickened, stirring once. Stir in snap peas; allow to heat through. If desired, serve over hot rice.

Nutrition Facts per serving: 216 cal., 3 g total fat (1 g sat. fat), 64 mg chol., 608 mg sodium, 16 g carbo., 3 g fiber, 29 g pro.

Prep: 20 minutes
Cook: Low 9 to 10 hours,
      High 4½ to 5 hours;
      plus 20 minutes
Makes: 6 servings
Slow Cooker: 3½- or 4-quart

1½ pounds boneless beef round steak, cut into 1-inch cubes
4 medium carrots, bias-sliced into ½-inch pieces
½ cup bias-sliced green onions
2 cloves garlic, minced
1½ cups water
2 tablespoons soy sauce
2 teaspoons grated fresh ginger
1½ teaspoons instant beef bouillon granules
¼ teaspoon crushed red pepper
3 tablespoons cornstarch
3 tablespoons cold water
½ cup chopped red sweet pepper
2 cups frozen sugar snap peas, thawed
Hot cooked brown rice (optional)

Beef with Broccoli

Brimming with all the flavors and fixings of a traditional stir-fry, this easy beef and veggie combo is draped in a sauce that begins with an envelope of gravy mix.

1 In a 3½- or 4-quart slow cooker place carrots, onions, beef strips, ginger, and garlic. Stir together water, soy sauce, and gravy mix. Pour over meat and vegetables.

2 Cover and cook on low-heat setting for 8 to 10 hours or on high-heat setting for 4 to 5 hours.

3 If using low-heat setting, turn to high-heat setting. Stir in broccoli. Cover and cook about 15 minutes more or until broccoli is crisp-tender. If desired, serve over hot cooked rice.

Nutrition Facts per serving: 213 cal., 3 g total fat (1 g sat. fat), 64 mg chol., 507 mg sodium, 16 g carbo., 5 g fiber, 29 g pro.

Prep: 20 minutes
Cook: Low 8 to 10 hours,
　　　High 4 to 5 hours;
　　　　　plus 15 minutes
Makes: 6 servings
Slow Cooker: 3½- or 4-quart

6	medium carrots, cut into 1-inch pieces
2	medium onions, cut into wedges
1½	pounds beef round steak, cut into ½-inch bias-sliced strips
1	tablespoon minced fresh ginger
2	cloves garlic, minced
½	cup water
2	tablespoons reduced-sodium soy sauce
1	¾-ounce envelope beef gravy mix
4	cups broccoli florets
	Hot cooked brown rice (optional)

Easy Italian Beef

Purchased spaghetti sauce simplifies the prep time for this beef dinner. If you like, sop up the sauce with whole wheat pasta.

1 In a 3½- or 4-quart slow cooker place beef, onions, and red sweet pepper. Add spaghetti sauce.

2 Cover and cook on low-heat setting for 9 to 10 hours or on high-heat setting for 5 hours.

3 If using low-heat setting, turn to high-heat setting. Add zucchini; cook for 1 hour more. Season to taste with salt and black pepper. If desired, serve over hot cooked pasta.

Nutrition Facts per serving: 350 cal., 15 g total fat (6 g sat. fat), 101 mg chol., 505 mg sodium, 20 g carbo., 3 g fiber, 32 g pro.

Prep: 25 minutes
Cook: Low 9 to 10 hours,
High 5 hours; plus 1 hour
Makes: 6 to 8 servings
Slow Cooker: 3½- or 4-quart

1 2-pound boneless beef chuck pot roast, trimmed and cut into 1-inch cubes
2 medium onions, cut into 1-inch chunks
1 large red sweet pepper, cut into ¾-inch pieces
1 14-ounce jar spaghetti sauce
1½ pounds zucchini, cut into ¾-inch chunks
Salt
Black pepper
Hot cooked whole wheat pasta (optional)

Beef Sandwiches with Avocado Aïoli

Slow cooked beef is so tender you can shred it with a fork. This shredded beef sandwich is topped with aïoli (ay-OH-lee), a French term for a garlic-flavored mayonnaise. This version is made from avocado.

1 Trim fat from meat. Sprinkle with salt and pepper. If necessary, cut roast to fit into a 3½- or 4-quart slow cooker. Place meat in cooker. Add onion, water, Worcestershire sauce, oregano, and garlic.

2 Cover and cook on low-heat setting for 8 to 10 hours or on high-heat setting for 4 to 5 hours. Remove meat from cooker, reserving juices. Use two forks to shred meat. Serve meat on rolls with Avocado Aïoli and shredded lettuce. If desired, drizzle meat with some of the reserved juices to moisten.

Avocado Aïoli: In a small bowl slightly mash 2 seeded and peeled ripe medium avocados with a fork. Stir in ⅔ cup finely chopped radishes; 2 tablespoons mayonnaise dressing or salad dressing; 1 tablespoon lemon juice; 1 clove garlic, minced; 2 teaspoons snipped fresh oregano or ½ teaspoon dried oregano, crushed; and ¼ teaspoon salt. Cover and chill for up to 24 hours. Makes 1¼ cups.

Nutrition Facts per serving: 307 cal., 13 g total fat (3 g sat. fat), 57 mg chol., 400 mg sodium, 23 g carbo., 3 g fiber, 25 g pro.

Prep: 25 minutes
Cook: Low 8 to 10 hours,
  High 4 to 5 hours
Makes: 12 to 16 servings
Slow Cooker: 3½- or 4-quart

1   2½- to 3-pound boneless beef chuck pot roast
    Salt
    Black pepper
½   cup finely chopped onion (1 medium)
½   cup water
3   tablespoons Worcestershire sauce
1   teaspoon dried oregano, crushed
3   cloves garlic, minced
12   to 16 whole wheat kaiser rolls or hamburger buns, split and toasted
1   recipe Avocado Aïoli
1   cup shredded lettuce

24 g carb

Southwestern Shredded Beef Sandwiches

Here's the top-ranked sandwich for tailgate picnics and other chilly-weather dining. Tote the spicy filling to the game in the slow cooker and assemble sandwiches on the spot.

1 Trim fat from meat. In a small bowl combine cumin, chili powder, salt, and black pepper. Rub mixture generously into both sides of meat. If necessary, cut roast to fit into a 4- or 4½-quart slow cooker. Place meat in cooker. Add onion, undrained tomatoes, chile peppers, and, if desired, jalapeño peppers.

2 Cover and cook on low-heat setting for 10 to 12 hours or on high-heat setting for 5 to 6 hours. Remove meat from cooker, reserving juices. Use two forks to shred the meat. Return meat to cooker; heat through. Stir in the cilantro.

3 To serve, sprinkle cheese over bottoms of rolls. Using a slotted spoon, place about ½ cup of the meat mixture on top of cheese on each roll. Add a lettuce leaf to each. Replace roll tops.

Nutrition Facts per serving: 298 cal., 11 g total fat (5 g sat. fat), 65 mg chol., 481 mg sodium, 24 g carbo., 3 g fiber, 26 g pro.

Prep: 25 minutes
Cook: Low 10 to 12 hours,
      High 5 to 6 hours
Makes: 16 servings
Slow Cooker: 4- or 4½-quart

1 3- to 3½-pound boneless beef chuck pot roast
1 tablespoon ground cumin
1 tablespoon chili powder
¼ teaspoon salt
⅛ teaspoon black pepper
1 cup coarsely chopped onion (1 large)
1 14½-ounce can stewed tomatoes, undrained
1 7-ounce can chopped green chile peppers or two 4½-ounce cans chopped green chile peppers, undrained
2 tablespoons chopped, pickled jalapeño peppers (optional)
¼ cup snipped fresh cilantro
2 cups shredded cheddar or Monterey Jack cheese (8 ounces)
16 whole wheat kaiser rolls or hamburger buns, split and toasted
   Lettuce leaves

Philadelphia Cheese Steak Wraps

The cheese steak sandwich is said to have originated in Philadelphia in the 1930s. This classic is updated by bundling the meat and cheese in tortillas.

1 Trim fat from meat. In a large skillet brown meat on both sides in hot oil. In a 4- to 5-quart slow cooker combine sweet pepper, onion, and Italian seasoning. Top with meat. Pour broth over meat.

2 Cover and cook on low-heat setting for 10 to 12 hours or on high-heat setting for 5 to 6 hours.

3 Transfer meat to a cutting board. Use two forks to shred the meat. In a small bowl combine mayonnaise dressing and horseradish. Evenly spread mayonnaise mixture on tortillas. Arrange meat along center of each tortilla. Using a slotted spoon, place onion mixture on meat. Top each with half of a slice of cheese. Roll up tightly.

Nutrition Facts per serving: 421 cal., 21 g total fat (7 g sat. fat), 48 mg chol., 900 mg sodium, 33 g carbo., 3 g fiber, 25 g pro.

Prep: 20 minutes
Cook: Low 10 to 12 hours,
High 5 to 6 hours
Makes: 6 servings
Slow Cooker: 4- to 5-quart

1	pound beef flank steak
1	tablespoon cooking oil
1	cup red sweet pepper strips
1	medium onion, cut into thin wedges
1½	teaspoons dried Italian seasoning, crushed
1	14-ounce can beef broth
½	cup light mayonnaise dressing or salad dressing
4	teaspoons prepared horseradish
6	9- to 10-inch whole wheat flour tortillas, warmed
3	slices provolone cheese, halved

Irish Grinders

These tasty corned beef and cabbage sandwiches are guaranteed to bring out the Irish in anyone. They're a must for St. Paddy's Day.

1 Trim fat from meat. Sprinkle spices from packet evenly over meat; rub in with your fingers. If necessary, cut meat to fit into a 3½- or 4-quart slow cooker. Place meat in the cooker. In a small bowl combine water, the ⅓ cup mustard, and horseradish. Pour mustard mixture over meat. Top with cabbage.

2 Cover and cook on low-heat setting for 8 to 10 hours or on high-heat setting for 4 to 5 hours.

3 Transfer meat to a cutting board. Thinly slice meat across the grain. Arrange meat slices on roll bottoms. With a slotted spoon, place some of the cooked cabbage on meat. Spread additional mustard on roll tops. Add roll tops.

Nutrition Facts per serving: 344 cal., 19 g total fat (4 g sat. fat), 58 mg chol., 312 mg sodium, 26 g carbo., 17 g fiber, 32 g pro.

Prep: 20 minutes
Cook: Low 8 to 10 **hours,**
High 4 to 5 **hours**
Makes: 8 **servings**
Slow Cooker: 3½- or 4-**quart**

1 2- to 3-pound corned beef brisket
    with spice packet
1 cup water
⅓ cup Dijon-style mustard
2 teaspoons prepared horseradish
4 cups coarsely shredded cabbage
8 whole wheat kaiser rolls or
    hamburger buns, split and toasted
    Dijon-style mustard

Spicy Sloppy Joes

There's nothing ho-hum about this familiar favorite! Jalapeño peppers give these joes a lively, spicy twist.

1 In a large skillet cook ground beef, onion, and garlic until meat is brown and onion is tender. Drain off fat.

2 Meanwhile, in a 3½- or 4-quart slow cooker combine vegetable juice, catsup, water, sugar substitute, jalapeño peppers (if desired), mustard, chili powder, and Worcestershire sauce. Stir in meat mixture.

3 Cover and cook on low-heat setting for 6 to 8 hours or high-heat setting for 3 to 4 hours. Spoon meat mixture onto buns halves. If desired, sprinkle with cheese.

For a 5- or 6-quart slow cooker: Double all ingredients; prepare as above. Makes 16 servings.

Nutrition Facts per serving: 310 cal., 13 g total fat (5 g sat. fat), 53 mg chol., 522 mg sodium, 27 g carbo., 3 g fiber, 21 g pro.

Prep: 20 minutes
Cook: Low 6 to 8 hours,
      High 3 to 4 hours
Makes: 8 servings
Slow Cooker: 3½- or 4-quart

1½ pounds lean ground beef
1 cup chopped onion (1 large)
1 clove garlic, minced
1 6-ounce can vegetable juice
½ cup catsup
½ cup water
2 tablespoons no-calorie, heat-stable, granular sugar substitute (Splenda)
2 tablespoons chopped, canned jalapeño peppers (optional)
1 tablespoon prepared mustard
2 teaspoons chili powder
1 teaspoon Worcestershire sauce
8 whole wheat hamburger buns, split and toasted
  Shredded cheddar cheese (optional)

Beef and Chipotle Burritos

Chipotle peppers are smoked jalapeños that lend a great flavor to foods. Find them at the supermarket next to the canned chile peppers.

1 Trim fat from meat. Cut meat into 6 pieces. In a 3½- or 4-quart slow cooker place meat, undrained tomatoes, onion, chipotle peppers, oregano, cumin, and garlic.

2 Cover and cook on low-heat setting for 8 to 10 hours or on high-heat setting for 4 to 5 hours. Remove meat from cooker. Use two forks to shred the meat. Place meat in a large bowl. Stir in cooking liquid to reach desired consistency. Spoon one-sixth of the meat onto each warm tortilla just below the center. Top with cheese, Pico de Gallo, and, if desired, jicama and sour cream. Roll up tortilla.

Pico de Gallo: In a bowl combine 2 finely chopped medium tomatoes; 2 tablespoons finely chopped onion; 2 tablespoons snipped fresh cilantro; and 1 fresh serrano chile pepper, seeded and finely chopped (see note, page 62). Cover and chill for several hours.

Nutrition Facts per serving: 386 cal., 13 g total fat (5 g sat. fat), 69 mg chol., 665 mg sodium, 33 g carbo., 3 g fiber, 33 g pro.

Prep: 20 minutes
Cook: Low 8 to 10 hours,
   High 4 to 5 hours
Makes: 6 servings
Slow Cooker: 3½- or 4-quart

1½ pounds boneless beef round steak, cut ¾ inch thick
1 14½-ounce can diced tomatoes, undrained
⅓ cup chopped onion (1 small)
1 to 2 canned chipotle peppers in adobo sauce, chopped
1 teaspoon dried oregano, crushed
¼ teaspoon ground cumin
1 clove garlic, minced
6 9- to 10-inch whole wheat flour tortillas, warmed
¾ cup shredded cheddar cheese (3 ounces)
1 recipe Pico de Gallo
Shredded jicama or radishes (optional)
Dairy sour cream (optional)

Beef Fajitas

The slow cooker produces unbelievably tender meat for this south-of-the-border favorite. Put the fajita mixture and the toppers out and let diners make their own.

1 Trim fat from meat. Cut meat into 6 pieces. In a 3½- or 4-quart slow cooker combine onion, sweet pepper, jalapeño pepper(s), cilantro, garlic, chili powder, cumin, coriander, and salt. Top with meat; add the undrained tomatoes.

2 Cover and cook on low-heat setting for 8 to 10 hours or on high-heat setting for 4 to 5 hours.

3 To heat tortillas, wrap them in foil and heat in a 350° oven for 10 to 15 minutes or until softened. Remove meat from cooker. Use two forks to shred meat. Return meat to cooker. Stir in lime juice.

4 To serve fajitas, use a slotted spoon to fill the warmed tortillas with the beef mixture. If desired, add shredded cheese, guacamole, sour cream, and salsa. Roll up tortillas.

Nutrition Facts per serving: 361 cal., 11 g total fat (4 g sat. fat), 56 mg chol., 690 mg sodium, 36 g carbo., 4 g fiber, 28 g pro.

Prep: 20 minutes
Cook: Low 8 to 10 hours,
    High 4 to 5 hours
Oven: 350°F
Makes: 6 servings
Slow Cooker: 3½- or 4-quart

1½ pounds beef flank steak
  1 cup chopped onion (1 large)
  1 green sweet pepper, cut into
       ½-inch pieces
  1 or 2 fresh jalapeño chile peppers,
       chopped (see tip, page 62)
  1 tablespoon snipped fresh cilantro
  2 cloves garlic, minced
  1 teaspoon chili powder
  1 teaspoon ground cumin
  1 teaspoon ground coriander
  ¼ teaspoon salt
  1 14½-ounce can stewed tomatoes,
       undrained
  6 9- to 10-inch whole wheat flour
       tortillas
  1 tablespoon lime juice
     Shredded cheddar cheese (optional)
     Guacamole (optional)
     Dairy sour cream (optional)
     Salsa (optional)

Pork & Lamb

33 g
carb

Apple Pork Roast
and Vegetables

Savory and slightly sweet from the apple juice concentrate, this pork roast makes a family-pleasing weeknight supper.

1 Trim fat from meat. If necessary, cut roast to fit into a 3½- or 4-quart slow cooker. In the cooker place parsnips, carrots, sweet pepper, and celery. Sprinkle with tapioca. Add juice concentrate, water, bouillon granules, and black pepper. Place meat on top of vegetables.

2 Cover and cook on low-heat setting for 10 to 12 hours or on high-heat setting for 5 to 6 hours.

3 To serve, transfer the meat and vegetables to a serving platter. Strain cooking juices; skim off fat. Drizzle some of the juices over the sliced meat and pass the remaining juices.

Nutrition Facts per serving: 269 cal., 7 g total fat (2 g sat. fat), 61 mg chol., 250 mg sodium, 33 g carbo., 4 g fiber, 19 g pro.

Prep: 25 minutes
Cook: Low 10 to 12 hours,
       High 5 to 6 hours
Makes: 6 to 8 servings
Slow Cooker: 3½- or 4-quart

1 2- to 2½-pound boneless pork shoulder roast
3 medium parsnips, cut into 1-inch pieces (2 cups)
3 medium carrots, cut into 1-inch pieces (1½ cups)
1 large green sweet pepper, cut into 1-inch strips
2 stalks celery, cut into 1-inch pieces (1 cup)
3 tablespoons quick-cooking tapioca
1 6-ounce can (⅔ cup) frozen apple juice concentrate, thawed
¼ cup water
1 teaspoon instant beef bouillon granules
¼ teaspoon black pepper

Apricot-Glazed Pork Roast

Just five ingredients are needed for this flavorful entrée. The pork shoulder roast becomes melt-in-your-mouth tender when slow cooked.

1 Trim fat from meat. If necessary, cut roast to fit into a 3½- to 6-quart slow cooker. Place meat in cooker. In a bowl combine apricot spread, broth, mustard, and onion; pour over meat.

2 Cover and cook on low-heat setting for 10 to 12 hours or on high-heat setting for 5 to 6 hours. Transfer meat to a serving plate. Skim fat from the cooking juices. Spoon some of the juices over meat; discard any remaining cooking juices.

Nutrition Facts per serving: 296 cal., 8 g total fat (3 g sat. fat), 82 mg chol., 176 mg sodium, 29 g carbo., 2 g fiber, 26 g pro.

Prep: 15 minutes
Cook: Low 10 to 12 hours,
        High 5 to 6 hours
Makes: 6 to 8 servings
Slow Cooker: 3½- to 6-quart

1   3- to 3½-pound boneless pork
    shoulder roast
1   15½-ounce jar low-sugar apricot
    spread
¼   cup chicken broth
2   tablespoons Dijon-style mustard
1   cup chopped onion (1 large)

17 g
carb

Pork Roast with Cherries

If you like, replace the dried cherries with other dried fruits, such as coarsely chopped cranberries, apricots, golden raisins, or dried mixed fruit. All work equally well.

1 Trim fat from meat. If necessary, cut roast to fit into a 3½- to 6-quart slow cooker. In a large skillet brown meat on all sides in hot oil. Drain off fat.

2 Place meat in the cooker. Sprinkle tapioca, dried thyme (if using), and pepper over meat. Add onion and dried cherries. Pour apple juice over all.

3 Cover and cook on low-heat setting for 7 to 9 hours or on high-heat setting for 3½ to 4½ hours. Transfer meat to serving platter; cover to keep warm.

4 For sauce, skim fat from cooking juices. If using, stir fresh thyme into juices. If desired, serve with hot cooked rice.

Nutrition Facts per serving: 242 cal., 8 g total fat (3 g sat. fat), 73 mg chol., 94 mg sodium, 17 g carbo., 1 g fiber, 23 g pro.

Prep: 20 minutes
Cook: Low 7 to 9 hours,
　　　High 3½ to 4½ hours
Makes: 8 servings
Slow Cooker: 3½- to 6-quart

1　2- to 2½-pound boneless pork shoulder roast
2　tablespoons cooking oil
1　tablespoon quick-cooking tapioca
1　tablespoon snipped fresh thyme or
　　1 teaspoon dried thyme, crushed
½　teaspoon black pepper
1　medium onion, sliced
1　cup dried cherries
½　cup apple juice or apple cider
　　Hot cooked brown rice (optional)

Curried Pork Roast with Apples

This pork roast integrates the traditional flavors of East Indian curries.

1 Trim fat from meat; cut roast into 1-inch cubes. Transfer pork to a 3½- or 4-quart slow cooker; sprinkle with tapioca. Add water, onion, raisins, curry powder, bouillon granules, and paprika.

2 Cover and cook on low-heat setting for 8½ to 9½ hours or on high-heat setting for 4 to 4½ hours. Stir in the apple slices; cover and cook 30 minutes more. If desired, serve over hot cooked rice.

Nutrition Facts per serving: 318 cal., 9 g total fat (3 g sat. fat), 98 mg chol., 680 mg sodium, 27 g carbo., 3 g fiber, 31 g pro.

Prep: 15 minutes
Cook: Low 8½ to 9½ hours,
High 4 to 4½ hours;
plus 30 minutes
Makes: 6 servings
Slow Cooker: 3½- or 4-quart

1 2-pound boneless pork shoulder roast
¼ cup quick-cooking tapioca
2 cups water
1 cup chopped onion (1 large)
½ cup raisins
2 tablespoons curry powder
1 tablespoon instant chicken bouillon
     granules
½ teaspoon paprika
2 medium cooking apples, cored
     and sliced
   Hot cooked brown rice (optional)

Pork Roast with Fennel

Fresh fennel is available from September through April. Choose firm, smooth bulbs without cracks or brown spots. Bright green fennel leaves may be used as garnish.

1 Trim fat from meat. In a small bowl combine crushed fennel seeds, garlic powder, oregano, and ¼ teaspoon pepper. Rub about 1 teaspoon of the seasoning mixture evenly over roast. In a Dutch oven brown meat on all sides in hot oil. Drain off fat.

2 In a 3½- or 4-quart slow cooker place potatoes and fennel. Sprinkle with remaining seasoning mixture. Stir together the 1½ cups water and bouillon granules; add to cooker. If necessary, cut meat to fit in the cooker. Place meat on vegetables.

3 Cover and cook on low-heat setting for 7 to 8 hours or on high-heat setting for 3½ to 4 hours.

4 For gravy, pour cooking juices into a large measuring cup; skim fat. Measure 1½ cups juice; transfer to a medium saucepan. Stir the ½ cup cold water into the flour; stir into juices in saucepan. Cook and stir until thickened and bubbly. Cook and stir 1 minute more. Season to taste with salt and pepper. Pass gravy with meat.

Nutrition Facts per serving: 360 cal., 14 g total fat (4 g sat. fat), 98 mg chol., 453 mg sodium, 23 g carbo., 8 g fiber, 34 g pro.

Prep: 25 minutes
Cook: Low 7 to 8 hours,
　　　High 3½ to 4 hours;
　　　　plus 10 minutes
Makes: 6 to 8 servings
Slow Cooker: 3½- or 4-quart

- 1 2- to 2½-pound boneless pork shoulder roast
- 1 teaspoon fennel seeds, crushed
- ½ teaspoon garlic powder
- ½ teaspoon dried oregano, crushed
- ¼ teaspoon black pepper
- 2 tablespoons cooking oil
- 1½ pounds small red-skin potatoes, halved
- 1 large fennel bulb, trimmed and cut into 1-inch pieces
- 1½ cups water
- 2 teaspoons instant chicken bouillon granules
- ½ cup cold water
- ¼ cup all-purpose flour
  Salt
  Black pepper

Caraway Pork Roast

Caraway and sour cream are the flavor stars in this pork roast. The savory juices are combined with the sour cream to make a gravy.

1 Trim fat from meat. If necessary, cut roast to fit into a 3½- to 6-quart slow cooker. In a small bowl combine caraway seeds, marjoram, salt, and pepper. Sprinkle evenly over meat; rub in with your fingers.

2 In a large skillet brown meat on all sides in hot oil. Drain off fat. Place meat in slow cooker. Add water to skillet. Bring to a gentle boil, stirring to loosen brown bits from bottom of skillet. Pour skillet juices and vinegar over meat.

3 Cover and cook on low-heat setting for 8 to 10 hours or on high-heat setting for 4 to 5 hours. Remove meat from cooker; keep warm.

4 For gravy, pour juices into a large measuring cup; skim fat. Measure 1¼ cups juices, adding water, if necessary. In a small bowl combine sour cream and cornstarch. In a small saucepan bring cooking juices to boiling; reduce heat; stir in sour cream mixture. Cook and stir until mixture is thickened and bubbly. Cook and stir for 2 minutes more. Slice meat; serve with gravy and, if desired, hot cooked pasta.

Nutrition Facts per serving: 255 cal., 15 g total fat (7 g sat. fat), 90 mg chol., 405 mg sodium, 4 g carbo., 0 g fiber, 24 g pro.

Prep: 25 minutes
Cook: Low 8 to 10 hours,
High 4 to 5 hours;
plus 10 minutes
Makes: 6 servings
Slow Cooker: 3½- to 6-quart

1	1½- to 2-pound boneless pork shoulder roast
2	teaspoons caraway seeds
1	teaspoon dried marjoram, crushed
¾	teaspoon salt
½	teaspoon black pepper
1	teaspoon olive oil
½	cup water
2	tablespoons white wine vinegar
1	8-ounce carton dairy sour cream
4	teaspoons cornstarch
	Hot cooked whole wheat pasta (optional)

4 g
carb

Sauerkraut and Pork Shoulder Roast

This pork roast is for the adventurous tongue. Beer, mustard, and sauerkraut each contribute to its robust flavor.

1 Place sauerkraut in a 3½- or 4-quart slow cooker. Trim fat from meat. If necessary, cut roast to fit into the slow cooker. Sprinkle lightly with salt and pepper. Spread mustard over meat. Place meat on top of the sauerkraut. Add the beer.

2 Cover and cook on low-heat setting for 8 to 10 hours or on high-heat setting for 4 to 5 hours.

3 Transfer meat to a cutting board; cool slightly. Slice meat; discard fat. Serve sauerkraut with meat.

Nutrition Facts per serving: 230 cal., 10 g total fat (3 g sat. fat), 92 mg chol., 546 mg sodium, 4 g carbo., 1 g fiber, 29 g pro.

Prep: 15 minutes
Cook: Low 8 to 10 hours,
        High 4 to 5 hours
Makes: 8 servings
Slow Cooker: 3½- or 4-quart

1 14½-ounce can sauerkraut with caraway seeds, rinsed and drained
1 2½-pound boneless pork shoulder roast or pork sirloin roast
   Salt
   Black pepper
2 tablespoons creamy Dijon-style mustard blend
1 cup beer or nonalcoholic beer

Seeded Pork Roast

This savory blend of anise, fennel, caraway, dill, and celery seeds creates a crustlike coating for this ultratender pork roast. The cooking liquid contains apple juice, which lends a pleasant subtle sweetness.

1 If necessary, cut roast to fit into a 3½- to 5-quart slow cooker. Remove netting from roast, if present. Trim fat from meat. Brush soy sauce over surface of roast. On a large piece of foil combine anise seeds, fennel seeds, caraway seeds, dill seeds, and celery seeds. Roll roast in seeds to coat evenly.

2 Place roast in cooker. Pour broth and ⅓ cup of the apple juice around roast.

3 Cover and cook on low-heat setting for 9 to 11 hours or on high-heat setting for 4½ to 5½ hours.

4 Transfer roast to a serving platter. for gravy, strain cooking juices and skim fat; transfer juices to small saucepan. Combine remaining apple juice and cornstarch; add to juices in saucepan. Cook and stir until thickened and bubbly. Cook and stir 2 minutes more. Pass gravy with roast.

Nutrition Facts per serving: 220 cal., 9 g total fat (3 g sat. fat), 92 mg chol., 285 mg sodium, 5 g carbo., 0 g fiber, 29 g pro.

Prep: 25 minutes
Cook: Low 9 to 11 hours,
High 4½ to 5½ hours:
plus 10 minutes
Makes: 8 servings
Slow Cooker: 3½- to 5-quart

- 1 2½- to 3-pound boneless pork shoulder roast
- 1 tablespoon soy sauce
- 2 teaspoons anise seeds, crushed
- 2 teaspoons fennel seeds, crushed
- 2 teaspoons caraway seeds, crushed
- 2 teaspoons dill seeds, crushed
- 2 teaspoons celery seeds, crushed
- ½ cup beef broth
- ⅔ cup apple juice
- 1 tablespoon cornstarch

39 g
carb

Dijon Pork Chops

For this tasty dish use ¾-inch-thick chops or ask a butcher to cut a bone-in top loin roast into ¾-inch-thick slices.

1 In a large bowl combine soup, wine, mustard, thyme, garlic, and pepper. Add potatoes and onion, stirring to coat. Transfer to a 4- to 5-quart slow cooker. Trim fat from chops. Place chops on potato mixture.

2 Cover and cook on low-heat setting for 7 to 8 hours or on high-heat setting for 3½ hours.

Nutrition Facts per serving: 385 cal., 12 g total fat (3 g sat. fat), 48 mg chol., 658 mg sodium, 39 g carbo., 4 g fiber, 26 g pro.

Prep: 20 minutes
Cook: Low 7 to 8 hours,
 High 3½ hours
Makes: 4 servings
Slow Cooker: 4- to 5-quart

1   10¾-ounce can condensed cream of
     mushroom soup
¼   cup dry white wine or chicken broth
¼   cup Dijon-style mustard
1   teaspoon dried thyme, crushed
1   clove garlic, minced
¼   teaspoon black pepper
5   medium potatoes, cut into ¼-inch
     slices (1⅔ pounds)
1   medium onion, sliced
4   pork loin chops, cut ¾ inch thick

Mushroom-Sauced Pork Chops

Mushroom soup and mushrooms give a double dose of earthy flavors to this comfort-food dish.

1 Trim fat from chops. In a skillet brown chops on both sides in hot oil. Drain fat. In a 3½- or 4-quart slow cooker place onion; add chops. Grind tapioca with a mortar and pestle. In a bowl combine the tapioca, soup, apple juice, mushrooms, Worcestershire sauce, thyme, and garlic powder; pour over chops.

2 Cover and cook on low-heat setting for 8 to 9 hours or on high-heat setting for 4 to to 4½ hours. If desired, serve with hot cooked rice.

For a 5- to 6-quart slow cooker: Use 6 pork loin chops, cut ¾ inch thick. Leave remaining ingredient amounts the same and prepare as above. Makes 6 servings.

Nutrition Facts per serving: 327 cal., 16 g total fat (4 g sat. fat), 63 mg chol., 732 mg sodium, 17 g carbo., 1 g fiber, 27 g pro.

Prep: 15 minutes
Cook: Low 8 to 9 hours,
High 4 to 4½ hours
Makes: 4 servings
Slow Cooker: 3½- or 4-quart

4	pork loin chops, cut ¾ inch thick
1	tablespoon cooking oil
1	small onion, thinly sliced
2	tablespoons quick-cooking tapioca
1	10¾-ounce can condensed cream of mushroom soup
½	cup apple juice
1	4-ounce can sliced mushrooms, drained
2	teaspoons Worcestershire sauce
¾	teaspoon dried thyme, crushed
¼	teaspoon garlic powder
	Hot cooked brown rice (optional)

Pork Chops with Orange Sauce

Orange marmalade and mustard team up for a glistening, piquant sauce for these chops and winter squash slices. Steam green beans or asparagus to serve alongside.

1 Cut squash in half lengthwise. Discard seeds and membranes. Cut each squash half into 3 wedges. In a 5- to 6-quart slow cooker place squash and onion. Trim fat from chops. Place chops on top of squash and onion.

2 In a small bowl stir together broth, marmalade spread, mustard, marjoram, and pepper. Pour broth mixture over chops and vegetables.

3 Cover and cook on low-heat setting for 5 to 6 hours or on high-heat setting for 2½ to 3 hours. Lift chops and vegetables from cooker to platter, reserving juices; cover meat and keep warm.

4 For sauce, strain cooking juices into a large measuring cup; skim off fat. Measure 1¾ cups juices, adding water, if necessary. Pour juices into a medium saucepan. Combine cornstarch and the cold water; stir into juices in saucepan. Cook and stir over medium heat until thickened and bubbly. Cook and stir for 2 minutes more. Serve sauce with the pork chops and vegetables.

Nutrition Facts per serving: 236 cal., 7 g total fat (2 g sat. fat), 59 mg chol., 194 mg sodium, 18 g carbo., 2 g fiber, 26 g pro.

Prep: 20 minutes
Cook: Low 5 to 6 hours,
High 2½ to 3 hours;
plus 10 minutes
Makes: 6 servings
Slow Cooker: 5- to 6-quart

2 small or medium acorn squash (1½ to 2 pounds total)
1 large onion, halved and sliced
6 pork chops, cut ¾ inch thick (2½ to 2 ¾ pounds total)
½ cup chicken broth
⅓ cup low-sugar orange marmalade spread
1 tablespoon Dijon-style mustard
1 teaspoon dried marjoram or thyme, crushed
¼ teaspoon black pepper
2 tablespoons cornstarch
2 tablespoons cold water

Spiced Fruit and Chops

Sweet and spicy describes this pork dish. Raisins, dried apples, and orange juice contribute to the sweetness while a jalapeño chile pepper supplies the heat.

1 Trim fat from chops. Sprinkle chops with salt and black pepper. In a large skillet brown chops in hot oil, turning once. Drain fat. Transfer chops to a 3½- or 4-quart slow cooker. Sprinkle apples, onion, and raisins over chops. In a bowl stir together orange juice, the ¾ cup broth, jalapeño pepper, garlic, ginger, and apple pie spice. Pour over meat and fruit.

2 Cover and cook on low-heat setting for 6 to 8 hours or on high-heat setting for 3 to 4 hours. Transfer chops and fruit to a platter; keep warm.

3 For sauce, pour cooking juices into a large measuring cup; skim fat. If necessary, add broth to cooking juices to make 1 cup. Place broth mixture in a saucepan. Combine the ¼ cup cold water and the cornstarch; stir into juices in saucepan. Cook and stir until thickened. Cook and stir 2 minutes more. Serve chops and fruit with sauce.

Nutrition Facts per serving: 340 cal., 10 g total fat (3 g sat. fat), 66 mg chol., 426 mg sodium, 41 g carbo., 5 g fiber, 24 g pro.

Prep: 20 minutes
Cook: Low 6 to 8 hours,
High 3 to 4 hours;
plus 10 minutes
Makes: 4 servings
Slow Cooker: 3½- or 4-quart

4   pork sirloin chops, cut ¾-inch thick (about 1½ pounds)
¼   teaspoon salt
¼   teaspoon black pepper
1   tablespoon cooking oil
1   6-ounce package dried apples
½   cup chopped onion (1 medium)
2   tablespoons golden raisins
¾   cup orange juice
¾   cup chicken broth
1   small fresh jalapeño chile pepper, seeded and finely chopped (see note, page 62)
1   clove garlic, minced
1   teaspoon grated fresh ginger
½   teaspoon apple pie spice
     Chicken broth
¼   cup water
2   teaspoons cornstarch

19 g
carb

Southwest Pork Chops

Pork chops from a slow cooker? Yes! Slow cookers are versatile as well as convenient. Four ingredients are all you need for this tasty dish.

1 Trim fat from chops. Place chops in the bottom of a 3½- or 4-quart slow cooker. Add chili beans and salsa.

2 Cover and cook on low-heat setting for 5 hours or on high-heat setting for 2½ hours.*

3 If using low-heat setting, turn to high. Stir in corn. Cover and cook 30 minutes more. If desired, serve over hot cooked rice and sprinkle with cilantro.

Nutrition Facts per serving: 265 cal., 7 g total fat (2 g sat. fat), 77 mg chol., 715 mg sodium, 19 g carbo., 4 g fiber, 32 g pro.

*Note: If you would like to cook this recipe for longer than 5 hours while you are at work, you'll need to substitute 8 boneless pork chops for the 6 rib chops. (If cooked too long, rib chops will break down and leave bony fragments in the cooked mixture.) To cook boneless chops, cover and cook on low-heat setting for 9½ hours. Turn cooker to high-heat setting. Stir in the corn. Cover and cook for 30 minutes more.

Prep: 15 minutes
Cook: Low 5 hours,
High 2½ hours;
plus 30 minutes
Makes: 6 servings
Slow Cooker: 3½- or 4-quart

6 pork rib chops, cut ¾-inch thick
(about 2½ pounds)
1 15-ounce can Mexican-style or
Tex-Mex-style chili beans
1¼ cups bottled salsa
1 cup frozen whole kernel corn
Hot cooked brown rice (optional)
Snipped fresh cilantro (optional)

German-Style Pork Chops

Try pork spareribs for a variation of this mouthwatering meal. If you prefer a milder flavor, rinse and drain the sauerkraut.

1 Trim fat from pork chops. In a 3½- to 5-quart slow cooker place potatoes, carrots, and onion; top with pork chops. In a small bowl combine apple cider, catsup, and caraway seeds; pour over pork chops.

2 Cover and cook on low-heat setting for 5 to 6 hours or on high-heat setting for 2½ to 3 hours.

3 If using low-heat setting, turn to high-heat setting. Add sauerkraut and apple slices; cover and cook 30 minutes more. Transfer to a serving dish. If desired, garnish with snipped fresh parsley.

Nutrition Facts per serving: 340 cal., 8 g total fat (3 g sat. fat), 76 mg chol., 1,005 mg sodium, 35 g carbo., 7 g fiber, 34 g pro.

Prep: 20 minutes
Cook: Low 5 to 6 hours,
    High 2½ to 3 hours;
        plus 30 minutes
Makes: 4 servings
Slow Cooker: 3½- to 5-quart

4 pork loin chops, cut ¾ inch thick
    (about 1½ pounds)
2 medium potatoes, peeled and cut into
    1-inch cubes
2 medium carrots, cut into ½-inch
    pieces
1 medium onion, thinly sliced
½ cup apple cider or apple juice
¼ cup catsup
½ teaspoon caraway seeds
1 16-ounce can sauerkraut, drained
2 small cooking apples, peeled, cored,
    and cut into ¼-inch slices
    (1½ cups)
    Snipped fresh parsley (optional)

Country-Style Pork Ribs

Enjoy BBQ at its best—without a grill! These pork ribs are fall-off-the-bone tender and delicious.

1 Place onion rings in a 3½- or 4-quart slow cooker. Trim fat from ribs. Place over onions in cooker. In a medium bowl combine the vegetable juice, tomato paste, sugar substitute, vinegar, dry mustard, salt, pepper, thyme, and rosemary. Reserve 1 cup of the mixture for the sauce; cover and chill. Pour remaining mixture over ribs in cooker.

2 Cover and cook on low-heat setting for 10 to 12 hours or on high-heat setting for 5 to 6 hours.

3 For sauce, in a small saucepan heat reserved mixture to boiling; reduce heat and simmer, uncovered, for 10 minutes, stirring occasionally. Remove ribs from cooker to a serving dish; discard cooking liquid. Serve sauce with ribs.

Nutrition Facts per serving: 304 cal., 16 g total fat (6 g sat. fat), 98 mg chol., 293 mg sodium, 9 g carbo., 1 g fiber, 30 g pro.

Prep: 15 minutes
Cook: Low 10 to 12 hours,
High 5 to 6 hours;
plus 10 minutes
Makes: 6 servings
Slow Cooker: 3½- or 4-quart

- 1 large onion, sliced and separated into rings
- 2½ to 3 pounds country-style pork ribs
- 1½ cups vegetable juice
- ½ of a 6-ounce can (⅓ cup) tomato paste
- ¼ cup no-calorie, heat-stable, granular sugar substitute (Splenda)
- 3 tablespoons vinegar
- 1 teaspoon dry mustard
- ¼ teaspoon salt
- ¼ teaspoon black pepper
- ⅛ teaspoon dried thyme, crushed
- ⅛ teaspoon dried rosemary, crushed

Tomato-Sauced Pork Ribs

The sauce for these scrumptious ribs contains hot pepper sauce for a kick of heat.

1 For sauce, in a 3½- or 4-quart slow cooker combine undrained tomatoes, celery, sweet pepper, onion, tapioca, sugar (if desired), dried basil (if using), salt, black pepper, hot pepper sauce, and garlic. Add ribs; stir to coat ribs with sauce.

2 Cover and cook on low-heat setting for 8 to 10 hours or on high-heat setting for 4 to 5 hours. Transfer meat to a serving platter. Skim fat from sauce. If using, stir fresh basil into sauce. Spoon some of the sauce over meat. Pass remaining sauce.

Nutrition Facts per serving: 303 cal., 12 g total fat (4 g sat. fat), 96 mg chol., 489 mg sodium, 16 g carbo., 3 g fiber, 32 g pro.

Prep: 20 minutes
Cook: Low 8 to 10 hours,
High 4 to 5 hours
Makes: 6 servings
Slow Cooker: 3½- or 4-quart

- 1 28-ounce can crushed tomatoes, undrained
- 2 stalks celery, chopped
- 1 medium green sweet pepper, chopped
- ½ cup chopped onion (1 medium)
- 2 tablespoons quick-cooking tapioca
- 1½ teaspoons sugar (optional)
- 1½ teaspoons snipped fresh basil or ½ teaspoon dried basil, crushed
- ½ teaspoon salt
- ¼ teaspoon black pepper
- ¼ teaspoon bottled hot pepper sauce
- 1 clove garlic, minced
- 2 pounds boneless country-style pork ribs

32 g
carb

Ribs with Apples and Sauerkraut

Quick browning in a skillet seals in natural juices, adding flavor and aroma to the country-style pork ribs.

1 In a large skillet brown pork ribs on both sides in hot oil over medium-high heat. In a 3½- or 4-quart slow cooker layer potatoes, carrots, onion, browned pork ribs, and sauerkraut. In a bowl combine apple cider, caraway seeds, and cloves. Pour over sauerkraut.

2 Cover and cook on low-heat setting for 8 to 10 hours or on high-heat setting for 4 to 5 hours. Remove meat and vegetables from cooker, reserving the juices in the cooker. Place meat and vegetables on serving platter; cover with foil to keep warm.

3 For gravy, strain juices into a large measuring cup. Skim off fat. Measure 1 cup cooking juices, adding water, if necessary; pour into a saucepan. In a small bowl stir flour into cold water until smooth. Stir flour mixture into the juices in saucepan. Cook and stir until thickened and bubbly. Stir in the apple. Cook and stir for 1 minute more. If desired, season to taste with salt and pepper. Stir in parsley just before serving. Serve gravy with ribs and vegetables.

Nutrition Facts per serving: 431 cal., 20 g total fat (7 g sat. fat), 103 mg chol., 371 mg sodium, 32 g carbo., 4 g fiber, 31 g pro.

Prep: 30 minutes
Cook: Low 8 to 10 hours,
  High 4 to 5 hours;
    plus 10 minutes
Makes: 4 servings
Slow Cooker: 3½- or 4-quart

2½ pounds country-style pork ribs, cut crosswise in half and cut into 1- to 2-rib portions
1 tablespoon cooking oil
2 medium potatoes, sliced ½ inch thick
2 medium carrots, sliced ¼ inch thick
1 medium onion, thinly sliced
1 8-ounce can sauerkraut, rinsed and drained
½ cup apple cider or apple juice
2 teaspoons caraway or fennel seeds
⅛ teaspoon ground cloves
1 tablespoon all-purpose flour
2 tablespoons cold water
½ of a large apple, cored and thinly sliced
  Salt (optional)
  Black pepper (optional)
1 tablespoon snipped fresh parsley

Lemon Pork

Scented with fresh basil and shallots, this one-dish dinner suits weeknight entertaining or weekend celebrations because it frees the cook to visit with guests.

1 In a plastic bag combine flour and pepper. Add pork, close bag, and shake until pork is coated with flour. In a large skillet brown half of the meat in 1 tablespoon of the oil. Remove from skillet. Brown remaining pork in remaining 1 tablespoon oil. Drain fat.

2 In a 3½- to 6-quart slow cooker place carrots, parsnips, shallots, lemon, and half of the basil. Place pork on top of vegetables. Pour broth over all.

3 Cover and cook on low-heat setting for 7 to 8 hours or on high-heat setting for 3½ to 4 hours. Discard lemon pieces.

4 Transfer pork and vegetables to a serving dish using a slotted spoon; reserve juices. Sprinkle with remaining fresh basil. If desired, serve pork and vegetables over hot cooked rice. Spoon some of the juices over each serving.

Nutrition Facts per serving: 339 cal., 14 g total fat (4 g sat. fat), 98 mg chol., 430 mg sodium, 20 g carbo., 4 g fiber, 32 g pro.

Prep: 30 minutes
Cook: Low 7 to 8 hours,
High 3½ to 4 hours
Makes: 6 servings
Slow Cooker: 3½- to 6-quart

2 pounds boneless pork shoulder, trimmed and cut into 1-inch pieces
¼ cup all-purpose flour
½ teaspoon black pepper
2 tablespoons cooking oil
1 16-ounce package peeled baby carrots
8 ounces parsnips, cut into ½-inch slices
2 medium shallots, sliced
1 lemon, quartered
¼ cup thinly sliced fresh basil
1 14-ounce can chicken broth
Hot cooked brown rice (optional)

12 g
carb

Pork and Mushroom Marengo

Marengo refers to the battle Napoléon Bonaparte won against Austria in 1800. To celebrate the victory, Napoléon's chef invented a dish similar to this one.

1 In a large skillet brown meat, half at a time, in hot oil. Drain off fat. In a 3½- to 5-quart slow cooker place mushrooms and onion. Add meat. In a bowl combine undrained tomatoes, the 1 cup water, the dried marjoram and thyme (if using), bouillon granules, salt, and pepper. Pour over all.

2 Cover and cook on low-heat setting for 8 to 10 hours or on high-heat setting for 4 to 5 hours.

3 If using low-heat setting, turn to high-heat setting. In a bowl stir together the ⅓ cup water and the flour. Stir flour mixture into pork mixture in cooker. Cover and cook on high-heat setting for 15 to 20 minutes or until thickened. If using, stir in fresh marjoram and thyme. If desired, serve over hot cooked rice.

Nutrition Facts per serving: 329 cal., 15 g total fat (4 g sat. fat), 110 mg chol., 718 mg sodium, 12 g carbo., 2 g fiber, 37 g pro.

Prep: 25 minutes
Cook: Low 8 to 10 hours,
High 4 to 5 hours;
plus 15 minutes
Makes: 4 servings
Slow Cooker: 3½- to 5-quart

1½   pounds boneless pork shoulder, trimmed and cut into 1-inch cubes
1   tablespoon cooking oil
8   ounces fresh mushrooms, sliced
½   cup chopped onion (1 medium)
1   14½-ounce can diced tomatoes, undrained
1   cup water
1   tablespoon snipped fresh marjoram or 1 teaspoon dried marjoram, crushed
1½   teaspoons snipped fresh thyme or ½ teaspoon dried thyme, crushed
1   teaspoon instant chicken bouillon granules
¼   teaspoon salt
    Dash black pepper
⅓   cup cold water
3   tablespoons all-purpose flour
    Hot cooked brown rice (optional)

Ginger Pork and Dried Plums

Apples and dried plums—along with ginger, cinnamon, and cloves—make this a fragrant and flavorful dish.

1 Trim fat from meat; cut pork into 1-inch pieces. Place pork in a 3½- or 4-quart slow cooker. Sprinkle tapioca over meat. Add apples, carrots, onion, dried plums, broth, apple juice, lemon juice, ginger, cinnamon, pepper, and cloves. Stir to combine.

2 Cover and cook on low-heat setting for 7 to 8 hours or on high-heat setting for 3½ to 4 hours. If desired, serve with hot cooked rice.

Nutrition Facts per serving: 389 cal., 12 g total fat (4 g sat. fat), 102 mg chol., 289 mg sodium, 39 g carbo., 5 g fiber, 31 g pro.

Prep: 20 minutes
Cook: Low 7 to 8 hours,
High 3½ to 4 hours
Makes: 6 servings
Slow Cooker: 3½- or 4-quart

- 1 **2-pound boneless pork shoulder roast**
- 3 **tablespoons quick-cooking tapioca**
- 2 **medium cooking apples, peeled, cored, and cut into ½-inch slices**
- 4 **medium carrots, bias-sliced into ½-inch pieces**
- 1 **medium onion, cut into 1-inch chunks**
- 1 **cup pitted dried plums (prunes), quartered**
- 1 **cup chicken broth**
- ¾ **cup apple juice**
- 1 **tablespoon lemon juice**
- 1 **teaspoon ground ginger**
- ¼ **teaspoon ground cinnamon**
- ¼ **teaspoon black pepper**
- ⅛ **teaspoon ground cloves**
  Hot cooked brown rice or whole wheat pasta (optional)

Pork Hocks and Black-Eyed Peas

Southerners eat black-eyed peas on New Year's Day to ensure good luck throughout the year. The legumes are tasty in this dish any time of year you choose to eat them.

1 Rinse black-eyed peas; place in a large saucepan. Add enough water to cover peas by 2 inches. Bring to boiling; reduce heat. Simmer, uncovered, for 10 minutes. Remove from heat. Cover and let stand for 1 hour. Drain and rinse peas.

2 In a 3½- to 5-quart slow cooker combine the black-eyed peas, pork hocks, broth, sweet pepper, onion, celery, bay leaves, and cayenne pepper.

3 Cover and cook on low-heat setting for 8 to 10 hours or on high-heat setting for 4 to 5 hours. Add okra. Cover; let stand about 10 minutes or until okra is tender. Remove pork hocks. When cool enough to handle, remove meat from bones; cut into bite-size pieces. Discard bones and bay leaves. To serve, stir meat into black-eyed pea mixture.

Nutrition Facts per serving: 191 cal., 3 g total fat (1 g sat. fat), 14 mg chol., 763 mg sodium, 28 g carbo., 7 g fiber, 15 g pro.

Prep: 25 minutes
Cook: Low 8 to 10 hours,
    High 4 to 5 hours
Stand: 1 hour 10 minutes
Makes: 6 servings
Slow Cooker: 3½- to 5-quart

1½ cups dry black-eyed peas
 4 small smoked pork hocks
    (1½ pounds)
 4 cups reduced-sodium chicken broth
¾ cup chopped green sweet pepper
    (1 medium)
½ cup chopped onion (1 medium)
½ cup chopped celery (1 stalk)
 2 bay leaves
¼ teaspoon cayenne pepper
 2 cups sliced okra or one 10-ounce
    package frozen whole okra, thawed
    and cut into ½-inch slices

Ham and Scalloped Potatoes

This no-fuss main dish is an old-fashioned favorite. Use leftover ham from Sunday's dinner or look for diced, cooked ham at your local supermarket. Some larger supermarket salad bars provide cubed ham.

1 In a 3½-quart slow cooker combine frozen hash brown potatoes, ham, pimiento, and pepper. In a medium bowl combine the soup and milk; pour over the potato mixture. Mix to combine.

2 Cover and cook on low-heat setting for 7 to 9 hours or on high-heat setting for 3½ to 4 hours. To serve, stir in parsley.

Nutrition Facts per serving: 241 cal., 9 g total fat (3 g sat. fat), 37 mg chol., 1,180 mg sodium, 30 g carbo., 3 g fiber, 16 g pro.

Prep: 10 minutes
Cook: Low 7 to 9 hours,
 High 3½ to 4 hours
Makes: 6 servings
Slow Cooker: 3½-quart

- 1 28-ounce package loose-pack frozen hash brown potatoes with onion and peppers
- 2 cups (10 ounces) diced fully cooked ham
- 1 2-ounce jar diced pimiento, drained
- ¼ teaspoon black pepper
- 1 11-ounce can condensed cheddar cheese soup
- ¾ cup milk
- 1 tablespoon snipped fresh parsley

34 g
carb

Simple Succotash
with Ham

Diced ham cooks with the vegetables in this slow cooker dish, giving it a delicious rich flavor.

1 In a 3½- or 4-quart slow cooker combine lima beans, corn, ham, sweet pepper, onion, celery, garlic, and black pepper. Pour broth over all.

2 Cover; cook on low-heat setting for 7 to 9 hours or on high heat setting for 3½ to 4½ hours. Use a slotted spoon to serve.

Nutrition Facts per serving: 255 cal., 6 g total fat (2 g sat. fat), 28 mg chol., 959 mg sodium, 34 g carbo., 7 g fiber, 20 g pro.

Prep: 20 minutes
Cook: Low: 7 to 9 hours,
        High: 3½ to 4½ hours
Makes: 8 to 10 servings
Slow Cooker: 3½- or 4-quart

1 16-ounce package frozen baby lima beans, thawed
1 16-ounce package frozen whole kernel corn, thawed
2 cups diced cooked ham (about 12 ounces)
1 cup coarsely chopped red or green sweet pepper
½ cup chopped onion
½ cup chopped celery
2 cloves garlic, minced
¼ teaspoon black pepper
1 14-ounce can chicken broth

Shredded Pork Tacos

Use this spicy pork filling for sandwiches, burritos, or tacos.

1 Trim fat from meat. If necessary, cut roast to fit into a 3½- or 4-quart slow cooker. Place meat in the cooker. Add water, onions, jalapeño peppers, garlic, coriander, cumin, oregano, salt, and black pepper.

2 Cover and cook on low-heat setting for 8 to 10 hours or on high-heat setting for 4 to 5 hours. Remove meat from cooker using a slotted spoon; discard cooking liquid. When cool enough to handle, use two forks to shred the meat.

3 To serve, place warm meat in taco shells. Top with lettuce, cheese, and, if desired, salsa and sour cream.

Nutrition Facts per taco: 283 cal., 13 g total fat (4 g sat. fat), 82 mg chol., 323 mg sodium, 14 g carbo., 3 g fiber, 26 g pro.

Prep: 15 minutes
Cook: Low 8 to 10 hours,
High 4 to 5 hours
Makes: 8 tacos
Slow Cooker: 3½- or 4-quart

1   2-pound boneless pork shoulder
    blade roast
1   cup water
2   large onions, quartered
3   fresh jalapeño chile peppers, cut up
    (see tip, page 62)
8   cloves garlic, minced
2   teaspoons ground coriander
2   teaspoons ground cumin
2   teaspoons dried oregano, crushed
½   teaspoon salt
½   teaspoon black pepper
8   corn taco shells
2   cups shredded lettuce
½   cup finely shredded Monterey Jack
    cheese (2 ounces)
    Bottled salsa (optional)
    Dairy sour cream (optional)

21 g
carb

Shredded Pork Sandwiches

These Southern-style barbecue sandwiches have just the right amount of heat. Cool it down with a side of coleslaw.

1 Remove string from meat, if present. Trim fat from meat. If necessary, cut roast to fit into a 3½- or 4-quart slow cooker. In a small bowl combine garlic powder, ginger, and thyme. Sprinkle mixture over meat and rub in with fingers. Place roast in the cooker. Pour broth over roast.

2 Cover and cook on low-heat setting for 8 to 10 hours or on high-heat setting for 4 to 5 hours.

3 Remove meat from cooker, reserving 1 cup of cooking juices. Use two forks to shred meat and place in a large bowl. Add the cooking liquid, the vinegar, and red pepper; toss to combine. Serve on buns.

Nutrition Facts per sandwich: 318 cal., 11 g total fat (3 g sat. fat), 89 mg chol., 394 mg sodium, 21 g carbo., 2 g fiber, 34 g pro.

Prep: 15 minutes
Cook: Low 8 to 10 hours,
         High 4 to 5 hours
Makes: 8 to 10 sandwiches
Slow Cooker: 3½- or 4-quart

1   2½- to 3-pound pork sirloin roast
½   teaspoon garlic powder
½   teaspoon ground ginger
½   teaspoon dried thyme, crushed
1   cup chicken broth
½   cup vinegar
½   teaspoon cayenne pepper
8   to 10 hamburger buns, split and
     toasted

Pork and Slaw Barbecue Buns

In eastern North Carolina, home of vinegar-sauced barbecued pork, coleslaw is a must-have accompaniment. Spoon some slaw onto the bun with the meat or serve it alongside.

1 Place meat in a 4- to 6-quart slow cooker. In a small bowl combine vinegar, sugar substitute, salt, red pepper, and black pepper. Pour over meat.

2 Cover and cook on low-heat setting for 10 to 12 hours or on high-heat setting for 5 to 6 hours.

3 Transfer meat to a cutting board; reserve cooking juices. When cool enough to handle, cut meat off bones and coarsely chop. In a medium bowl combine meat and as much of the juices as desired to moisten. Serve meat in buns. Serve with coleslaw.

Nutrition Facts per sandwich: 244 cal., 8 g total fat (2 g sat. fat), 46 mg chol., 336 mg sodium, 28 g carbo., 3 g fiber, 17 g pro.

Prep: 10 minutes
Cook: Low 10 to 12 hours,
          High 5 to 6 hours
Makes: 16 sandwiches
Slow Cooker: 4- to 6-quart

1	4- to 5-pound pork shoulder roast or pork shoulder blade Boston roast (Boston butt)
¾	cup cider vinegar
2	tablespoons no-calorie, heat-stable, granular sugar substitute (Splenda)
½	teaspoon salt
½	teaspoon crushed red pepper
¼	teaspoon black pepper
16	whole grain hamburger buns or kaiser rolls, split and toasted
8	cups purchased or homemade coleslaw

Down-South Barbecue

This feeds a crowd of hungry tailgaters. An old Southern trick is to toast the buns to keep them from getting soggy when the barbecue is added.

1 Trim fat from beef and pork roasts. If necessary, cut roasts to fit into a 3½- or 4-quart slow cooker. Place meat in the cooker. In a small bowl combine tomato paste, sugar substitute, vinegar, water, chili powder, Worcestershire sauce, salt, and dry mustard. Pour over meat in cooker.

2 Cover and cook on low-heat setting for 10 to 12 hours or on high-heat setting for 5 to 6 hours. Remove meat from slow cooker, reserving sauce. Use two forks to shred meat. Stir together shredded meat and reserved sauce in cooker. Use a slotted spoon to transfer meat mixture to toasted buns.

Nutrition Facts per sandwich: 241 cal., 7 g total fat (2 g sat. fat), 53 mg chol., 430 mg sodium, 23 g carbo., 2 g fiber, 22 g pro.

Prep: 20 minutes
Cook: Low 10 to 12 hours, High 5 to 6 hours
Makes: 16 sandwiches
Slow Cooker: 3½- or 4-quart

1 1½-pound boneless pork shoulder roast
1 1½-pound boneless beef chuck pot roast
1 6-ounce can tomato paste
½ cup no-calorie, heat-stable, granular sugar substitute (Splenda)
¼ cup cider vinegar
¼ cup water
2 tablespoons chili powder
2 teaspoons Worcestershire sauce
½ teaspoon salt
1 teaspoon dry mustard
16 whole grain hamburger buns, split and toasted

Cuban Pork

32 g
carb

Shredded tender pork and onions stuff these tortilla wraps. For even more Caribbean flavor, spoon on fresh tomato salsa and avocado dip.

1 For marinade, in a small bowl combine lime juice, water, grapefruit juice, garlic, oregano, salt, cumin, pepper, and bay leaves. Trim fat from meat. If necessary, cut roast to fit into a 3½- to 5-quart slow cooker. With a large fork, pierce meat in several places. Place meat in a large plastic bag set in a deep bowl or a baking dish. Pour marinade over meat. Close bag. Marinate in the refrigerator for 6 to 24 hours, turning occasionally.

2 Place onion in the cooker. Top with meat and marinade mixture. Cover and cook on low-heat setting for 10 to 12 hours or on high-heat setting for 5 to 6 hours.

3 Transfer meat to a cutting board; cool slightly. Skim fat from juices; keep warm. Discard bay leaves. Use two forks to shred meat. Transfer shredded meat to a serving platter. With a slotted spoon, remove onion from juices. Transfer onions to same serving platter. Serve meat and onions in tortillas with small bowls of the hot juices and Tomato Salsa. If desired, pass lettuce and guacamole.

Tomato Salsa: In a bowl combine 2 peeled and finely chopped medium tomatoes, 2 tablespoons finely chopped red onion, 2 tablespoons snipped fresh cilantro, 1 teaspoon lime juice, and ⅛ teaspoon salt. Mix well. Cover; chill for at least 2 hours or overnight. Makes about 1¼ cups.

Prep: 25 minutes
Marinate: 6 to 24 hours (meat)
Chill: 2 hours (Pico de Gallo)
Cook: Low 10 to 12 hours,
     High 5 to 6 hours
Makes: 8 to 10 servings
Slow Cooker: 3½- to 5-quart

½ cup lime juice
¼ cup water
¼ cup grapefruit juice
3 cloves garlic, minced
1 teaspoon dried oregano, crushed
½ teaspoon salt
½ teaspoon ground cumin
¼ teaspoon black pepper
2 bay leaves
1 3-pound boneless pork shoulder roast
1 cup sliced onion (1 large)
8 to 10 whole wheat flour tortillas
   (9 to 10 inches)
1 recipe Tomato Salsa or bottled salsa
   Shredded lettuce (optional)
   Purchased guacamole (optional)

Nutrition Facts per serving: 400 cal., 13 g total fat (4 g sat. fat), 110 mg chol., 706 mg sodium, 32 g carbo., 3 g fiber, 38 g pro.

23 g
carb

Jerk Pork Sandwiches with Lime Mayo

Mango, onions, and sweet pepper complement the jerk seasoning. The lime mayo adds a citrus flavor.

1 Trim fat from meat. Rub jerk seasoning evenly over roast. Place meat in a 3½- or 4-quart slow cooker. Sprinkle with the thyme. Pour water over meat.

2 Cover and cook on low-heat setting for 8 to 10 hours or on high-heat setting for 4 to 5 hours. Remove meat from cooker, reserving juices. Use two forks to shred meat; discard any fat. Skim fat from juices. Add enough of the juices to moisten meat (about ½ cup). Stir lime juice into meat.

3 To serve, use a slotted spoon to transfer pork mixture to bun bottoms. If desired, add lettuce leaves, sweet pepper rings, and mango slices. Spoon Lime Mayo onto each sandwich; add bun tops.

Lime Mayo: In a bowl stir together ½ cup light mayonnaise dressing or regular mayonnaise, ¼ cup finely chopped red onion, ¼ teaspoon finely shredded lime peel, 1 tablespoon lime juice, and 1 clove garlic, minced. Cover; chill until ready to serve.

Nutrition Facts per serving: 341 cal., 16 g total fat (4 g sat. fat), 80 mg chol., 561 mg sodium, 23 g carbo., 2 g fiber, 27 g pro.

Prep: 30 minutes
Cook: Low 8 to 10 hours,
High 4 to 5 hours
Makes: 6 to 8 sandwiches
Slow Cooker: 3½- or 4-quart

1 1½-to 2-pound boneless pork
   shoulder roast
1 tablespoon Jamaican jerk seasoning
¼ teaspoon dried thyme, crushed
1 cup water
1 tablespoon lime juice
6 to 8 whole grain hamburger buns or
   kaiser rolls, split and toasted
6 to 8 lettuce leaves (optional)
6 thinly sliced red or green sweet
   pepper rings (optional)
1 medium mango, peeled and thinly
   sliced (optional)
1 recipe Lime Mayo

Five-Spice Pork Sandwiches

Five-spice powder is the dominant flavor in this shredded pork sandwich. The cooking juices are used for dipping the sandwiches, similar to French dip sandwiches.

1 Trim fat from meat. If necessary, cut roast to fit into a 3½- or 4-quart slow cooker. Place meat in cooker. In a small bowl combine apple juice, soy sauce, hoisin sauce, and five-spice powder. Pour over meat.

2 Cover and cook on low-heat setting for 10 to 12 hours or on high heat setting for 5½ to 6 hours.

3 Remove meat from cooker, reserving juices. Remove meat from bone; discard bone. Use two forks to shred meat. Place meat on bun bottoms. Top with shredded Chinese cabbage; add bun tops. Skim fat from juices. Serve juices in serving bowls for dipping.

Nutrition Facts per sandwich: 297 cal., 9 g total fat (3 g sat. fat), 68 mg chol., 653 mg sodium, 27 g carbo., 2 g fiber, 26 g pro.

Prep: 25 minutes
Cook: Low 10 to 12 **hours,**
      High 5½ to 6 **hours**
Makes: 6 to 8 **sandwiches**
Slow Cooker: 3½- or 4-**quart**

1	2½- to 3-pound pork shoulder roast
1	cup apple juice or apple cider
2	tablespoons soy sauce
2	tablespoons hoisin sauce
1½	teaspoons five-spice powder*
6	to 8 whole grain hamburger buns or kaiser rolls, split and toasted
1½	to 2 cups shredded Chinese cabbage (napa) or packaged shredded broccoli (broccoli slaw mix)

*To make Five-Spice Powder: In a blender container combine 3 tablespoons ground cinnamon, 6 star anise or 2 teaspoons anise seeds, 1½ teaspoons fennel seeds, 1½ teaspoons whole Szechwan pepper or whole black pepper, and ¾ teaspoon ground cloves. Cover and blend to a fine powder. Store in a tightly covered container at room temperature. Makes ⅓ cup.

23 g
carb

Hot Pepper Pork Sandwiches

You can adjust the heat level by varying the number of jalapeños you use. Want to turn up the heat? Don't seed the peppers.

1 Trim fat from meat. If necessary, cut roast to fit into a 3½- or 4-quart slow cooker. Place meat in the cooker. Sprinkle meat with the fajita seasoning. Add peppers and enchilada sauce.

2 Cover and cook on low-heat setting for 11 to 12 hours or on high-heat setting for 5½ to 6 hours. Transfer roast to a cutting board. Use two forks to shred meat. Stir shredded meat into juices in slow cooker. Use a slotted spoon to transfer shredded meat mixture to toasted buns.

Nutrition Facts per sandwich: 262 cal., 9 g total fat (3 g sat. fat), 58 mg chol., 778 mg sodium, 23 g carbo., 3 g fiber, 22 g pro.

Prep: 20 minutes
Cook: Low 11 to 12 hours,
       High 5½ to 6 hours
Makes: 8 sandwiches
Slow Cooker: 3½- or 4-quart

1   2½- to 3-pound boneless pork shoulder roast
2   teaspoons fajita seasoning
1   or 2 fresh jalapeño chile peppers, seeded, if desired, and finely chopped (see note, page 62)
2   10-ounce cans enchilada sauce
8   whole grain hamburger buns or kaiser rolls, split and toasted

Saucy Sausage Sandwiches

If you like Italian sausage, this is the sandwich for you. Mushrooms, olives, tomato sauce, and cheese make this like a pizza on a bun.

1 In a large skillet cook sausage, ground beef, and onion until meat is brown and onion is tender. Drain off fat.

2 Meanwhile, in a 3½- or 4-quart slow cooker combine the drained tomatoes, tomato sauce, mushrooms, olives, tapioca, sugar (if desired), oregano, pepper, and garlic powder. Stir in meat mixture.

3 Cover and cook on low-heat setting for 8 to 10 hours or on high-heat setting for 4 to 5 hours. Spoon meat mixture onto bottom halves of buns. Top with cheese. Cover with bun tops.

For a 5- or 6-quart cooker: Double the ingredients. Prepare as above. Makes 16 sandwiches.

Nutrition Facts per sandwich: 362 cal., 18 g total fat (7 g sat. fat), 53 mg chol., 807 mg sodium, 27 g carbo., 3 g fiber, 19 g pro.

Prep: 20 minutes
Cook: Low 8 to 10 hours,
High 4 to 5 hours
Makes: 10 sandwiches
Slow Cooker: 3½- or 4-quart

1 pound bulk Italian sausage
½ pound lean ground beef
1 cup chopped onion (1 large)
1 14½-ounce can diced tomatoes, drained
1 8-ounce can tomato sauce
1 4½-ounce jar sliced mushrooms, drained
½ cup sliced, pitted ripe olives
4 teaspoons quick-cooking tapioca
1 teaspoon sugar (optional)
1 teaspoon dried oregano, crushed
⅛ teaspoon black pepper
Dash garlic powder
10 whole grain hamburger buns or kaiser rolls, split and toasted
5 ounces sliced mozzarella cheese

Chorizo Sandwiches

Chorizo is a spicy pork sausage often used in Mexican or Spanish cuisines. Be sure to remove the casing before cooking.

1 Remove casing from chorizo (if using). In a large skillet cook sausage and ground turkey, half at a time, until meat is no longer pink. Drain off fat. In a 5- to 6-quart slow cooker combine onion, tomato sauce, undrained tomatoes, tapioca, jalapeño peppers, sugar (if desired), and oregano. Stir in the meat.

2 Cover and cook on low-heat setting for 8 to 10 hours or on high-heat setting for 4 to 5 hours. Spoon meat mixture into buns. If desired, serve with sliced olives, shredded cheese, and/or cherry peppers.

Nutrition Facts per sandwich: 306 cal., 14 g total fat (4 g sat. fat), 64 mg chol., 557 mg sodium, 25 g carbo., 2 g fiber, 19 g pro.

Prep: 25 minutes
Cook: Low 8 to 10 hours,
High 4 to 5 hours
Makes: 16 to 20 sandwiches
Slow Cooker: 5- to 6-quart

1 pound chorizo or bulk Italian sausage
2 pounds uncooked ground turkey or lean ground beef
2 cups chopped onion (2 large)
1 15-ounce can tomato sauce
1 14½-ounce can diced tomatoes, undrained
2 tablespoons quick-cooking tapioca
2 tablespoons finely chopped, seeded fresh jalapeño chile peppers (see note, page 62)
2 teaspoons sugar (optional)
2 teaspoons dried oregano, crushed
16 to 20 whole grain hamburger buns or kaiser rolls, split and toasted
Sliced, pitted ripe olives; shredded Monterey Jack cheese; and/or mild sliced cherry peppers (optional)

Spicy Lamb Shanks

Lamb shanks are an underutilized and wonderfully flavorful cut of lamb. Ideal for the crockery cooker, the meat literally falls off the bone. Infused with orange and spices, this dish is the perfect warming supper for chilly days.

1 Using a vegetable peeler, remove the orange part of the peel from 1 of the oranges. Cut peel into thin strips (should have about ¼ cup); set aside. Squeeze juice from both oranges to make about ⅔ cup. In a small bowl stir together orange juice, broth, cardamom, cumin, salt, turmeric, and pepper. Set aside.

2 Place carrots, onions, and garlic in the bottom of a 5- to 6-quart slow cooker. Top with lamb shanks, strips of orange peel, and cinnamon sticks. Pour orange juice mixture over all. Cover and cook on low-heat setting for 8 to 9 hours.

3 Transfer the lamb shanks and vegetables to a serving dish using a slotted spoon. Pour cooking juices into a large measuring cup; skim fat. Discard the cinnamon sticks. Measure 1½ cups juices; transfer to a small saucepan. Combine water and cornstarch; stir into juices in saucepan. Cook and stir over medium heat until thickened and bubbly. Cook and stir 2 minutes more. Spoon sauce over lamb and vegetables. Sprinkle with olives and cilantro.

Nutrition Facts per serving: 461 cal., 21 g total fat (8 g sat. fat), 150 mg chol., 760 mg sodium, 22 g carbo., 6 g fiber, 44 g pro.

*Note: To peel onions more easily, place onions in a saucepan with water. Bring to boiling and cook for 30 seconds. Slice off the root ends and squeeze onions from peels.

Prep: 25 minutes
Cook: Low 8 to 9 hours
plus 10 minutes
Makes: 4 to 6 servings
Slow Cooker: 5- to 6-quart

2	large oranges
1¼	cups beef broth
1½	teaspoons ground cardamom
1	teaspoon ground cumin
½	teaspoon salt
½	teaspoon ground turmeric
½	teaspoon black pepper
5	carrots, peeled and cut into 2-inch lengths
1½	cups boiling onions, peeled*
4	large cloves garlic, thinly sliced
4	pounds lamb foreshanks (3 to 4)
2	3-inch cinnamon sticks
2	tablespoons water
4	teaspoons cornstarch
⅓	cup pitted kalamata or other black olives, halved if desired
1	tablespoon snipped fresh cilantro

Mediterranean Lamb Shanks

When purchasing lamb shanks for this Greek-inspired dinner, make sure they'll fit in your slow cooker. If they're too large, have the butcher cut them in half crosswise.

1 In a small bowl combine oregano, garlic, and salt. Sprinkle evenly over meat; rub in with your fingers.

2 In a 4½- to 6-quart slow cooker combine garbanzo beans, undrained tomatoes, onion, lemon juice, allspice, and pepper. Top with meat.

3 Cover and cook on low-heat setting for 7 to 9 hours or on high-heat setting for 3½ to 4½ hours. Remove meat; cover with foil to keep warm.

4 Stir spinach into bean mixture. In a small bowl combine yogurt, cucumber, and mint. Divide bean mixture among 4 shallow bowls; top each with a shank. Top each serving with some of the yogurt mixture.

Nutrition Facts per serving: 455 cal., 20 g total fat (8 g sat. fat), 117 mg chol., 850 mg sodium, 28 g carbo., 9 g fiber, 40 g pro.

Prep: 15 minutes
Cook: Low 7 to 9 hours,
High 3½ to 4½ hours
Makes: 4 servings
Slow Cooker: 4½- to 6-quart

- 1 tablespoon dried oregano, crushed
- 4 cloves garlic, minced
- ¼ teaspoon salt
- 4 meaty lamb shanks (about 3½ to 4 pounds)
- 1 14½-ounce can garbanzo beans (chickpeas), rinsed and drained
- 1 14½-ounce can diced tomatoes, undrained
- ½ cup chopped onion (1 medium)
- 2 tablespoons lemon juice
- ½ teaspoon ground allspice
- ½ teaspoon black pepper
- 7 cups coarsely chopped fresh spinach
- ½ cup plain yogurt
- ¼ cup chopped cucumber
- 1 tablespoon snipped fresh mint

Spicy Fruited Lamb

Dried fruit—apricots, plums, and raisins—plump up to create a delicious sauce for these lamb shanks.

1 Sprinkle lamb shanks with salt and pepper. Dredge in flour. In a large skillet brown shanks on all sides in hot oil. Drain off fat. In a 3½- or 4-quart slow cooker combine apricots, plums, raisins, broth, sugar substitute, vinegar, lemon juice, allspice, and cinnamon. Add browned lamb shanks.

2 Cover and cook on low-heat setting for 9 to 10 hours or on high-heat setting for 4½ to 5 hours. Remove shanks from cooker; keep warm.

3 For gravy, strain cooking juices into a large measuring cup, reserving fruit. Skim fat. Measure juices, adding enough water, if necessary, to equal 1½ cups. Pour into a medium saucepan. Combine cornstarch and cold water; stir into juices in saucepan. Cook and stir over medium heat until thickened and bubbly. Cook and stir 2 minutes more. Stir in reserved fruit. Heat through. Serve lamb shanks with gravy and, if desired, hot cooked rice.

Nutrition Facts per serving: 378 cal., 11 g total fat (3 g sat. fat), 115 mg chol., 266 mg sodium, 32 g carbo., 3 g fiber, 39 g pro.

Prep: 25 minutes
Cook: Low 9 to 10 hours,
High 4½ to 5 hours;
plus 10 minutes
Makes: 6 servings
Slow Cooker: 3½- or 4-quart

3½ pounds lamb shanks, halved crosswise (3 to 4 shanks)
    Salt
    Black pepper
¼ cup all-purpose flour
2 tablespoons cooking oil
½ cup dried apricots
½ cup pitted dried plums (prunes), halved
½ cup raisins
¾ cup beef broth
2 tablespoons no-calorie, heat-stable, granular sugar substitute (Splenda)
2 tablespoons vinegar
2 tablespoons lemon juice
½ teaspoon ground allspice
½ teaspoon ground cinnamon
1 tablespoon cornstarch
1 tablespoon cold water
    Hot cooked brown rice (optional)

Lamb Shanks with Rosemary and Olives

Purchase lamb foreshanks, which are smaller than hindshanks, for this flavorful Mediterranean dish.

1 In a 5- to 6-quart slow cooker place onions and olives. Arrange lamb in cooker. Sprinkle with garlic, rosemary, salt, and pepper. Pour broth over all.

2 Cover and cook on low-heat setting for 11 to 12 hours or on high-heat setting for 5½ to 6 hours. Use a slotted spoon to transfer lamb, onions, and olives to a serving dish; reserve cooking juices. Skim fat from juices. If desired, strain juices; pass with meat. Garnish with parsley.

Nutrition Facts per serving: 238 cal., 7 g total fat (1 g sat. fat), 95 mg chol., 842 mg sodium, 12 g carbo., 3 g fiber, 31 g pro.

Prep: 15 minutes
Cook: Low 11 to 12 hours,
        High 5½ to 6 hours
Makes: 4 to 6 servings
Slow Cooker: 5- to 6-quart

- 1   pound boiling onions, peeled
- ½   cup pitted Kalamata olives
- 4   meaty lamb foreshanks (about 4 pounds) or meaty veal shank crosscuts (about 3 pounds)
- 4   cloves garlic, minced
- 2   teaspoons dried rosemary, crushed
- ½   teaspoon salt
- ¼   teaspoon black pepper
- 1   cup chicken broth
    Snipped fresh flat-leaf parsley

Lamb Shanks with Barley

Perfect for a simple Sunday supper, the lamb shanks cook while you take a hike in the woods, play a game of tag football, or snuggle up to watch your favorite movie.

1 In a large skillet brown the lamb shanks in hot oil over medium heat. Drain off fat.

2 In a 5- to 6-quart slow cooker combine barley, onion, carrots, celery, broth, undrained tomatoes, water, and pepper. Add lamb shanks.

3 Cover and cook on low-heat setting for 7 to 9 hours. Transfer lamb shanks to a serving platter. Skim off fat from vegetable-barley mixture. If desired, stir in balsamic vinegar. Serve with lamb.

Nutrition Facts per serving: 370 cal., 8 g total fat (2 g sat. fat), 99 mg chol., 529 mg sodium, 36 g carbo., 7 g fiber, 37 g pro.

Prep: 20 minutes
Cook: Low 7 to 9 hours
Makes: 6 to 8 servings
Slow Cooker: 5- to 6-quart

3 to 3½ pounds lamb shanks or beef
    shank crosscuts
1 tablespoon cooking oil
1 cup regular barley
½ cup chopped onion (1 medium)
4 carrots, cut into ½-inch slices
    (2 cups)
3 stalks celery, cut into ½-inch slices
    (1½ cups)
1 14-ounce can chicken broth
1 14½-ounce can diced tomatoes,
    undrained
⅓ cup water
½ teaspoon black pepper
2 tablespoons balsamic vinegar
    (optional)

Lamb and Sausage Cassoulet

Cassoulet (ka-soo-LAY) is a classic French dish consisting of white beans and a variety of meats—sausage, pork, duck, or goose. The combination varies according to the region. Lamb and kielbasa are used in this version.

1 Rinse beans; place in a large saucepan. Add enough water to cover by 2 inches. Bring to boiling; reduce heat. Simmer, uncovered, for 10 minutes. Remove from heat. Cover and let stand for 1 hour. Drain and rinse beans.

2 Meanwhile, in a large skillet brown lamb in hot oil. Drain off fat. In a 3½- to 5-quart slow cooker combine the beans, lamb, broth, kielbasa, dried thyme (if using), garlic, peppercorns, and bay leaf.

3 Cover and cook on low-heat setting for 8 to 10 hours or on high-heat setting for 4 to 5 hours.

4 If using low-heat setting, turn to high-heat setting. Stir in the eggplant, sweet pepper, and tomato paste. Cover and cook for 30 minutes more. Discard bay leaf. If using, stir in fresh thyme. Season to taste with salt and black pepper. If desired, serve over hot cooked rice.

Nutrition Facts per serving: 369 cal., 16 g total fat (7 g sat. fat), 62 mg chol., 686 mg sodium, 30 g carbo., 9 g fiber, 26 g pro.

Prep: 25 minutes
Stand: 1 hour
Cook: Low 8 to 10 hours,
  High 4 to 5 hours;
  plus 30 minutes
Makes: 6 servings
Slow Cooker: 3½- to 5-quart

- 1 cup dry Great Northern beans or dry navy beans
- 12 ounces lamb stew meat, cut into 1-inch cubes
- 1 tablespoon cooking oil
- 2 cups beef broth
- 8 ounces cooked kielbasa, cut into ¼-inch slices
- 1 tablespoon snipped fresh thyme or 1 teaspoon dried thyme, crushed
- 3 cloves garlic, minced
- ¼ teaspoon whole black peppercorns
- 1 bay leaf
- 1 small eggplant, peeled and chopped
- 1 large green or red sweet pepper, coarsely chopped
- 1 6-ounce can tomato paste
  Salt
  Black pepper
  Hot cooked brown rice (optional)

Lemon-Mustard Lamb Roast

Spoon golden mustard-and-lemon-flavor cooking juices over this tender lamb and roasted vegetables.

1 Trim fat from meat. If necessary, cut roast to fit into a 3½- or 4-quart slow cooker. In a small bowl combine lemon-pepper seasoning and dry mustard. Sprinkle evenly over entire lamb roast; rub lightly with fingers. In a large skillet brown the roast on all sides in hot oil.

2 Place potatoes and carrots in slow cooker. Place the meat on vegetables. In a small bowl combine broth, mustard, tapioca, lemon juice, rosemary, lemon peel, pepper, and garlic; pour broth mixture over meat and vegetables.

3 Cover and cook on low-heat setting for 8 to 10 hours or on high-heat setting for 4 to 5 hours.

4 If using low-heat setting, turn to high-heat setting. Add artichoke hearts. Cover and cook 30 minutes more. Remove roast from cooker and remove string or netting, if present. Skim fat from cooking juices. Serve juices with meat and vegetables.

Nutrition Facts per serving: 539 cal., 19 g total fat (5 g sat. fat), 148 mg chol., 694 mg sodium, 40 g carbo., 8 g fiber, 51 g pro.

Prep: 25 minutes
Cook: Low 8 to 10 hours,
High 4 to 5 hours;
plus 30 minutes
Makes: 4 servings
Slow Cooker: 3½- or 4-quart

- 1 2- to 2½-pound boneless lamb shoulder roast
- ½ teaspoon lemon-pepper seasoning
- ½ teaspoon dry mustard
- 1 tablespoon cooking oil
- 4 medium potatoes, quartered
- 1½ cups whole tiny carrots
- 1 cup chicken broth
- ½ cup Dijon-style mustard
- 2 tablespoons quick-cooking tapioca
- 1 tablespoon lemon juice
- ½ teaspoon dried rosemary, crushed
- ½ teaspoon finely shredded lemon peel
- ½ teaspoon black pepper
- 2 cloves garlic, minced
- 1 9-ounce package frozen artichoke hearts, thawed

29 g
carb

Lamb and Vegetables with Spiced Sauce

The combination of spices and flavors adds exotic richness to this roast. For convenience, leave the skin on the potatoes.

1 Remove a narrow strip of peel from the center of each new potato, or peel (if desired) and quarter each medium potato. In a 3½- to 5-quart slow cooker place potatoes, carrots, and onions. Drizzle with honey (if desired) and sprinkle with ginger, salt, anise seeds, cinnamon, and cayenne pepper.

2 Trim the fat from meat. If necessary, cut roast to fit into the cooker. Place meat on top of vegetables. Pour broth over meat and vegetables.

3 Cover and cook on low-heat setting for 10 to 12 hours or on high-heat setting for 5 to 6 hours.

4 Use a slotted spoon to transfer meat and vegetables to a serving platter; reserve cooking juices. Cover meat and vegetables to keep warm.

5 For gravy, pour juices into a large measuring cup; skim fat. Measure 1½ cups juices. In a small saucepan, combine the cold water, flour, and orange peel. Stir in reserved 1½ cups juices. Cook and stir until thickened and bubbly. Cook and stir for 1 minute more. Season to taste with salt and black pepper. Pass gravy with the meat and vegetables.

Nutrition Facts per serving: 364 cal., 8 g total fat (3 g sat. fat), 119 mg chol., 518 mg sodium, 29 g carbo., 4 g fiber, 42 g pro.

Prep: 15 minutes
Cook: Low 10 to 12 hours, High 5 to 6 hours; plus 10 minutes
Makes: 6 to 8 servings
Slow Cooker: 3½- to 5-quart

1½ pounds tiny new potatoes or
    5 medium potatoes
2 cups packaged, peeled baby carrots
2 small onions, cut into wedges
1 tablespoon honey (optional)
1 tablespoon grated fresh ginger or
    ¾ teaspoon ground ginger
½ teaspoon salt
½ teaspoon anise seeds or ¼ teaspoon ground allspice
½ teaspoon ground cinnamon
⅛ to ¼ teaspoon cayenne pepper
1 2½- to 3-pound boneless lamb shoulder roast
1¼ cups beef broth
½ cup cold water
¼ cup all-purpose flour
1 teaspoon finely shredded orange peel

Brown Rice Risotto with Lamb

Curry adds intrigue to this colorful main dish. Round out the meal with a salad of fresh spinach, cucumber, and tomato.

1 Trim fat from meat. If necessary, cut roast to fit into a 3½- or 4-quart slow cooker. In a large skillet brown meat on all sides in hot oil. In the slow cooker combine vegetable juice, uncooked rice, curry powder, and salt. Add carrots. Place meat over carrots.

2 Cover and cook on low-heat setting for 8 to 9 hours or on high-heat setting for 4 to 4½ hours.

3 Add the sweet pepper to the cooker. Cover and let stand 5 to 10 minutes.

Nutrition Facts per serving: 299 cal., 12 g total fat (3 g sat. fat), 99 mg chol., 537 mg sodium, 15 g carbo., 2 g fiber, 32 g pro.

Prep: 15 minutes
Cook: Low 8 to 9 hours,
High 4 to 4½ hours
Stand: 5 minutes
Makes: 6 servings
Slow Cooker: 3½- or 4-quart

1	2- to 2½-pound boneless lamb shoulder roast
1	tablespoon cooking oil
2½	cups hot-style vegetable juice
1	cup regular brown rice
1	teaspoon curry powder
¼	teaspoon salt
2	medium carrots, diced
1	medium green sweet pepper, finely chopped

30 g
carb

Greek Lamb with Spinach

The sunny flavors of the Mediterranean come alive in this robust dish of chunks of lamb tossed with spinach and feta cheese.

1 Trim fat from meat. If necessary, cut roast to fit into a 3½- to 6-quart slow cooker. In a small bowl combine oregano, lemon peel, garlic, and salt. Sprinkle evenly over meat; rub lightly with fingers. Place lamb in cooker. Sprinkle lamb with lemon juice.

2 Cover and cook on low-heat setting for 8 to 10 hours or on high-heat setting for 4 to 5 hours.

3 Remove lamb from cooker. Remove meat from bones; discard bones and fat. Chop meat; set aside. Add spinach to cooking juices in cooker, stirring until spinach is wilted. Add cooked rice, feta cheese, and lamb; stir to mix.

Nutrition Facts per serving: 313 cal., 9 g total fat (4 g sat. fat), 80 mg chol., 352 mg sodium, 30 g carbo., 5 g fiber, 28 g pro.

Prep: 20 minutes
Cook: Low 8 to 10 hours,
    High 4 to 5 hours;
        plus 5 minutes
Makes: 8 servings
Slow Cooker: 3½- to 6-quart

 1 3- to 3½-pound lamb shoulder roast
        (bone-in)
 1 tablespoon dried oregano, crushed
 1 tablespoon finely shredded lemon peel
 4 cloves garlic, minced
 ¼ teaspoon salt
 ¼ cup lemon juice
 1 10-ounce bag prewashed fresh
        spinach, chopped
 5 cups hot cooked brown rice
 4 ounces crumbled feta cheese

Lemony Lamb Pitas

Reminiscent of gyros, but much simpler, these lamb sandwiches are a welcome change from daily fare. Serve them with wedges of fresh melon.

1 Trim fat from meat. In a small bowl combine the ½ teaspoon lemon-pepper seasoning and the dry mustard. Sprinkle evenly over roast; rub lightly with your fingers. Place meat in a 3½- or 4-quart slow cooker. In a bowl combine broth, lemon peel, lemon juice, rosemary, and garlic. Pour over meat.

2 Cover and cook on low-heat setting for 8 to 10 hours or on high-heat setting for 4 to 5 hours.

3 In a bowl stir together yogurt, cucumber, and the ¼ teaspoon lemon-pepper seasoning. Set aside. Remove meat from cooker. Cool slightly. Use two forks to shred meat. To serve, open pita bread halves to form pockets. Place a lettuce leaf in each pita half. Spoon lamb into pita halves. Top meat with yogurt mixture and chopped tomato.

Nutrition Facts per serving: 231 cal., 6 g total fat (2 g sat. fat), 73 mg chol., 471 mg sodium, 18 g carbo., 3 g fiber, 28 g pro.

Prep: 20 minutes
Cook: Low 8 to 10 hours,
High 4 to 5 hours
Makes: 6 servings
Slow Cooker: 3½- or 4-quart

1 1½- to 2-pound boneless lamb
    shoulder roast
½ teaspoon lemon-pepper seasoning
½ teaspoon dry mustard
½ cup chicken broth
¼ teaspoon finely shredded lemon peel
1 tablespoon lemon juice
1 teaspoon snipped fresh rosemary or
    ¼ teaspoon dried rosemary,
    crushed
2 cloves garlic, minced
½ cup plain yogurt
¼ cup chopped, seeded cucumber
¼ teaspoon lemon-pepper seasoning
3 large whole wheat pita bread rounds,
    halved crosswise
6 lettuce leaves
1 small tomato, seeded and chopped

Mediterranean Lamb Pitas

An exotic mix of garlic, wine, allspice, mint, and yogurt flavors the lamb. Serve it in pitas with lettuce, tomato, and cumin-spiked yogurt.

1 Trim fat from meat. If necessary, cut roast to fit into a 3½- or 4-quart slow cooker. In a large skillet brown the lamb on all sides in hot oil.

2 In the slow cooker combine garbanzo beans, wine, tomato paste, water, onion, garlic, allspice, mint, salt, and pepper. Place meat on top of beans.

3 Cover and cook on low-heat setting for 8 to 10 hours or on high-heat setting for 4 to 5 hours. Remove meat from cooker. Use two forks to shred meat; return meat to the cooker. Cover and cook 15 minutes more. Remove meat and beans with a slotted spoon.

4 To serve, open pita bread halves to form pockets. Line pitas with lettuce and/or cucumber. Combine yogurt and ground cumin. Spoon meat mixture, then yogurt mixture into pitas. Sprinkle with chopped tomato.

Nutrition Facts per serving: 241 cal., 5 g total fat (1 g sat. fat), 49 mg chol., 397 mg sodium, 25 g carbo., 5 g fiber, 23 g pro.

Prep: 25 minutes
Cook: Low 8 to 10 hours,
High 4 to 5 hours;
plus 15 minutes
Makes: 12 servings
Slow Cooker: 3½- or 4-quart

- 1 2-pound portion boneless lamb leg roast
- 1 tablespoon olive oil
- 1 15-ounce can garbanzo beans (chickpeas), rinsed and drained
- ¾ cup dry red wine
- ½ of a 6-ounce can (⅓ cup) tomato paste
- ¼ cup water
- 1 cup chopped onion (1 large)
- 4 cloves garlic, minced
- ½ teaspoon ground allspice
- ½ teaspoon dried mint, crushed
- ¼ teaspoon salt
- ¼ teaspoon black pepper
- 6 large whole wheat pita bread rounds, halved crosswise
  Lettuce leaves and/or thinly sliced cucumber
- 1 8-ounce carton plain yogurt
- ¼ teaspoon ground cumin
- 1 medium tomato, chopped

Poultry

Barbecue-Style Chicken

Chicken thighs and drumsticks generally are a meat department bargain. Cooked in a robust barbecue sauce, they're as tasty as they are economical.

1 In a 3½- or 4-quart slow cooker place the potatoes, sweet pepper, and onion. Sprinkle tapioca over potato mixture. Place chicken on top of vegetables. For sauce, in a small bowl stir together tomato sauce, sugar substitute, Worcestershire sauce, mustard, garlic, and salt. Pour sauce over chicken.

2 Cover and cook on low-heat setting for 10 to 12 hours or on high-heat setting for 5 to 6 hours.

3 Transfer chicken and vegetables to a large serving bowl. Skim fat from sauce. Spoon sauce over chicken and vegetables.

Nutrition Facts per serving: 259 cal., 5 g total fat (1 g sat. fat), 107 mg chol., 668 mg sodium, 25 g carbo., 3 g fiber, 29 g pro.

Prep: 25 minutes
Cook: Low 10 to 12 hours,
High 5 to 6 hours
Makes: 4 to 5 servings
Slow Cooker: 3½- or 4-quart

2   medium unpeeled potatoes, cut into ½-inch pieces
1   large green sweet pepper, cut into strips
1   medium onion, sliced
1   tablespoon quick-cooking tapioca
2   pounds chicken thighs or drumsticks, skinned
1   8-ounce can tomato sauce
2   tablespoons no-calorie, heat-stable, granular sugar substitute (Splenda)
1   tablespoon Worcestershire sauce
1   tablespoon prepared mustard
1   clove garlic, minced
¼   teaspoon salt

Chicken and Vegetables in Wine Sauce

Chicken and hearty vegetables are simmered in a delicately flavored wine sauce. Choose dark meat chicken—legs, thighs, or drumsticks—for this dish.

1 In a 5- to 6-quart slow cooker place potatoes, carrots, celery, and onion. Place chicken pieces on top of vegetables. Sprinkle with parsley, salt, rosemary, thyme, pepper, and garlic; add broth and wine.

2 Cover and cook on low-heat setting for 8 to 9 hours or on high-heat setting for 4 to 4½ hours. Use a slotted spoon to transfer chicken and vegetables to a serving platter; cover with foil to keep warm.

3 For gravy, skim fat from cooking juices; strain juices. In a large saucepan, melt butter. Stir in flour; cook for 1 minute. Add cooking juices. Cook and stir until thickened and bubbly. Cook and stir 2 minutes more. Pass the gravy with the chicken and vegetables.

Nutrition Facts per serving: 328 cal., 11 g total fat (5 g sat. fat), 124 mg chol., 544 mg sodium, 24 g carbo., 3 g fiber, 29 g pro.

Prep: 20 minutes
Cook: Low 8 to 9 hours,
High 4 to 4½ hours;
plus 10 minutes
Makes: 6 servings
Slow Cooker: 5- to 6-quart

- 4 medium red-skin potatoes, quartered
- 4 medium carrots, cut into ½-inch pieces
- 2 stalks celery, cut into 1-inch pieces
- 1 small onion, sliced
- 3 pounds chicken thighs or drumsticks, skinned
- 1 tablespoon snipped fresh parsley
- ½ teaspoon salt
- ½ teaspoon dried rosemary, crushed
- ½ teaspoon dried thyme, crushed
- ¼ teaspoon black pepper
- 1 clove garlic, minced
- 1 cup chicken broth
- ½ cup dry white wine
- 3 tablespoons butter or margarine
- 3 tablespoons all-purpose flour

11 g

carb

Chicken in Red Wine

To peel the pearl onions, submerge the unpeeled onions in boiling water for about three minutes. Cut off the root end and gently press the onions. The skins will slip off.

1 In a 3½- or 4-quart slow cooker place mushrooms and onions. Stir in the ½ cup broth, the wine, tomato paste, garlic salt, rosemary, thyme, pepper, and bay leaf. Add chicken legs.

2 Cover and cook on low-heat setting for 7 to 8 hours or on high-heat setting for 3½ to 4 hours. Transfer chicken to a serving platter; keep warm.

3 For sauce, transfer vegetables and cooking liquid to a medium saucepan. Combine the ¼ cup broth and the flour; stir into mixture in saucepan. Cook and stir until thickened and bubbly; cook and stir 1 minute more. Discard bay leaf. Spoon some of the sauce over chicken; pass remaining sauce. If desired, sprinkle with parsley.

Nutrition Facts per serving: 231 cal., 6 g total fat (1 g sat. fat), 103 mg chol., 429 mg sodium, 11 g carbo., 2 g fiber, 30 g pro.

Prep: 25 minutes
Cook: Low 7 to 8 hours,
       High 3½ to 4 hours;
       plus 10 minutes
Makes: 4 servings
Slow Cooker: 3½- or 4-quart

  8 ounces mushrooms, halved
 16 pearl onions (1⅓ cups), peeled
 ½ cup chicken broth
 ¼ cup dry red wine
  2 tablespoons tomato paste
 ½ teaspoon garlic salt
 ½ teaspoon dried rosemary, crushed
 ½ teaspoon dried thyme, crushed
 ¼ teaspoon black pepper
  1 bay leaf
  4 small chicken legs (drumstick-thigh portion) (about 2 pounds total), skinned
 ¼ cup chicken broth
  2 tablespoons all-purpose flour
    Snipped fresh parsley (optional)

Chicken Merlot with Mushrooms

To ensure proper doneness, always place ingredients in your crockery cooker in the order given in the recipe. Generally, vegetables are added first and the meat is last.

1 In a 3½- to 5-quart slow cooker place mushrooms, onion, and garlic. Place chicken on top of vegetables. In a bowl combine broth, tomato paste, wine, tapioca, dried basil (if using), sugar (if using), salt, and pepper. Pour over chicken.

2 Cover and cook on low-heat setting for 7 to 8 hours or on high-heat setting for 3½ to 4 hours. If using, stir in fresh basil. If desired, serve over pasta. Sprinkle with Parmesan cheese.

Nutrition Facts per serving: 306 cal., 12 g total fat (5 g sat. fat), 89 mg chol., 595 mg sodium, 13 g carbo., 2 g fiber, 35 g pro.

Prep: 25 minutes
Cook: Low 7 to 8 hours,
High 3½ to 4 hours
Makes: 6 servings
Slow Cooker: 3½- to 5-quart

3 cups sliced fresh mushrooms
1 cup chopped onion (1 large)
2 cloves garlic, minced
2½ to 3 pounds meaty chicken pieces (breasts, thighs, and drumsticks), skinned
¾ cup chicken broth
1 6-ounce can tomato paste
¼ cup dry red wine (such as Merlot) or chicken broth
2 tablespoons quick-cooking tapioca
2 tablespoons snipped fresh basil or 1½ teaspoons dried basil, crushed
2 teaspoons sugar or no-calorie, heat-stable, granular sugar substitute (Splenda)(optional)
¼ teaspoon salt
¼ teaspoon black pepper
Hot cooked whole wheat pasta (optional)
3 tablespoons finely shredded Parmesan cheese

19 g
carb

Mediterranean Chicken

Tender chicken pieces and chunks of vegetables make up this Mediterranean-flavored dish that can be served over pasta.

1 In a 3½- or 4-quart slow cooker combine the mushrooms, tomatoes, undrained artichoke hearts (cut up large pieces), and olives. Sprinkle with tapioca. Place the chicken pieces on top of vegetables. Sprinkle with Italian seasoning and salt. Add broth and wine.

2 Cover and cook on low-heat setting for 7 to 8 hours or on high-heat setting for 3½ to 4 hours. If desired, serve with hot pasta.

Nutrition Facts per serving: 287 cal., 11 g total fat (2 g sat. fat), 107 mg chol., 1,009 mg sodium, 19 g carbo., 2 g fiber, 30 g pro.

Prep: 30 minutes
Cook: Low 7 to 8 hours,
    High 3½ to 4 hours
Makes: 4 to 6 servings
Slow Cooker: 3½- or 4-quart

- 2 cups sliced fresh mushrooms
- 1 14½-ounce can whole tomatoes, drained and cut up
- 1 6-ounce jar marinated artichoke hearts, undrained
- 1 2½-ounce can sliced, pitted ripe olives, drained
- 3 tablespoons quick-cooking tapioca
- 2 to 2½ pounds chicken thighs and/or drumsticks, skinned
- 1 tablespoon dried Italian seasoning, crushed
- ½ teaspoon salt
- ¾ cup chicken broth
- ¼ cup dry white wine or chicken broth
  Hot cooked whole wheat pasta (optional)

Cacciatore-Style Drumsticks

Like the stove top version, this one is brimming with onions, mushrooms, and tomatoes perfectly seasoned with herbs.

1 In a 5- to 6-quart slow cooker combine mushrooms, celery, carrots, onions, sweet pepper, and garlic. Place chicken on top of vegetables. In a small bowl combine broth, wine, tapioca, bay leaves, oregano, sugar (if desired), salt, and black pepper; pour over chicken.

2 Cover and cook on low-heat setting for 6 to 7 hours or on high-heat setting for 3 to 3½ hours. Remove chicken and keep warm. Discard bay leaves.

3 If using low-heat setting, turn to high-heat setting. Stir in undrained tomatoes and tomato paste. Cover and cook 15 minutes more. To serve, spoon vegetable mixture over chicken. If desired, serve with pasta.

Nutrition Facts per serving: 268 cal., 6 g total fat (1 g sat. fat), 114 mg chol., 531 mg sodium, 17 g carbo., 3 g fiber, 34 g pro.

Prep: 25 minutes
Cook: Low 6 to 7 hours,
High 3 to 3½ hours;
plus 15 minutes
Makes: 6 servings
Slow Cooker: 5- to 6-quart

- 2 cups sliced fresh mushrooms
- 1 cup sliced celery (2 stalks)
- 1 cup chopped carrots (2 medium)
- 2 medium onions, cut into wedges
- 1 green, yellow, or red sweet pepper, cut into strips
- 4 cloves garlic, minced
- 12 chicken drumsticks, skinned (about 3½ pounds)
- ½ cup chicken broth
- ¼ cup dry white wine
- 2 tablespoons quick-cooking tapioca
- 2 bay leaves
- 1 teaspoon dried oregano, crushed
- 1 teaspoon sugar (optional)
- ½ teaspoon salt
- ¼ teaspoon black pepper
- 1 14½-ounce can diced tomatoes, undrained
- ⅓ cup tomato paste
  Hot cooked whole wheat pasta or brown rice (optional)

Easy Italian Chicken

An easy-to-make dinner, this chicken dish goes together in just 10 minutes. Use your family's favorite spaghetti sauce.

1 In a 3½- to 6-quart slow cooker place cabbage wedges, onion, and mushrooms. Sprinkle tapioca over vegetables. Place chicken pieces on top of vegetables. Pour spaghetti sauce over chicken.

2 Cover and cook on low-heat setting for 6 to 7 hours or on high-heat setting for 3 to 3½ hours. Transfer to a serving platter. Sprinkle with Parmesan cheese.

Nutrition Facts per serving: 300 cal., 9 g total fat (3 g sat. fat), 94 mg chol., 662 mg sodium, 24 g carbo., 4 g fiber, 35 g pro.

Prep: 10 minutes
Cook: Low 6 to 7 hours,
 High 3 to 3½ hours
Makes: 4 to 6 servings
Slow Cooker: 3½- to 6-quart

½ of a medium head cabbage, cut into wedges (about 12 ounces)
1 medium onion, sliced and separated into rings
1 4½-ounce jar sliced mushrooms, drained
2 tablespoons quick-cooking tapioca
2 to 2½ pounds meaty chicken pieces (breasts, thighs, and drumsticks), skinned
2 cups meatless spaghetti sauce
Grated Parmesan cheese

Alfredo Chicken

Purchased Alfredo sauce makes this classic dish a weeknight keeper.

1 In a 3½- or 4-quart slow cooker place the chicken pieces. Sprinkle lightly with salt and pepper. Pour sauce over chicken.

2 Cover and cook on low-heat setting for 6 to 7 hours or on high heat setting for 3 to 3½ hours, adding green beans for the last 30 minutes of cooking.

3 Remove chicken and green beans to a serving platter. Stir cooked pasta into sauce in cooker. Transfer chicken and pasta to a serving platter. If desired, sprinkle with Parmesan cheese.

Nutrition Facts per serving: 392 cal., 15 g total fat (7 g sat. fat), 123 mg chol., 680 mg sodium, 26 g carbo., 3 g fiber, 36 g pro.

Prep: 20 minutes
Cook: Low 6 to 7 hours,
       High 3 to 3½ hours
Makes: 6 servings
Slow Cooker: 3½- or 4-quart

3 pounds meaty chicken pieces, skinned
Salt
Black pepper
1 16-ounce jar light Parmesan Alfredo pasta sauce
1 9-ounce package frozen Italian green beans, thawed
3 cups hot cooked whole wheat pasta
Finely shredded Parmesan cheese (optional)

Chicken Cassoulet

Navy beans, meaty chicken pieces, and Polish sausage combine with vegetables for this hearty and satisfying cassoulet.

1 Rinse beans; place in a medium saucepan. Add enough water to cover beans by 2 inches. Bring to boiling; reduce heat. Simmer, uncovered, for 10 minutes. Remove from heat. Cover; let stand for 1 hour. (Or place the beans in a large bowl. Cover with water to about 2 inches above beans. Allow to soak in a cool place overnight.) Drain and rinse beans.

2 Skin the chicken; set aside. Halve sausage lengthwise and cut into 1-inch pieces. In a medium bowl combine drained beans, sausage, tomato juice, Worcestershire sauce, bouillon granules, basil, oregano, and paprika. Set aside.

3 In a 3½- or 4-quart crockery cooker combine the carrot, celery, and onion. Place chicken pieces on top. Pour bean mixture over chicken. Cover; cook on low-heat setting for 9 to 11 hours or on high-heat setting for 4½ to 5½ hours. Remove chicken and sausage from cooker using a slotted spoon. Mash bean mixture slightly. Serve chicken, sausage, and beans in soup bowls.

Nutrition Facts per serving: 381 cal., 16 g total fat (5 g sat. fat), 88 mg chol., 720 mg sodium, 26 g carbo., 4 g fiber, 32 g pro.

Prep: 1 hour 50 minutes
Cook: Low 9 to 11 hours,
  High 4½ to 5½ hours
Makes: 6 servings
Slow Cooker: 3½- or 4-quart

1	cup dry navy beans (7 to 8 ounces)
2½	to 3 pounds meaty chicken pieces (breasts, thighs, and/or drumsticks)
8	ounces cooked Polish sausage
1	cup tomato juice
1	tablespoon Worcestershire sauce
1	teaspoon instant beef or chicken bouillon granules
½	teaspoon dried basil, crushed
½	teaspoon dried oregano, crushed
½	teaspoon paprika
½	cup chopped carrot
½	cup chopped celery
½	cup chopped onion

Spicy Chicken with Peppers and Olives

Spicy red pepper sauce is the choice for this recipe. If you can't find it, use your favorite variety of pasta sauce.

1 In a 3½- or 4-quart slow cooker place the chicken. Sprinkle lightly with salt and black pepper. Add sweet pepper and olives to cooker. Pour sauce over mixture in cooker.

2 Cover and cook on low-heat setting for 6 to 7 hours or on high-heat setting for 3 to 3½ hours. If desired, serve chicken and sauce over hot pasta.

Nutrition Facts per serving: 239 cal., 10 g total fat (2 g sat. fat), 77 mg chol., 592 mg sodium, 10 g carbo., 3 g fiber, 27 g pro.

Prep: 20 minutes
Cook: Low 6 to 7 hours,
        High 3 to 3½ hours
Makes: 6 servings
Slow Cooker: 3½- or 4-quart

2½ to 3 pounds meaty chicken pieces (breasts, thighs, and drumsticks), skinned
    Salt
    Black pepper
1   small yellow sweet pepper, coarsely chopped
½   cup sliced, pitted ripe olives and/or pimiento-stuffed green olives
1   26-ounce jar spicy red pepper pasta sauce
    Hot cooked whole wheat pasta (optional)

3 g
carb

Thyme and Garlic Chicken Breasts

Thyme, garlic, a little orange juice, and a splash of balsamic vinegar flavor these moist, fork-tender chicken breasts.

1 Sprinkle garlic and thyme over chicken. Place chicken pieces in a 3½- or 4-quart slow cooker. Pour orange juice and vinegar over chicken.

2 Cover and cook on low-heat setting for 5 to 6 hours or on high-heat setting for 2½ to 3 hours.

3 Remove chicken from cooker; cover with foil to keep warm. Skim off fat from cooking juices. Strain juices into a saucepan. Bring to boiling; reduce heat. Boil gently, uncovered, about 10 minutes or until reduced to 1 cup. Pass juices with chicken.

Nutrition Facts per serving: 178 cal., 2 g total fat (0 g sat. fat), 85 mg chol., 78 mg sodium, 3 g carbo., 0 g fiber, 34 g pro.

Prep: 15 minutes
Cook: Low 5 to 6 hours,
High 2½ to 3 hours;
plus 10 minutes
Makes: 6 to 8 servings
Slow Cooker: 3½- or 4-quart

6 cloves garlic, minced
1½ teaspoons dried thyme, crushed
3 to 4 pounds whole chicken breasts (with bone), halved and skinned
¼ cup orange juice
1 tablespoon balsamic vinegar

Saffron Chicken and Sausage

Saffron threads—the dried stigmas of the crocus flower—are traditionally used in such dishes as Spanish paella. However, ground turmeric can be substituted.

1 In a large skillet brown chicken pieces, half at a time, in hot oil. Drain off fat. In a 3½- to 5-quart slow cooker place chicken pieces, turkey sausage, and onion. Sprinkle with garlic, dried thyme (if using), black pepper, and saffron. Pour broth and water over all.

2 Cover and cook on low-heat setting for 7 to 8 hours or on high-heat setting for 3½ to 4 hours. Stir in the tomatoes, sweet peppers, peas, and, if using, the fresh thyme. Cover; let stand for 5 minutes. If desired, serve over hot rice.

Nutrition Facts per serving: 304 cal., 12 g total fat (3 g sat. fat), 102 mg chol., 582 mg sodium, 14 g carbo., 3 g fiber, 34 g pro.

Prep: 30 minutes
Cook: Low 7 to 8 hours,
      High 3½ to 4 hours
Stand: 5 minutes
Makes: 6 servings
Slow Cooker: 3½- to 5-quart

2½   to 3 pounds meaty chicken pieces (breasts, thighs, and drumsticks), skinned
1   tablespoon cooking oil
8   ounces cooked smoked turkey sausage, halved lengthwise and sliced
1   large onion, sliced
3   cloves garlic, minced
2   tablespoons snipped fresh thyme or 2 teaspoons dried thyme, crushed
¼   teaspoon black pepper
⅛   teaspoon thread saffron or ¼ teaspoon ground turmeric
1   14-ounce can reduced-sodium chicken broth
½   cup water
2   cups chopped tomatoes (4 medium)
2   yellow or green sweet peppers, cut into very thin bite-size strips
1   cup frozen green peas
    Hot cooked brown rice (optional)

Mole with Chicken

Mole (MOH-lay), a spicy sauce traditionally made with chiles and chocolate, is a treat for the taste buds. For a more traditional garnish, sprinkle with toasted pepitas (pumpkin seeds) instead of the almonds.

1 For mole sauce, in a blender container or food processor bowl combine undrained tomatoes, onion, ¼ cup almonds, garlic, jalapeño peppers, cocoa powder, raisins, sesame seeds, sugar (if desired), salt, and the spices. Cover and blend or process until mixture is a coarse puree.

2 In a 3½- or 4-quart slow cooker place tapioca. Add chicken and then sauce.

3 Cover and cook on low-heat setting for 9 to 11 hours or on high-heat setting for 4½ to 5½ hours. Remove the chicken from slow cooker; arrange on a serving platter. Stir sauce; pour sauce over chicken. Sprinkle with the 2 tablespoons almonds. If desired, serve with hot rice.

Nutrition Facts per serving: 329 cal., 11 g total fat (2 g sat. fat), 95 mg chol., 562 mg sodium, 22 g carbo., 3 g fiber, 34 g pro.

Prep: 25 minutes
Cook: Low 9 to 11 hours,
**   High 4½ to 5½ hours**
Makes: 4 to 6 servings
Slow Cooker: 3½- or 4-quart

1   14½-ounce can diced tomatoes, undrained
½   cup chopped onion (1 medium)
¼   cup slivered almonds, toasted
3   cloves garlic, quartered
2   canned jalapeño chile peppers, drained
3   tablespoons unsweetened cocoa powder
3   tablespoons raisins
1   tablespoon sesame seeds
1   teaspoon sugar (optional)
¼   teaspoon salt
¼   teaspoon ground cinnamon
⅛   teaspoon ground nutmeg
⅛   teaspoon ground coriander
2   tablespoons quick-cooking tapioca
1   2½- to 3-pound broiler-fryer chicken, cut up and skinned
2   tablespoons slivered almonds, toasted
    Hot cooked brown rice (optional)

Zesty Ginger-Tomato Chicken

Chicken drumsticks or thighs are great for the slow cooker. They stay moist and tender during the long cooking times.

1 Place chicken pieces in a 3½- or 4-quart slow cooker.

2 Drain 1 can of tomatoes; chop tomatoes from both cans. For sauce, in a medium bowl combine chopped tomatoes and the juice from 1 can, tapioca, ginger, cilantro, garlic, brown sugar (if using), crushed red pepper, and salt. Pour sauce over chicken.

3 Cover and cook on low-heat setting for 6 to 7 hours or on high-heat setting for 3 to 3½ hours. Skim fat from sauce. Serve chicken with sauce in shallow bowls. If desired, serve with hot rice.

Nutrition Facts per serving: 168 cal., 4 g total fat (1 g sat. fat), 81 mg chol., 472 mg sodium, 10 g carbo., 1 g fiber, 23 g pro.

Prep: 20 minutes
Cook: Low 6 to 7 hours,
     High 3 to 3½ hours
Makes: 6 servings
Slow Cooker: 3½- or 4-quart

12   chicken drumsticks and/or thighs, skinned (2½ to 3 pounds)
2   14½-ounce cans tomatoes
2   tablespoons quick-cooking tapioca
1   tablespoon grated fresh ginger
1   tablespoon snipped fresh cilantro or parsley
4   cloves garlic, minced
2   teaspoons brown sugar (optional)
½   teaspoon crushed red pepper
½   teaspoon salt
    Hot cooked brown rice (optional)

31 g
carb

Spiced Chicken and Vegetables

An intriguing blend of spices makes this slowly simmered chicken and potato dish sizzle with flavors typical of Indian cuisine.

1 In 3½- to 6-quart slow cooker place potatoes, sweet pepper, and onion. Place chicken on top of vegetables. In a medium bowl combine tomatoes, coriander, paprika, ginger, salt, red pepper, turmeric, cinnamon, and cloves; stir in broth. Pour over chicken in cooker.

2 Cover and cook on low-heat setting for 8 to 10 hours or on high-setting for 4 to 5 hours.

3 If using low-heat setting, turn to high-heat setting. Combine cold water and cornstarch; stir into mixture in cooker. Cover and cook 15 to 20 minutes more or until slightly thickened and bubbly.

Nutrition Facts per serving: 246 cal., 2 g total fat (0 g sat. fat), 53 mg chol., 609 mg sodium, 31 g carbo., 5 g fiber, 26 g pro.

Prep: 30 minutes
Cook: Low 8 to 10 hours,
High 4 to 5 hours;
plus 15 minutes
Makes: 5 servings
Slow Cooker: 3½- to 6-quart

5	medium potatoes, cut into 1-inch chunks (1½ pounds)
1	medium green sweet pepper, cut into 1-inch pieces (¾ cup)
1	medium onion, sliced
1	pound skinless, boneless chicken breast halves or thighs, cut into 1-inch pieces
1½	cups chopped tomatoes (3 medium)
1	tablespoon ground coriander
1½	teaspoons paprika
1	teaspoon grated fresh ginger or ¼ teaspoon ground ginger
¾	teaspoon salt
¼	to ½ teaspoon crushed red pepper
½	teaspoon ground turmeric
¼	teaspoon ground cinnamon
⅛	teaspoon ground cloves
1	cup chicken broth
2	tablespoons cold water
4	teaspoons cornstarch

Chicken Curry

In India, curry powder is ground fresh each day and combines as many as 16 to 20 spices. You can skip that step by using your favorite ready-to-use blend.

1 In a large plastic bag combine the flour, curry powder, cumin, and salt. Add chicken, a few pieces at a time; seal bag. Shake bag to coat.

2 In a 3½- or 4-quart slow cooker combine potatoes, carrots, apple, onion, garlic, jalapeño pepper, and bouillon granules. Top with chicken. Pour water over all.

3 Cover and cook on low-heat setting for 6 to 8 hours or on high-heat setting for 3 to 4 hours.

4 If using low-heat setting turn to high-heat setting. Stir coconut milk into chicken mixture. Cover and cook for 30 minutes more. If desired, serve over hot rice. Sprinkle each serving with peanuts.

Nutrition Facts per serving: 292 cal., 14 g total fat (10 g sat. fat), 49 mg chol., 484 mg sodium, 20 g carbo., 4 g fiber, 24 g pro.

Prep: 30 minutes
Cook: Low 6 to 8 hours,
High 3 to 4 hours;
plus 30 minutes
Makes: 8 servings
Slow Cooker: 3½- or 4-quart

3 tablespoons all-purpose flour
3 tablespoons curry powder
1½ teaspoons ground cumin
1 teaspoon salt
1½ pounds boneless, skinless chicken breast halves or thighs, cut into 1-inch pieces
2 cups peeled and chopped potatoes
1½ cups bias-sliced carrots
1 cup coarsely chopped cooking apple
¾ cup chopped onion
2 cloves garlic, minced
1 fresh jalapeño chile pepper, seeded and finely chopped (see note, page 62)
1 teaspoon instant chicken bouillon granules
½ cup water
1 13½-ounce can unsweetened coconut milk
Hot cooked brown rice (optional)
¼ cup chopped peanuts

Apricot Chicken

Apricot and mustard flavors come together for this chicken dish. Soak up the flavorful juices by serving with brown rice.

1 In a very large skillet brown chicken, half at a time, in hot oil. (Add more oil, if necessary.) Set aside.

2 In a 3½- or 4-quart slow cooker combine onions and carrots. Top with chicken. Sprinkle chicken with salt and pepper. In a small bowl stir together broth, apricot spread, tapioca, mustard, and allspice. Pour over chicken and vegetables in cooker.

3 Cover and cook on low-heat setting for 8 to 9 hours or on high-heat setting for 4 to 4½ hours. Serve chicken and vegetables with some of the cooking juices. If desired, serve with hot rice.

Nutrition Facts per serving: 247 cal., 8 g total fat (2 g sat. fat), 113 mg chol., 234 mg sodium, 13 g carbo., 2 g fiber, 29 g pro.

Prep: 25 minutes
Cook: Low 8 to 9 **hours,**
      High 4 to 4½ **hours**
Makes: 8 **servings**
Slow Cooker: 3½- or 4-**quart**

2½ pounds skinless, boneless chicken thighs
1 tablespoon cooking oil
2 cups frozen small whole onions, thawed
4 medium carrots, bias-sliced ½ inch thick
   Salt
   Black pepper
½ cup chicken broth
⅓ cup low-sugar apricot spread
2 tablespoons quick-cooking tapioca, ground if desired
1 to 2 tablespoons Dijon-style mustard
⅛ teaspoon ground allspice
   Hot cooked brown rice (optional)

Chicken and Shrimp with Feta

Serve this festive dish for the holidays with a baby greens salad and a white wine, such as a Gewürztraminer.

1 In a 3½- to 5-quart slow cooker place the onion and garlic. Top with the chicken pieces. In a bowl combine the undrained tomatoes, port, lemon juice, tomato paste, bay leaves, salt, and crushed red pepper. Pour over all.

2 Cover and cook on low-heat setting for 6 to 7 hours or on high-heat setting for 3 to 3½ hours.

3 If using low-heat setting, turn to high-heat setting. Discard bay leaves. Stir shrimp and artichoke hearts into chicken mixture in cooker. Cover; cook for 5 minutes more. Spoon chicken and shrimp mixture into bowls. Sprinkle with feta cheese. If desired, serve with hot pasta.

Nutrition Facts per serving: 347 cal., 8 g total fat (3 g sat. fat), 166 mg chol., 1,168 mg sodium, 26 g carbo., 6 g fiber, 35 g pro.

Prep: 15 minutes
Cook: Low 6 to 7 hours,
High 3 to 3½ hours;
plus 5 minutes
Makes: 4 to 5 servings
Slow Cooker: 3½- to 5-quart

- 1 cup chopped onion (1 large)
- 3 cloves garlic, minced
- 12 ounces skinless, boneless chicken thighs, cut into quarters
- 1 14½-ounce can diced tomatoes with basil, garlic, and oregano; or diced tomatoes with onion and garlic; undrained
- ½ cup port wine or chicken broth
- 2 tablespoons lemon juice
- 2 tablespoons tomato paste
- 2 bay leaves
- ½ teaspoon salt
- ¼ teaspoon crushed red pepper
- 1 8-ounce package frozen, peeled, cooked shrimp, thawed and drained
- 1 9-ounce package frozen artichoke hearts, thawed and coarsely chopped
- ½ cup crumbled feta cheese (2 ounces)
Hot cooked whole wheat pasta or brown rice (optional)

Italian Chicken

These boneless chicken thighs are tender and juicy and full of flavor. Mushrooms, Italian-style green beans, and onion all add flavor to this tomato-based sauce.

1 In a 3½- or 4-quart slow cooker place green beans, mushrooms, and onion. Place chicken on vegetables. In a small bowl combine undrained tomatoes, tomato paste, Italian seasoning, and garlic. Pour over chicken.

2 Cover and cook on low-heat setting for 5 to 6 hours or on high-heat setting for 2½ to 3 hours. If desired, serve over hot pasta. Sprinkle with Parmesan cheese.

Nutrition Facts per serving: 334 cal., 12 g total fat (5 g sat. fat), 86 mg chol., 1,094 mg sodium, 24 g carbo., 3 g fiber, 31 g pro.

Prep: 15 minutes
Cook: Low 5 to 6 hours,
High 2½ to 3 hours
Makes: 4 servings
Slow Cooker: 3½- or 4-quart

1   9-ounce package frozen Italian-style green beans
1   cup fresh mushrooms, quartered
1   small onion, sliced ¼ inch thick
12 ounces skinless, boneless chicken thighs, cut into 1-inch pieces
1   14½-ounce can Italian-style stewed tomatoes, undrained
1   6-ounce can Italian-style tomato paste
1   teaspoon dried Italian seasoning, crushed
2   cloves garlic, minced
    Hot cooked whole wheat pasta (optional)
3   tablespoons finely shredded or grated Parmesan cheese

Plum-Sauced Chicken in Tortillas

Hoisin sauce is a Chinese condiment that can be found in the Asian foods section of the supermarket. The reddish-brown sauce adds a sweet-and-spicy flavor to the chicken.

1 Remove pits from plums. Place plums in a blender container or food processor bowl. Cover and blend or process until smooth. Transfer plums to a 3½- or 4-quart slow cooker. Stir in vegetable juice, hoisin sauce, tapioca, ginger, and five-spice powder. Cut chicken into strips. Stir chicken into cooker.

2 Cover and cook on low-heat setting for 4 to 5 hours or on high-heat setting for 2 to 2½ hours. Remove chicken from cooker, reserving juices.

3 Spoon about ⅓ cup chicken mixture onto each warm tortilla just below the center. Drizzle with the reserved juices and top with ⅓ cup shredded broccoli. Roll up tortilla.

Nutrition Facts per serving: 271 cal., 6 g total fat (2 g sat. fat), 36 mg chol., 539 mg sodium, 38 g carbo., 2 g fiber, 13 g pro.

Prep: 15 minutes
Cook: Low 4 to 5 hours,
   High 2 to 2½ hours
Makes: 6 servings
Slow Cooker: 3½- or 4-quart

1 16-ounce can whole, unpitted purple plums, drained
1 cup hot-style vegetable juice
¼ cup hoisin sauce
4½ teaspoons quick-cooking tapioca
2 teaspoons grated fresh ginger
½ teaspoon five-spice powder
1 pound skinless, boneless chicken thighs
6 7- to 8-inch flour tortillas, warmed
2 cups packaged shredded broccoli (broccoli slaw mix) or packaged shredded cabbage with carrot (coleslaw mix)

15 g carb

Chicken with Artichokes and Olives

If you think you've served chicken in every way imaginable, you'll love this dish. The flavors of artichokes, olives, and thyme lend a Mediterranean accent.

1 In a 3½- or 4-quart slow cooker combine the mushrooms, undrained tomatoes, frozen artichoke hearts, broth, onion, olives, and wine. Stir in tapioca, curry powder, thyme, salt, and pepper. Add chicken; spoon some of the tomato mixture over the chicken.

2 Cover and cook on low-heat setting for 7 to 8 hours or on high-heat setting for 3½ to 4 hours. If desired, serve with rice.

Nutrition Facts per serving: 227 cal., 4 g total fat (1 g sat. fat), 66 mg chol., 578 mg sodium, 15 g carbo., 4 g fiber, 29 g pro.

Prep: 20 minutes
Cook: Low 7 to 8 hours,
      High 3½ to 4 hours
Makes: 6 servings
Slow Cooker: 3½- or 4-quart

2	cups sliced fresh mushrooms
1	14½-ounce can diced tomatoes, undrained
1	8- or 9-ounce package frozen artichoke hearts
1	cup chicken broth
½	cup chopped onion (1 medium)
½	cup sliced, pitted ripe olives or ¼ cup capers, drained
¼	cup dry white wine or chicken broth
3	tablespoons quick-cooking tapioca
2	to 3 teaspoons curry powder
¾	teaspoon dried thyme, crushed
¼	teaspoon salt
¼	teaspoon black pepper
1½	pounds skinless, boneless chicken breast halves and/or thighs
	Hot cooked brown rice (optional)

Chicken with Creamy Chive Sauce

A rich and creamy sauce, consisting of mushroom soup and cream cheese, makes this chicken dish full of flavor. Serve it over pasta, if you like.

1 Place chicken in a 3½- or 4-quart slow cooker. In a medium saucepan melt the butter. Stir in the dry Italian salad dressing mix. Stir in mushroom soup, wine, and cream cheese until combined. Pour over the chicken.

2 Cover and cook on low-heat setting for 4 to 5 hours. Serve chicken with sauce. If desired, serve with hot pasta and sprinkle with chives.

Nutrition Facts per serving: 310 cal., 17 g total fat (9 g sat. fat), 110 mg chol., 1,043 mg sodium, 6 g carbo., 0 g fiber, 28 g pro.

Prep: 15 minutes
Cook: Low 4 to 5 hours
Makes: 6 servings
Slow Cooker: 3½- or 4-quart

6 skinless, boneless chicken breast halves (about 1½ pounds)
¼ cup butter
1 0.7-ounce package Italian salad dressing mix
1 10¾-ounce can condensed golden mushroom soup
½ cup dry white wine
½ of an 8-ounce tub cream cheese with chives and onion
   Hot cooked whole wheat pasta (optional)
   Snipped fresh chives (optional)

10 g
carb

Rosemary Chicken

Twelve cloves of garlic may sound like a lot, but the garlic mellows as it slowly envelops the chicken in a delightful flavor.

1 In a small skillet cook garlic and onion in hot oil over medium heat, stirring occasionally, 5 minutes or until tender.

2 In a 3½- or 4-quart slow cooker combine the garlic mixture, frozen artichoke hearts, sweet pepper, broth, tapioca, rosemary, lemon peel, and black pepper. Add chicken; spoon some of the garlic mixture over chicken.

3 Cover and cook on low-heat setting for 6 to 7 hours or on high-heat setting for 3 to 3½ hours. If desired, serve with rice.

Nutrition Facts per serving: 197 cal., 4 g total fat (1 g sat. fat), 66 mg chol., 172 mg sodium, 10 g carbo., 3 g fiber, 28 g pro.

Prep: 20 minutes
Cook: Low 6 to 7 hours,
    High 3 to 3½ hours
Makes: 6 servings
Slow Cooker: 3½- or 4-quart

12 cloves garlic, minced
½   cup chopped onion (1 medium)
1   tablespoon olive oil
1   8- or 9-ounce package frozen
    artichoke hearts
1   red sweet pepper, cut into strips
½   cup chicken broth
1   tablespoon quick-cooking tapioca
2   teaspoons dried rosemary, crushed
1   teaspoon finely shredded lemon peel
½   teaspoon black pepper
1½ pounds skinless, boneless chicken
    breast halves or thighs
    Hot cooked brown rice (optional)

Teriyaki Chicken with Orange

Here's a sauce that is full of flavor. Use orange sections or slices to garnish the dish.

1 In a 3½- or 4-quart slow cooker place frozen vegetables. Sprinkle tapioca over vegetables. Stir to combine. Place chicken pieces on vegetable mixture.

2 For sauce, in a small bowl combine broth, marmalade spread, teriyaki sauce, mustard, and ginger. Pour sauce over chicken pieces.

3 Cover and cook on low-heat setting for 4 to 5 hours or on high-heat setting for 2 to 2½ hours. If desired, serve with rice.

Nutrition Facts per serving: 218 cal., 2 g total fat (1 g sat. fat), 66 mg chol., 596 mg sodium, 18 g carbo., 3 g fiber, 29 g pro.

Prep: 15 minutes
Cook: Low 4 to 5 hours,
  High 2 to 2½ hours
Makes: 4 servings
Slow Cooker: 3½- or 4-quart

1 16-ounce package loose-pack frozen broccoli, baby carrots, and water chestnuts
2 tablespoons quick-cooking tapioca
1 pound skinless, boneless chicken breast halves or thighs, cut into 1-inch pieces
¾ cup chicken broth
3 tablespoons low-sugar orange marmalade spread
2 tablespoons teriyaki sauce
1 teaspoon dry mustard
½ teaspoon ground ginger
   Hot cooked brown rice (optional)

Cashew Chicken

As easy as carry-out, this savory dish is a fun way to celebrate the Chinese New Year—or any red-letter day.

1 In a 3½- or 4-quart slow cooker combine soup, soy sauce, and ginger. Stir in chicken tenders, mushrooms, celery, carrots, and water chestnuts.

2 Cover and cook on low-heat setting for 6 to 8 hours or on high-heat setting for 3 to 4 hours.

3 Stir cashews into chicken mixture. If desired, serve over hot rice.

Nutrition Facts per serving: 253 cal., 9 g total fat (2 g sat. fat), 68 mg chol., 859 mg sodium, 15 g carbo., 2 g fiber, 31 g pro.

Prep: 15 minutes
Cook: Low 6 to 8 hours,
High 3 to 4 hours
Makes: 6 servings
Slow Cooker: 3½- or 4-quart

- 1 10¾-ounce can condensed golden mushroom soup
- 2 tablespoons soy sauce
- ½ teaspoon ground ginger
- 1½ pounds chicken tenders
- 1 cup sliced fresh mushrooms or one 4-ounce can sliced mushrooms, drained
- 1 cup sliced celery (2 stalks)
- 1 cup shredded carrots
- 1 8-ounce can sliced water chestnuts, drained
- ½ cup cashews
  Hot cooked brown rice (optional)

Turkey Chablis

Rosemary and wine flavor this turkey dish. The addition of half-and-half makes a creamy sauce for the turkey.

1 In a 3½- to 6-quart slow cooker combine wine, onion, garlic, and bay leaf. If turkey is wrapped in netting; remove and discard netting. If gravy packet is present, remove and refrigerate for another use. Combine rosemary and pepper. Rub turkey with rosemary mixture. Place turkey in cooker.

2 Cover and cook on low-heat setting for 9 to 10 hours or on high-heat setting for 4½ to 5 hours. Remove turkey; cover to keep warm.

3 For gravy, strain cooking juices into a large measuring cup; discard solids. Skim fat from juices. Measure 1⅓ cups juices into a small saucepan. Combine half-and-half and cornstarch; stir into juices. Cook and stir until thickened and bubbly. Cook and stir 2 minutes more. Slice turkey. Spoon some gravy over turkey. Pass remaining gravy with turkey.

Nutrition Facts per serving: 365 cal., 9 g total fat (3 g sat. fat), 176 mg chol., 193 mg sodium, 5 g carbo., 0 g fiber, 58 g pro.

Prep: 15 minutes
Cook: Low 9 to 10 hours,
High 4½ to 5 hours;
plus 10 minutes
Makes: 6 to 8 servings
Slow Cooker: 3½- to 6-quart

¾ cup Chablis or other dry white wine
½ cup chopped onion (1 medium)
1 clove garlic, minced
1 bay leaf
1 3½- to 4-pound frozen boneless turkey roast, thawed
1 teaspoon dried rosemary, crushed
¼ teaspoon black pepper
⅓ cup half-and-half, light cream, or milk
2 tablespoons cornstarch

25 g
carb

Fruited Turkey in Red Wine Sauce

The delicious combination of dried apricots, plums, and red wine scented with garlic and thyme dresses up turkey thighs.

1 In a large skillet brown turkey in hot oil. Transfer turkey to a 3½- or 4-quart slow cooker. Place dried plums and apricots on top of turkey. Stir together orange juice, wine, garlic, lemon peel, thyme, and salt. Pour orange juice mixture over turkey.

2 Cover and cook on low-heat setting for 6 to 7 hours or on high-heat setting for 3 to 3½ hours.

3 Use a slotted spoon to transfer turkey and fruit to a serving platter; cover with foil to keep warm. Pour cooking juices into a large measuring cup; skim fat from juices. For sauce, measure 1¼ cups juices. Transfer to a saucepan. Combine the cornstarch and cold water; stir into juices in saucepan. Cook and stir over medium heat until thickened and bubbly. Cook and stir for 2 minutes more. Spoon sauce over turkey. If desired, serve with hot rice.

Nutrition Facts per serving: 350 cal., 10 g total fat (3 g sat. fat), 120 mg chol., 331 mg sodium, 25 g carbo., 3 g fiber, 36 g pro.

Prep: 30 minutes
Cook: Low 6 to 7 hours,
High 3 to 3½ hours;
plus 10 minutes
Makes: 5 servings
Slow Cooker: 3½- or 4-quart

3 pounds turkey thighs, skinned
1 tablespoon cooking oil
½ cup pitted dried plums (prunes)
½ cup dried apricot halves
½ cup orange juice
¼ cup dry red wine
4 cloves garlic, minced
1 tablespoon finely shredded lemon peel
2 teaspoons dried thyme, crushed
½ teaspoon salt
1 tablespoon cornstarch
1 tablespoon cold water
Hot cooked brown rice (optional)

Maple-Mustard-Sauced Turkey Thighs

Turkey offers good nutrition year-round—not just during the holidays. Complement this easy-to-prepare meal with steamed green beans.

1 In a 3½- or 4-quart slow cooker place parsnips. Place turkey on parsnips. In a small bowl stir together mustard, syrup, and tapioca. Pour over turkey.

2 Cover and cook on high-heat setting for 3 to 3½ hours.

Nutrition Facts per serving: 308 cal., 8 g total fat (2 g sat. fat), 100 mg chol., 439 mg sodium, 27 g carbo., 5 g fiber, 32 g pro.

Prep: 20 minutes
Cook: High 3 to 3½ hours
Makes: 4 servings
Slow Cooker: 3½- or 4-quart

- 1 pound parsnips, cut into 1-inch pieces
- 2 to 2½ pounds turkey thighs (about 2 thighs), skinned
- ⅓ cup coarse-grain brown mustard
- ¼ cup light maple-flavored syrup product made with heat-stable sweetener (Splenda)
- 1 tablespoon quick-cooking tapioca

Sweet 'n' Spicy Turkey

Now that you can buy turkey parts, rather than the whole bird, it's economical to use turkey in your favorite dishes. Here two thighs serve six people.

1 In a 3½- or 4-quart slow cooker place turkey. Add onion. In a bowl combine cranberry juice, mustard, and cayenne pepper. Pour over turkey and onion.

2 Cover and cook on low-heat setting for 5 to 6 hours or on high-heat setting for 2½ to 3 hours. Remove turkey; cover with foil to keep warm.

3 For sauce, strain cooking juices into a large measuring cup. If necessary, add water to make 1½ cups. In a small saucepan combine the juices and cranberries. Stir together 1 tablespoon water and cornstarch; add to mixture in saucepan. Cook and stir over medium heat until thickened and bubbly. Cook and stir for 2 minutes more. To serve, toss cooked barley with nectarine. Serve turkey and sauce over barley mixture.

Nutrition Facts per serving: 436 cal., 11 g total fat (3 g sat. fat), 116 mg chol., 365 mg sodium, 41 g carbo., 6 g fiber, 42 g pro.

Prep: 15 minutes
Cook: Low 5 to 6 hours,
    High 2½ to 3 hours;
      plus 10 minutes
Makes: 6 servings
Slow Cooker: 3½- or 4-quart

- 2 turkey thighs (2½ to 2¾ pounds), skinned
- ⅔ cup chopped onion
- ¾ cup light cranberry juice cocktail (sweetened with Slenda)
- ¼ cup Dijon-style mustard
- ¼ teaspoon cayenne pepper
- ½ cup dried cranberries or cherries
- 1 tablespoon water
- 2 teaspoons cornstarch
- 3 cups hot cooked barley
- 1 medium nectarine or pear, cored and chopped

Turkey Thighs in Barbecue Sauce

Who needs a grill for barbecue? These shapely, saucy thighs hold their form nicely during slow heat cooking and can hold their own among other grilled turkey dishes.

1 In a 3½- or 4-quart slow cooker combine catsup, sugar substitute, tapioca, vinegar, Worcestershire sauce, cinnamon, and red pepper. Place turkey thighs, meaty side down, on catsup mixture.

2 Cover and cook on low-heat setting for 10 to 12 hours or high-heat setting for 5 to 6 hours. Transfer turkey to a serving dish. Pour cooking juices into a small bowl; skim off fat. Serve turkey with cooking juices and, if desired, hot rice.

For a 5- or 6-quart slow cooker: Use ¾ cup catsup; 3 tablespoons no-calorie, heat-stable, granular sugar substitute (Splenda) or sugar; 4 teaspoons quick-cooking tapioca; 4 teaspoons vinegar; 2 teaspoons Worcestershire sauce; ¼ teaspoon ground cinnamon; ¼ teaspoon crushed red pepper; and 3 to 3½ pounds turkey thighs or meaty chicken pieces, skinned. Prepare as above. Makes 6 to 8 servings.

Nutrition Facts per serving: 225 cal., 6 g total fat (2 g sat. fat), 100 mg chol., 444 mg sodium, 12 g carbo., 1 g fiber, 30 g pro.

Prep: 15 minutes
Cook: Low 10 to 12 hours,
   High 5 to 6 hours
Makes: 4 to 6 servings
Slow Cooker: 3½- or 4-quart

- ½ cup catsup
- 2 tablespoons no-calorie, heat-stable, granular sugar substitute (Splenda)
- 1 tablespoon quick-cooking tapioca
- 1 tablespoon vinegar
- 1 teaspoon Worcestershire sauce
- ¼ teaspoon ground cinnamon
- ¼ teaspoon crushed red pepper
- 2 to 2½ pounds turkey thighs (about 2 thighs) or meaty chicken pieces (breasts, thighs, and drumsticks), skinned
- Hot cooked brown rice or whole wheat pasta (optional)

Texas Turkey Bonanza

The lime sour cream sauce is optional but is a perfect addition to this black-eyed pea dish. On the fly? Use dairy sour cream without adding lime.

1 Sort through peas to remove any pebbles or other foreign matter. Rinse peas. In a large saucepan combine peas and 5 cups of the water. Bring to boiling; reduce heat. Cook, uncovered, for 10 minutes. Remove from heat. Drain and rinse peas.

2 In a 4- or 4½-quart slow cooker combine peas, the remaining 3 cups water, the quartered jalapeño peppers, sage, and salt. Top with meat.

3 Cover and cook on low-heat setting for 8 to 10 hours or on high-heat setting for 4 to 5 hours.

4 If using low-heat setting, turn to high-heat setting. Stir squash into mixture in cooker. Cover and cook for 30 minutes more. Sprinkle each serving with red onion and cilantro. If desired, top with Lime Sour Cream and chopped jalapeño pepper.

Lime Sour Cream: In a small bowl combine ½ cup dairy sour cream, ½ teaspoon finely shredded lime peel, and 1 tablespoon lime juice. Cover and chill before serving.

Nutrition Facts per serving: 144 cal., 1 g total fat (0 g sat. fat), 47 mg chol., 423 mg sodium, 13 g carbo., 4 g fiber, 21 g pro.

Prep: 20 minutes
Cook: Low 8 to 10 hours,
High 4 to 5 hours;
plus 30 minutes
Makes: 6 servings
Slow Cooker: 4- or 4½-quart

2 cups dry black-eyed peas
8 cups water
1 to 3 fresh jalapeño chile peppers, seeded and quartered lengthwise (see note, page 62)
1½ teaspoons dried leaf sage, crushed
1 teaspoon salt
1 pound turkey or pork tenderloin, cut into 1½-inch pieces
2 medium yellow summer squash, cut into wedges
½ cup finely chopped red onion (1 medium)
⅓ cup snipped fresh cilantro
1 recipe Lime Sour Cream or dairy sour cream (optional)
Finely chopped fresh jalapeño chile pepper (optional)

11 g
carb

Turkey Meatballs and Gravy

No one will believe the rich tasting gravy starts with a mix. The best part is that you don't even have to make the meatballs. They are available frozen, which makes this a swift dish to put together.

1 Place thawed meatballs in a 3½- or 4-quart slow cooker. In a small bowl combine soup, water, gravy mix, and thyme. Pour soup mixture over meatballs.

2 Cover and cook on low-heat setting for 6 to 8 hours or on high-heat setting for 3 to 4 hours. If desired, serve with hot noodles. Sprinkle with parsley.

Nutrition Facts per serving: 362 cal., 26 g total fat (12 g sat. fat), 75 mg chol., 1,140 mg sodium, 11 g carbo., 4 g fiber, 19 g pro.

Prep: 10 minutes
Cook: Low 6 to 8 hours, High 3 to 4 hours
Makes: 9 servings
Slow Cooker: 3½- or 4-quart

3　12-ounce packages Italian-style turkey meatballs, thawed
1　10¾-ounce can condensed cream of mushroom soup
1　cup water
1　0.95-ounce envelope turkey gravy mix
½　teaspoon dried thyme, crushed
　　Hot cooked whole wheat noodles (optional)
2　tablespoons snipped fresh parsley

47 g
carb

Mexican-Style Sausage and Beans

Let the salsa—mild, medium, or hot—determine the heat of this bean and sausage combo. The trio of beans contribute a whopping 12 grams of fiber to this dish, leaving 35 grams of available carbohydrate.

1 In a 3½- or 4-quart crockery cooker combine sweet pepper, onion, garlic, beans, corn, salsa, cumin, and sausage.

2 Cover and cook on low-heat setting for 6 to 7 hours or on high-heat setting for 3 to 3½ hours.

Nutrition Facts per serving: 307 cal., 8 g total fat (2 g sat. fat), 47 mg chol., 1,213 mg sodium, 47 g carbo., 12 g fiber, 28 g pro.

Prep: 15 minutes
Cook: Low 6 to 7 hours,
      High 3 to 3½ hours
Makes: 6 servings
Slow Cooker: 3½- or 4-quart

1   cup chopped green sweet pepper
1   cup chopped onion (1 large)
3   cloves garlic, minced
1   15-ounce can white kidney beans (cannellini), rinsed and drained
1   15-ounce can black beans, rinsed and drained
1   15-ounce can red kidney beans, rinsed and drained
1½   cups frozen whole kernel corn
1½   cups bottled salsa
1   teaspoon ground cumin
1   pound smoked turkey sausage, sliced

Quick Sides

Asparagus with Almond Sauce

Asparagus adds elegance to any meal. The addition of this sauce takes it to glamourous.

1 Snap off and discard woody bases from fresh asparagus. If desired, scrape off scales. Cook asparagus, covered, in a small amount of boiling lightly salted water for 3 to 5 minutes or until crisp-tender. (Or cook frozen asparagus according to package directions.) Drain; transfer to a serving platter.

2 Meanwhile, for sauce, melt butter in a small saucepan; add almonds. Cook and stir over medium-low heat for 3 to 5 minutes or until golden. Stir in cornstarch. Add water, lemon juice, bouillon granules, and pepper. Cook and stir until thickened and bubbly. Cook and stir 2 minutes more. Spoon sauce over cooked asparagus.

Nutrition Facts per serving: 73 cal., 6 g total fat (2 g sat. fat), 8 mg chol., 179 mg sodium, 3 g carbo., 1 g fiber, 3 g pro.

Start to Finish: 13 minutes
Makes: 4 servings

1 **pound asparagus spears or one 10-ounce package frozen asparagus spears**
1 **tablespoon butter or margarine**
2 **tablespoons sliced almonds**
1¼ **teaspoons cornstarch**
½ **cup water**
2 **teaspoons lemon juice**
½ **teaspoon instant chicken bouillon granules**
  Dash black pepper

Roasted Asparagus Parmesan

This dish is so simple! Roast the asparagus and toss with cheese. It's great with any kind of meal.

1 Snap off and discard woody bases from asparagus spears. If desired, scrape off scales. Place asparagus in a 15×10×1-inch baking pan. Drizzle with olive oil, tossing gently to coat. Spread out in a single layer. Sprinkle with salt and pepper.

2 Bake in a 400° oven about 15 minutes or until asparagus is crisp-tender. Transfer to a serving platter; sprinkle with Parmesan cheese.

Prep: 10 minutes
Bake: 15 minutes
Oven: 400°F
Makes: 6 servings

2 pounds fresh asparagus spears
2 tablespoons olive oil
   Salt
   Black pepper
½ cup finely shredded Parmesan cheese

Nutrition Facts per serving: 95 cal., 7 g total fat (2 g sat. fat), 8 mg chol., 102 mg sodium, 4 g carbo., 2 g fiber, 5 g pro.

4 g
carb

Broccoli and Peppers

If you don't have a steamer basket, improvise with a metal colander to prepare this dish.

1 Place broccoli and sweet pepper in a steamer basket over simmering water. Steam, covered, for 8 to 12 minutes or until vegetables are crisp-tender. Arrange vegetables on a serving platter.

2 Meanwhile, in a saucepan melt butter. Stir in lemon peel, lemon juice, and black pepper. Drizzle over vegetables.

Nutrition Facts per serving: 55 cal., 4 g total fat (3 g sat. fat), 11 mg chol., 54 mg sodium, 4 g carbo., 2 g fiber, 2 g pro.

Prep: 10 minutes
Cook: 8 minutes
Makes: 6 servings

1 pound broccoli, cut into florets
1 red or yellow sweet pepper, cut into
     1-inch pieces
2 tablespoons butter or margarine
1 teaspoon finely shredded lemon peel
1 tablespoon lemon juice
⅛ teaspoon black pepper

Broccoli-Carrot Stir-Fry

A wok is nice, but not necessary. If you'll be stir-frying more than 4 cups of ingredients, as in this recipe, you'll need a 12-inch skillet.

1 For sauce, in a bowl stir together broth, balsamic vinegar, and cornstarch; set aside.

2 Pour oil into a wok or large skillet. (Add more oil as necessary during cooking.) Preheat over medium-high heat. Stir-fry ginger in hot oil for 15 seconds. Add carrots; stir-fry 1 minute. Add broccoli and stir-fry 3 to 4 minutes or until vegetables are crisp-tender. Push vegetables from center of wok.

3 Stir sauce; add sauce to center of wok. Cook and stir until thickened and bubbly. Stir all ingredients together to coat with sauce. Cook and stir about 1 minute more or until heated through. Sprinkle with nuts.

Nutrition Facts per serving: 94 cal., 6 g total fat (1 g sat. fat), 0 mg chol., 111 mg sodium, 9 g carbo., 3 g fiber, 3 g pro.

Start to Finish: 25 minutes
Makes: 4 servings

⅓ cup chicken broth or vegetable broth
1 tablespoon balsamic vinegar
1 teaspoon cornstarch
1 tablespoon cooking oil
1 teaspoon grated fresh ginger
1½ cups thinly bias-sliced carrots
     (3 medium)
2 cups broccoli florets
2 tablespoons chopped walnuts, toasted

Citrus Brussels Sprouts

Brussels sprouts pair up with sweet, mild carrots in a delicate orange sauce. Fresh Brussels sprouts are available between October and April. Avoid large sprouts because their flavor is bitter; small, vivid green sprouts taste sweet.

1 Halve Brussels sprouts. In a covered large saucepan cook Brussels sprouts and carrots in a small amount of boiling water for 10 to 12 minutes or until vegetables are crisp-tender. Drain in colander.

2 In the same saucepan combine orange juice, cornstarch, salt, and, if desired, nutmeg. Add Brussels sprouts and carrots. Cook and stir until thickened and bubbly. Cook and stir for 2 minutes more.

Nutrition Facts per serving: 50 cal., 0 g total fat (0 g sat. fat), 0 mg chol., 172 mg sodium, 11 g carbo., 3 g fiber, 2 g pro.

Prep: 15 minutes
Cook: 14 minutes
Makes: 4 servings

2 cups fresh Brussels sprouts or one 10-ounce package frozen Brussels sprouts, thawed
3 medium carrots, quartered lengthwise and cut into 1-inch pieces
⅓ cup orange juice
1 teaspoon cornstarch
¼ teaspoon salt
¼ teaspoon ground nutmeg (optional)

Green Beans with Caramelized Onions

Onions turn golden, sweet, and delicious when cooked long and slow. They add an interesting flavor twist to plain green beans.

1 In a covered medium saucepan cook beans in boiling lightly salted water for 12 to 15 minutes or until crisp-tender; drain.

2 Meanwhile, in a large skillet cook the onion and garlic, covered, in hot oil over medium-low heat for 12 to 15 minutes or until onions are tender, stirring occasionally. Uncover; cook and stir over medium-high heat for 3 to 5 minutes or until onions are golden, stirring once or twice. Remove from heat.

3 Add the tomato, oregano, salt, and pepper to mixture in skillet. Stir in beans. To serve, transfer to a serving dish.

Nutrition Facts per serving: 83 cal., 4 g total fat (1 g sat. fat), 0 mg chol., 140 mg sodium, 12 g carbo., 4 g fiber, 3 g pro.

Start to Finish: 30 minutes
Makes: 4 servings

- 1 pound green beans, trimmed
- 1 medium white or red onion, sliced
- 1 clove garlic, minced
- 1 tablespoon olive oil
- 1 medium tomato, seeded and chopped
- 1 teaspoon snipped fresh oregano or
     ¼ teaspoon dried oregano, crushed
- ¼ teaspoon salt
- ⅛ teaspoon black pepper

Feta-Stuffed Mushrooms

Portobello mushrooms are giant, making them great for holding stuffings. One taste of the feta, olives, and oil-packed tomatoes and you'll deem this dish a keeper.

1 Remove and discard mushroom stems. Place mushroom caps, stemmed side up, on a cookie sheet. Brush with olive oil (if desired, use the oil from the tomatoes); set aside.

2 For filling, in a small bowl stir together cheese, olives, and tomatoes. Divide filling among the mushrooms.

3 Bake in a 425° oven about 10 minutes or until heated through.

Nutrition Facts per serving: 161 cal., 11 g total fat (5 g sat. fat), 25 mg chol., 408 mg sodium, 8 g carbo., 4 g fiber, 8 g pro.

Prep: 20 minutes
Bake: 10 minutes
Oven: 425°F
Makes: 4 servings

4 portobello mushrooms (5 to 6 ounces each)
1 tablespoon olive oil
1 4-ounce package crumbled feta cheese with garlic and herb or crumbled feta cheese
¼ cup chopped pitted ripe olives
2 tablespoons snipped oil-packed dried tomatoes

Snow Peas and Tomatoes

Many main dishes benefit from a colorful side dish to perk them up. This side dish—with an Asian influence—is not only fast, but pretty to look at too.

1 In a 12-inch skillet cook shallot in hot oils over medium heat until tender. Add snow peas and teriyaki sauce. Cook and stir for 2 to 3 minutes or until peas are crisp-tender. Add tomatoes; cook 1 minute more.

2 Transfer mixture to a serving bowl. Sprinkle with sesame seeds.

Nutrition Facts per serving: 63 cal., 2 g total fat (0 g sat. fat), 0 mg chol., 120 mg sodium, 8 g carbo., 2 g fiber, 3 g pro.

Start to Finish: 10 minutes
Makes: 6 servings

- 1 large shallot, peeled and sliced
- 2 teaspoons peanut oil
- ¼ teaspoon toasted sesame oil
- 6 cups fresh snow peas, strings removed (about 1 pound)
- 1 tablespoon teriyaki sauce
- ½ cup grape tomatoes or cherry tomatoes, halved
- 2 teaspoons sesame seeds, toasted

15 g
carb

Sugar Snap Peas with Orange-Ginger Butter

Sugar snap peas (sometimes called sugar peas) are sweet, tender pods that have fully developed, plump, rounded peas inside. The quick glaze of marmalade and ginger complements them perfectly.

1 Remove strings and tips from fresh peas (if using). Cook fresh peas, covered, in a small amount of boiling salted water for 2 to 4 minutes or until crisp-tender. (Or cook frozen peas according to package directions.) Drain peas well.

2 Meanwhile, in a small saucepan cook ginger in hot butter for 1 minute. Stir in marmalade spread, vinegar, and pepper; cook and stir until marmalade melts. Pour marmalade mixture over hot peas; toss to coat.

Nutrition Facts per serving: 109 cal., 3 g total fat (2 g sat. fat), 8 mg chol., 50 mg sodium, 15 g carbo., 4 g fiber, 4 g pro.

Start to Finish: 25 minutes
Makes: 4 servings

3 cups fresh sugar snap peas or frozen loose-pack sugar snap peas
1 teaspoon grated fresh ginger
1 tablespoon butter or margarine
1 tablespoon low-sugar orange marmalade spread
1 teaspoon cider vinegar
⅛ teaspoon black pepper

Herbed Soybeans

Green soybeans are available fresh or frozen, in their pods or shelled at major markets or health food stores. They may also be labeled as edamame.

1 In a medium skillet melt butter over medium heat. Add soybeans to skillet; cook and stir about 5 minutes or until tender. Stir in mint, basil, and salt to taste.

Nutrition Facts per serving: 140 cal., 7 g total fat (2 g sat. fat), 4 mg chol., 123 mg sodium, 10 g carbo., 4 g fiber, 11 g pro.

Start to Finish: 10 minutes
Makes: 6 servings

2 teaspoons butter or margarine
3 cups shelled fresh soybeans or frozen soybeans, thawed
3 tablespoons fresh whole small mint leaves
1 tablespoon snipped fresh basil
   Salt

Wilted Spinach with Walnuts and Blue Cheese

Buy fresh spinach already washed and ready to eat, if you like. Baby fresh spinach also is readily available in most supermarket produce sections.

1 Thoroughly clean spinach. Drain well. Cut into 1-inch strips. In a large skillet heat oil over medium-high heat. Add walnuts. Cook and stir for 2 minutes. Add spinach. Cook and stir, uncovered, for 1 minute or just until wilted. Remove from heat.

2 Divide among 4 bowls. Top each serving with some crumbled blue cheese and sprinkle with pepper.

Nutrition Facts per serving: 58 cal., 5 g total fat (1 g sat. fat), 2 mg chol., 97 mg sodium, 1 g carbo., 5 g fiber, 3 g pro.

Start to Finish: 13 minutes
Makes: 4 servings

- 8 ounces fresh spinach or Swiss chard leaves
- 2 teaspoons cooking oil
- 2 tablespoons chopped walnuts
- 1 tablespoon crumbled blue cheese such as Gorgonzola, Stilton, French, or Danish blue
- ¼ teaspoon coarse ground black pepper

Roasted Summer Squash with Peppers

When you have lots of squash on hand and don't know what to do with it, here's a side dish that will surely please. A Greek- or Mediterranean-style seasoning gives the rather bland vegetable a punch of flavor.

1 Place the squash pieces and sweet pepper strips in a large shallow roasting pan. Drizzle with oil and sprinkle with seasoning and pepper, tossing to coat.

2 Roast vegetables, uncovered, in a 425° oven about 15 minutes or just until tender, stirring once.

Nutrition Facts per serving: 66 cal., 5 g total fat (1 g sat. fat), 0 mg chol., 25 mg sodium, 6 g carbo., 2 g fiber, 2 g pro.

Prep: 15 minutes
Roast: 15 minutes
Oven: 425°F
Makes: 6 servings

- 2 pounds yellow summer squash and/or zucchini, cut into bite-size chunks
- 1 sweet pepper, cut into strips
- 2 tablespoons olive oil
- 1½ teaspoons Greek-style or Mediterranean-style seasoning blend
- ¼ teaspoon black pepper

6 g
carb

Teeny Zucchini with Onions

Three main ingredients and less than 10 minutes in the skillet reward you with a side dish that's sensational.

1 Rinse and trim zucchini. If using medium zucchini, cut in half lengthwise and then into ½-inch slices.

2 In a large nonstick skillet heat olive oil over medium heat. Add zucchini and onion. Cook, stirring occasionally, for 6 to 8 minutes or just until vegetables are tender.

3 Add walnuts, oregano, salt, and pepper. Cook and stir for 1 minute more.

Nutrition Facts per serving: 106 cal., 9 g total fat (1 g sat. fat), 0 mg chol., 146 mg sodium, 6 g carbo., 1 g fiber, 4 g pro.

Start to Finish: 17 minutes
Makes: 4 to 6 servings

1 pound baby zucchini or 3 medium zucchini
1 tablespoon olive oil
1 small onion, cut into thin wedges
¼ cup chopped walnuts
½ teaspoon dried oregano, crushed
¼ teaspoon salt
¼ teaspoon black pepper

Zucchini alla Romana

Here's a quintessential Italian recipe that combines classic Italian ingredients: fresh herbs, garlic, olive oil, and Parmesan.

1 In a large skillet cook whole garlic cloves in hot oil until light brown; discard garlic.

2 Add zucchini, dried mint (if using), salt, and pepper to oil in skillet. Cook, uncovered, over medium heat about 5 minutes or until zucchini is crisp-tender, stirring occasionally.

3 To serve, sprinkle with cheese and fresh mint (if using).

Nutrition Facts per serving: 35 cal., 2 g total fat (1 g sat. fat), 2 mg chol., 130 mg sodium, 3 g carbo., 1 g fiber, 2 g pro.

Start to Finish: 15 minutes
Makes: 6 servings

- 2 cloves garlic
- 2 teaspoons olive oil
- 4 small zucchini, sliced (4 cups)
- 1 teaspoon dried mint or dried basil, crushed, or 1 tablespoon snipped fresh mint or fresh basil
- ¼ teaspoon salt
  Dash black pepper
- 2 tablespoons finely shredded Romano or Parmesan cheese

Avocado, Grapefruit, and Spinach Salad

This offers an interesting combination of flavors. Avocado, grapefruit, raspberry, and spinach taste great together.

1 On salad plates arrange the spinach, raspberries, grapefruit sections, and avocado slices. Sprinkle with chili powder.

2 In a small bowl whisk together vinegar and avocado oil. Drizzle over salads.

Nutrition Facts per serving: 169 cal., 14 g total fat (2 g sat. fat), 0 mg chol., 37 mg sodium, 11 g carbo., 6 g fiber, 2 g pro.

Start to Finish: 20 minutes
Makes: 6 servings

- 1 6-ounce package fresh baby spinach or 8 cups fresh baby spinach and/or assorted torn greens
- 1 cup fresh raspberries
- 2 grapefruits, peeled and sectioned
- 1 avocado, peeled, pitted, and sliced
  Several dashes chili powder
- ¼ cup raspberry vinegar
- ¼ cup avocado oil or olive oil

B.L.T. Salad

Inspired by the classic sandwich, this salad is simple and delicious with its grape tomatoes and bacon.

1 Place greens in a large salad bowl. Top with tomatoes, bacon, and chopped egg. Drizzle with dressing. Toss well.

Start to Finish: 20 minutes
Makes: 8 servings

5   cups torn washed greens or spinach
2   cups grape tomatoes, halved
½   pound bacon, crisp-cooked, drained, and crumbled (about 10 slices)
2   hard-cooked eggs, peeled and chopped
⅓   cup bottled ranch salad dressing

Nutrition Facts per serving: 139 cal., 12 g total fat (3 g sat. fat), 62 mg chol., 299 mg sodium, 4 g carbo., 1 g fiber, 5 g pro.

Fennel and Orange Salad

Fennel bulb, with its licorice flavor, is a nice complement to oranges. Use blood oranges, if you can find them, to add an exotic flair to the salad.

1 Cut off and discard upper stalks of fennel bulbs, reserving some of the feathery leaves. Cut off a thin slice from base of fennel bulbs. Remove and discard any wilted outer layers. Wash fennel and cut each bulb into ¼-inch slices, discarding core. Set aside.

2 Working over a bowl, section oranges, catching juice in bowl. For dressing, in the same bowl whisk together orange juice, olive oil, vinegar, and chervil.

3 Line 4 salad plates with lettuce leaves. Arrange the fennel slices and orange sections on lettuce; sprinkle with green onion. Drizzle dressing over salads. If desired, garnish salads with reserved fennel leaves.

Nutrition Facts per serving: 159 cal., 14 g total fat (2 g sat. fat), 0 mg chol., 31 mg sodium, 10 g carbo., 15 g fiber, 1 g pro.

Start to Finish: 15 minutes
Makes: 4 servings

2 medium fennel bulbs
2 medium blood oranges or oranges
¼ cup olive oil
2 tablespoons balsamic vinegar
1 tablespoon snipped fresh chervil or
    ½ teaspoon dried chervil, crushed
  Bibb lettuce leaves
1 green onion, sliced

Insalata Mista

This Italian-inspired salad is generously topped with fresh mozzarella, a specialty cheese worth seeking for its hallmark sweet flavor and soft texture. Look for it at Italian markets and cheese shops.

1 In a large salad bowl toss together the mixed greens, tomatoes, snipped basil, and olives. Drizzle Italian Vinaigrette over salad; toss to coat. Top with mozzarella cheese.

Italian Vinaigrette: In a screw-top jar combine 2 tablespoons olive oil or salad oil, 2 tablespoons balsamic vinegar, 2 teaspoons snipped fresh oregano or basil, ⅛ teaspoon salt, and ⅛ teaspoon black pepper. Cover the jar; shake well. Serve immediately or cover and store in the refrigerator up to 2 weeks. Shake before serving. Makes about ¼ cup.

Nutrition Facts per serving: 169 cal., 14 g total fat (4 g sat. fat), 16 mg chol., 255 mg sodium, 7 g carbo., 2 g fiber, 6 g pro.

Start to Finish: 15 minutes
Makes: 4 servings

- 4 cups torn mixed greens (such as radicchio, spinach, arugula, and/or chicory)
- 1 cup yellow and/or red cherry tomatoes, halved
- ¼ cup snipped fresh basil
- ½ cup kalamata olives
- 1 recipe Italian Vinaigrette
- 3 ounces fresh mozzarella cheese, thinly sliced

4 g
carb

Mozzarella Caprese

Fresh mozzarella is the cheese of choice for this side dish. It is a must for those who pick their own tomatoes fresh from the vine.

1 Cut tomatoes into ½-inch slices. Cut mozzarella into ¼-inch slices. Arrange tomato and cheese slices on a platter. Drizzle with vinaigrette. Sprinkle basil strips on top. Season to taste with salt and pepper.

Nutrition Facts per serving: 64 cal., 4 g total fat (2 g sat. fat), 11 mg chol., 174 mg sodium, 4 g carbo., 1 g fiber, 3 g pro.

Start to Finish: 10 minutes
Makes: 8 servings

4   medium or 6 plum tomatoes
4   ounces fresh mozzarella balls
2   tablespoons bottled balsamic
     vinaigrette salad dressing
½   cup loosely packed fresh basil leaves,
     thinly sliced
     Salt
     Fresh cracked black pepper

Tomato-Herb Salad

Bottled Italian dressing provides a shortcut and gets an added spark with a generous sprinkling of snipped fresh herbs.

1 Arrange tomato slices on a large platter. If desired, sprinkle with raisins.

2 In a small bowl combine Italian dressing and fresh herbs; drizzle over tomatoes. Serve immediately or cover and chill for up to 2 hours.

Nutrition Facts per serving: 117 cal., 10 g total fat (1 g sat. fat), 0 mg chol., 164 mg sodium, 8 g carbo., 1 g fiber, 1 g pro.

Start to Finish: 15 minutes
Makes: 4 to 6 servings

4 medium red and/or yellow tomatoes, sliced
⅓ cup raisins and/or golden raisins, chopped (optional)
⅓ cup bottled Italian salad dressing
2 teaspoons snipped chives
2 teaspoons snipped fresh basil
1 teaspoon snipped fresh thyme
1 teaspoon snipped fresh marjoram

Ginger-Sesame Slaw

To make carrot ribbons for this salad, scrape the length of carrot with a vegetable peeler. The ribbons add interest to an otherwise simple salad.

1 In a large bowl stir together the bok choy, carrot, radish, and ginger. Add enough dressing to moisten. Serve immediately or cover and chill up to 1 hour.

Nutrition Facts per serving: 71 cal., 4 g total fat (1 g sat. fat), 0 mg chol., 106 mg sodium, 9 g carbo., 2 g fiber, 2 g pro.

Start to Finish: 25 minutes
Makes: 6 servings

4 cups thinly bias-sliced bok choy
2 cups carrot ribbons
1 daikon radish (8 ounces), shredded, or
    1 cup sliced radishes
1 tablespoon finely chopped pickled
    ginger or 2 teaspoons grated fresh
    ginger
¼ to ½ cup bottled Oriental sesame
    salad dressing

Ruby and Gold Grapefruit Cocktail

Rosemary and cracked black pepper release a remarkable flavor in this winter-fresh citrus dish that's a refreshing predinner course.

1 In a medium bowl combine red and white grapefruit sections, oil, and pepper. Toss gently to coat. Divide evenly among 6 small bowls. Sprinkle with snipped rosemary. If desired, garnish with rosemary sprigs.

Nutrition Facts per serving: 60 cal., 3 g total fat (0 g sat. fat), 0 mg chol., 1 mg sodium, 8 g carbo., 1 g fiber, 1 g pro.

Start to Finish: 25 minutes
Makes: 6 servings

1⅓	cups red grapefruit sections
1⅓	cups white grapefruit sections
4	teaspoons rosemary-flavored oil or olive oil
½	teaspoon cracked black pepper
	Snipped fresh rosemary
	Rosemary sprigs (optional)

Index

Metric Information

The charts on this page provide a guide for converting measurements from the U.S. customary system, which is used throughout this book, to the metric system.

Product Differences

Most of the ingredients called for in the recipes in this book are available in most countries. However, some are known by different names. Here are some common American ingredients and their possible counterparts:

- Sugar (white) is granulated, fine granulated, or castor sugar.
- Powdered sugar is icing sugar.
- All-purpose flour is enriched, bleached or unbleached white household flour. When self-rising flour is used in place of all-purpose flour in a recipe that calls for leavening, omit the leavening agent (baking soda or baking powder) and salt.
- Light-colored corn syrup is golden syrup.
- Cornstarch is cornflour.
- Baking soda is bicarbonate of soda.
- Vanilla or vanilla extract is vanilla essence.
- Green, red, or yellow sweet peppers are capsicums or bell peppers.
- Golden raisins are sultanas.

Volume and Weight

The United States traditionally uses cup measures for liquid and solid ingredients. The chart below shows the approximate imperial and metric equivalents. If you are accustomed to weighing solid ingredients, the following approximate equivalents will be helpful.

- 1 cup butter, castor sugar, or rice = 8 ounces = ½ pound = 250 grams
- 1 cup flour = 4 ounces = ¼ pound = 125 grams
- 1 cup icing sugar = 5 ounces = 150 grams

Canadian and U.S. volume for a cup measure is 8 fluid ounces (237 ml), but the standard metric equivalent is 250 ml.

1 British imperial cup is 10 fluid ounces.

In Australia, 1 tablespoon equals 20 ml, and there are 4 teaspoons in the Australian tablespoon.

Spoon measures are used for smaller amounts of ingredients. Although the size of the tablespoon varies slightly in different countries, for practical purposes and for recipes in this book, a straight substitution is all that's necessary. Measurements made using cups or spoons always should be level unless stated otherwise.

Common Weight Range Replacements

Imperial / U.S.	Metric
½ ounce	15 g
1 ounce	25 g or 30 g
4 ounces (¼ pound)	115 g or 125 g
8 ounces (½ pound)	225 g or 250 g
16 ounces (1 pound)	450 g or 500 g
1¼ pounds	625 g
1½ pounds	750 g
2 pounds or 2¼ pounds	1,000 g or 1 Kg

Oven Temperature Equivalents

Fahrenheit Setting	Celsius Setting*	Gas Setting
300°F	150°C	Gas Mark 2 (very low)
325°F	160°C	Gas Mark 3 (low)
350°F	180°C	Gas Mark 4 (moderate)
375°F	190°C	Gas Mark 5 (moderate)
400°F	200°C	Gas Mark 6 (hot)
425°F	220°C	Gas Mark 7 (hot)
450°F	230°C	Gas Mark 8 (very hot)
475°F	240°C	Gas Mark 9 (very hot)
500°F	260°C	Gas Mark 10 (extremely hot)
Broil	Broil	Grill

*Electric and gas ovens may be calibrated using celsius. However, for an electric oven, increase celsius setting 10 to 20 degrees when cooking above 160°C. For convection or forced air ovens (gas or electric) lower the temperature setting 25°F/10°C when cooking at all heat levels.

Baking Pan Sizes

Imperial / U.S.	Metric
9×1½-inch round cake pan	22- or 23×4-cm (1.5 L)
9×1½-inch pie plate	22- or 23×4-cm (1 L)
8×8×2-inch square cake pan	20×5-cm (2 L)
9×9×2-inch square cake pan	22- or 23×4.5-cm (2.5 L)
11×7×1½-inch baking pan	28×17×4-cm (2 L)
2-quart rectangular baking pan	30×19×4.5-cm (3 L)
13×9×2-inch baking pan	34×22×4.5-cm (3.5 L)
15×10×1-inch jelly roll pan	40×25×2-cm
9×5×3-inch loaf pan	23×13×8-cm (2 L)
2-quart casserole	2 L

U.S. / Standard Metric Equivalents

⅛ teaspoon = 0.5 ml
¼ teaspoon = 1 ml
½ teaspoon = 2 ml
1 teaspoon = 5 ml
1 tablespoon = 15 ml
2 tablespoons = 25 ml
¼ cup = 2 fluid ounces = 50 ml
⅓ cup = 3 fluid ounces = 75 ml
½ cup = 4 fluid ounces = 125 ml
⅔ cup = 5 fluid ounces = 150 ml
¾ cup = 6 fluid ounces = 175 ml
1 cup = 8 fluid ounces = 250 ml
2 cups = 1 pint = 500 ml
1 quart = 1 litre